Productivity Spillovers from
Foreign Direct Investment

European University Studies
Europäische Hochschulschriften
Publications Universitaires Européennes

Series V
Economics and Management

Reihe V Série V
Volks- und Betriebswirtschaft
Sciences économiques, gestion d'entreprise

Vol./Bd. 2759

PETER LANG
Frankfurt am Main · Berlin · Bern · Bruxelles · New York · Oxford · Wien

Katarzyna Zukowska-Gagelmann

Productivity Spillovers from Foreign Direct Investment

The case of Poland

PETER LANG
Europäischer Verlag der Wissenschaften

Die Deutsche Bibliothek - CIP-Einheitsaufnahme

Zukowska-Gagelmann, Katarzyna:

Productivity spillovers from foreign direct investment : the case of Poland / Katarzyna Zukowska-Gagelmann. - Frankfurt am Main ; Berlin ; Bern ; Bruxelles ; New York ; Oxford ; Wien : Lang, 2001

(European university studies : Ser. 5, Economics and Management ; Vol. 2759)

Zugl.: Saarbrücken, Univ., Diss., 2000

ISBN 3-631-37441-0

D 291

ISSN 0531-7339

ISBN 3-631-37441-0

US-ISBN 0-8204-4762-5

www.peterlang.de

Productivity Spillovers from Foreign Direct Investment: The case of Poland

Dissertation zur Erlangung eines Doktors der Wirtschaftswissenschaft

(Doctoris rerum politicarum)

der

Rechts- und Wirtschaftswissenschaftlichen Fakultät

der Universität des Saarlandes

vorgelegt von

Katarzyna Zukowska-Gagelmann

Tag der Disputation: 28. Juli 2000

Dekan: Univ.-Prof. Dr. Klaus Grupp

Erstberichterstatter: Univ.-Prof. Dr. Robert Holzmann

Zweitberichterstatter: Univ.-Prof. Dr. Christian Keuschnigg

Acknowledgements

This book was being written while I was working as a teaching and research assistant at the University of Saarland in Saarbrücken, Germany. I am particularly indebted to my Ph.D. supervisor Prof. Robert Holzmann for fruitful discussions and comments, as well as to the member of my thesis committee Prof. Christian Keuschnigg. I want to thank my colleagues and friends Dr. Roland Demmel, Dr. Jarko Fidrmuc, Dr. Gesa Miehe-Nordmeyer and particularly, Dr. Yves Hervé for many helpful comments, valuable criticism and discussions within the four years. I owe lots of thanks to Dr. Andrzej Cieslik from the University of Warsaw, Poland for providing me with data.

Last but not least, I want to thank my husband Christian for his extraordinary engagement and help in growing up our little daughter Lidia. I dedicate this book to him.

Katarzyna Zukowska-Gagelmann

Table of Contents

List of Figures

List of Tables

Chapter 1:
Introduction

1.1 Motivation

Ten years ago, Poland as the first of the Central and Eastern European (CEE) countries started radical transformation towards a market economy in the hope of achieving economic growth sufficient to increase living standards. Given the legacy of central planning, restructuring and modernisation of the economy resulting in higher efficiency both at the macro- and the microeconomic level was necessary to approach this objective. Apart from privatisation, foreign direct investment (FDI) was viewed as one of the main tools for restructuring the CEE economies.

From the perspective of the transition countries, FDI is especially attractive since it seems to provide simultaneous solutions to many problems these economies faced at the beginning of the reforms. Firstly, due to capital inflows associated with FDI, these countries can gain access to foreign savings to fund investment which is necessary to restructure incumbent enterprises and the economy as a whole. Capital infusion is important because domestic savings in relation to estimated capital needs are highly insufficient, the domestic financial sector is underdeveloped and the access to international capital market is constrained. Compared to portfolio investment, FDI flows tend to be much less volatile and less likely to decline in the face of financial shocks. Another positive consequence of FDI consists of state revenues from privatisation to foreign investors. This may help reduce public debt, leading to a reduction of the country-specific risk premium and hence lowering of the cost of other types of foreign financing. Additionally, revenues from taxing of the activity of foreign investors would allow to reduce the tax burden on locally-owned firms during the period of their restructuring and help finance, for example, social programmes backing restructuring.

Secondly, the role of FDI goes beyond mere capital inflows. It may be a channel for modern technology transfer through which production techniques, managerial know-how, marketing skills and training of domestic workers flow into the transition countries. This helps upgrade technological levels in the sectors hosting FDI. Along with this process, firms with foreign ownership become more productive than the rest of the industry, and the sectors as a whole modernise and become more efficient.

Indeed, there is broad evidence with regards to the first years of transition confirming that substantial restructuring and new investment is the highest in foreign-owned firms (EBRD, 1995). Especially in the case of large industrial enterprises, restructuring led by a foreign strategic investor has proved the most effective way to enhance performance of an enterprise (EBRD, 1999). Firms with foreign ownership tend to perform better than locally-owned enterprises: they are more productive, use more recent technology and contribute over-proportionally to fixed investment (Hunya, 1997).

Apart from its direct contribution to industrial restructuring, FDI was expected to have an indirect positive impact on the modernisation of locally-owned firms. One important reason is that foreign firms may stimulate competition in the domestic industry especially in sectors characterised by inherited high concentration, with low penetration of imports and slow creation of *de novo* local firms. Dunning (1992) formulated this viewpoint in the following way:

> *'Indeed in the last resort, it may be that the pressures of competition to modify and improve a product range, production and/or transportation costs, and to introduce new marketing and distribution methods, are the most significant positive influences of inbound MNE (multinational enterprise) activity.' (p. 465)*

Hence, the role of FDI may be to *initialise* adjustment of the locally-owned firms aiming at productivity improvement.

Apart from being a spark for the process, the presence of foreign firms is also believed to *facilitate* restructuring. There is some evidence from less developed host countries showing how FDI may generate positive technological spillovers for the local firms (Blomström/Kokko, 1997). These effects manifest themselves in increased access to modern technology, improvement in labour skills, diffusion of marketing skills, easier access to foreign markets and development of local suppliers and distribution networks. Spillovers are particularly important if technologies used by foreign affiliates are not available in a country or cannot be obtained through market transactions.

Taking into account both the direct and the indirect channel through which FDI helps promote growth, opening to FDI inflows seems to be a very promising transition strategy. It can ensure the acquisition of up-to-date technology by foreign affiliates employing local labour and the simultaneous creation of a modern, locally-owned commercial and industrial sector. Hence, if spillovers to local firms are automatic, incumbent local firms in transition countries have no reason to fear competition from FDI: they would become benefactors of the foreign presence. This would also imply that essential efforts including fiscal incentives offered to foreign direct investors by prospective host countries in order to attract the highest possible capital inflows are appropriate policy measures.

However, this view on the double contribution of FDI to industrial restructuring in the transition countries may be too optimistic. Most reservations against FDI stem from the fact that, in general, locally-owned firms are too weak to compete effectively against foreign affiliates. Since the latter ones have superior access to information, human capital and financial resources, the competition is on a very unequal base. This would mean that technologically backward local firms will be crowded out of the market before technological spillovers have materialised. According to this criticism, the conflict arises between restructuring of the industry as a whole, for which the most efficient (or sometimes only) way is opening to FDI, and restructuring of the existing locally-owned firms within the industry. The destruction of indigenous firms may lead to high social costs and national resentments because of over-reliance on multinationals. The perceived danger is that the host economy over a very short period of time may loose its attractiveness as a base for multinational investment when cheaper external locations become available.

Despite that FDI has been a hotly debated issue in transition countries, far-going liberalisation of FDI inflows was adapted in most of them in the early 1990s. Along with this opening, the competition for foreign capital has grown steadily. However, with a few exceptions, the scope of FDI inflows has been rather disappointing. Today, it is hard to imagine that FDI will provide a major net source of funds to these countries in the near future. Meanwhile, indirect external effects of FDI on the locally-owned firms in transition countries gain increasing importance. Does the presence of foreign firms result in technological spillovers which translate into productivity improvement? Or, is the detrimental competition effect on technologically inferior local firms dominating? In this thesis, we want to shed some light on this issue through a systematic, empirical examination of productivity spillovers in Poland during the first decade of transition.

The competitiveness of the local firms in relation to firms stemming from the industrialised countries is an essential issue in view of the targeted accession of the transition countries to the EU. The Copenhagen summit of 1993 laid down two sub-criteria for the economic progress required from candidates to qualify for EU membership. The criteria are (i) the existence of a functioning market economy, and (ii) the capacity to withstand competitive pressures and market forces within the Union countries. For the evaluation of the second economic criterion, the key question is whether local firms have the necessary capacity to adapt, and whether the economic environment in the transition country supports further adjustment (EC, 1997). Since a proper assessment would require a perfect forecast of future developments, the European Commission relies heavily on a catalogue of indicators, including the level of physical infrastructure and education, competition policy, the level of trade integration with the EU, the wage level and the proportion of small firms. However, the Commission admits that the method is quite imperfect.

With our empirical investigation of the FDI impact on local firms, we propose another approach to evaluate a future competitiveness of CEE countries in confrontation with technologically advanced rivals within the EU. We argue that the response of the indigenous firms to the competitive pressure from foreign affiliates may provide a first test and interesting insights into the adjustment capacity of local firms and their environment.

1.2 Objectives of the thesis

The main objective of the thesis is the empirical investigation of the contribution of FDI to the restructuring in a transition economy. The analysis focuses on the generation of productivity spillovers in domestic firms without participation of foreign capital and verifies the view of FDI being a catalyst for their restructuring.

We investigate both the extent to which the activity of foreign firms affects the productivity growth of local firms and whether it facilitates convergence in productivity between the foreign- and the locally-owned part of the domestic industry. In order to explain the measured differences in the scope of spillovers, we test various hypotheses concerning their determinants. We apply an econometric approach and use a comprehensive data set covering about 90 per cent of all domestic firms. Contrary to the case-study literature, we are hence able to examine whether there is a systematic relationship between FDI and the performance of local firms.

The empirical analysis refers to the presence of foreign-owned firms in Poland over the period 1993-97. The reasons for our focus on Poland are manifold. It was the first transition country to introduce deep macroeconomic and structural reforms as early as in 1990, and the first one to overcome the transitional recession. The investigated period is characterised by a remarkable macro-economic recovery for which efficiency gains turned out to be a main driving force (Zukowski, 1998). The progress in transition as measured by the EBRD transition indicators is high in all respects (EBRD, 1999). The country is one of the leaders in attracting FDI inflows which are spread across a wide range of industries. But the direct contribution of FDI to restructuring through privatisation of state firms is relatively low. Apart from foreign and state firms, there is a dynamic locally-owned private sector which developed intensively during the transition period. The economic structure is well diversified with local firms operating in all industries in which foreign investors are engaged. Hence, the country provides a convenient framework to test the external effects of FDI. In addition, the European Commission considered Poland to satisfy the competitiveness criterion for the EU accession (EC, 1997). Hence, we may also check whether our quantitative analysis supports this evaluation. Last but not least, the analysis of spillovers for Poland was feasible due to the availability of statistical data on firms by various ownership types.

At the theoretical level, the main objective of the present thesis is to elaborate a unified framework in order to present the actual state-of-the-art of the theoretical economic literature on spillovers from FDI. Our survey fills the existing gap and gives a systematic review of the models elaborated in the 1990s, most of which are still unpublished. We identify shortcomings of these models and suggest theoretical extensions. The presentation serves also as a convenient tool to derive empirical hypotheses to be tested in the following empirical part of the thesis.

The present work is one of the first attempts to identify spillovers in a transition country and the first one for Poland. With our analysis, we aim to add empirical facts to the continuing debate on the benefits of FDI in the transition countries. In addition, by comparing our results to the few existing studies for developing countries which liberalised FDI in the 1980s, we want to clarify whether the pattern of FDI impact is general and whether these countries provide valuable lessons to the transition countries in CEE.

This analysis is unique in studying the role of the competition level - both from domestic firms and imports - and of the ownership status for the ability of local firms to reap productivity spillovers. Hence, our results contribute to the present discussion of the relative dynamism of different ownership sectors in transition countries.

1.3 Structure of the thesis

The plan of the thesis is as follows: in Chapter 2, we briefly present the main features of the FDI phenomenon world-wide and compare them to FDI developments in the CEE transition countries. Based on this evidence, we draw tentative conclusions about the role of FDI in the restructuring and modernisation of transition economies.

Chapter 3 discusses the differences between FDI and other sorts of capital inflows, like portfolio investment or foreign aid. The feature that makes it more attractive from the viewpoint of less developed countries is its nature as a bundle of assets, capital being only the easiest measurable part of it. The other components of this package include resources in the form of innovative technology, managerial and organisational know-how, reputation for product quality, access to export markets and more. FDI must be understood as a mode of capital and technology transfer within the network of a multinational company. That is why FDI has the potential to initialise *productivity spillovers* in the form of unintended technological transfer from foreign affiliates to local firms in the host country.

In Chapter 4, we survey empirical evidence concerning productivity spillovers from FDI in less developed countries. We summarise findings both from case-studies and from econometric research. The first sort of evidence helps isolate channels for the diffusion of productivity spillovers to locally-owned firms. Econometric studies provide tests for three hypotheses about the determinants of the scope of spillovers: the contagion, the technology gap and the competition hypothesis. According to these hypotheses, productivity spillovers increase with a higher intra-industrial foreign presence, with a higher relative technological backwardness of local firms, and with higher intra-industrial competition. We show that the existing econometric evidence is only partially consistent with the above hypotheses. The explanation of this discrepancy is given in Chapter 5 by a theoretical investigation of the creation process of productivity spillovers.

Chapter 5 reviews the just emerging theoretical literature on technology transfer through FDI. We present various models of interaction between foreign firms possessing superior technology and local firms. Each of these models focuses on a single channel through which FDI might exercise impact on local firms of the host economy. Within the presented theoretical framework, we discuss determinants of positive spillovers. Next, we investigate the support given by the models to each of the three tested hypotheses. We find out that the theoretical literature surveyed here derives predictions that are partially at odds with the above hypotheses. The emergence of positive spillovers depends heavily on the type of linkages between foreign and local firms. We close the chapter by giving some suggestions for further theoretical research.

In Chapter 6, we examine productivity spillovers from FDI in Poland over the period between 1993 and 1997. Using comprehensive data for Polish manufacturing firms, we study the effect of a higher foreign presence on productivity change of locally-owned firms. Following the existing empirical literature, we test econometrically whether the scope of productivity spillovers is properly described by the three standard hypotheses. The results suggest that Polish manufacturing benefits from a higher presence of foreign firms which are more productive than the local ones. However, we generally detect an adverse impact of FDI on the performance of local firms. The effect differs between groups of firms and groups of industries. The ownership status of a local firm seems to be an important determinant of the emergence of spillovers. The technology gap between local and foreign firms and the competition status of the industry are important determinants of the scope of the impact.

Chapter 7 summarises and comments upon the empirical findings. Finally, we will draw some policy recommendations for transition countries on how to strengthen the contribution of FDI to the transition and the EU accession.

Chapter 2:
FDI and international production by multinationals

2.1 Introduction

A striking feature of recent decades has been the rapid growth of international production by multinational companies. In the second half of the 1980s, foreign direct investment (FDI) and international capital flows increased immensely. At that time, many governments, previously quite hostile to multinationals, liberalised their policies seeking to attract FDI. Starting in the early 1990s, transition countries in Central and Eastern Europe radically changed their general attitude and regulatory framework in order to facilitate FDI inflows. In doing so, they joined a group of numerous countries all over the world with a view that FDI will help them cope with domestic structural as well as macroeconomic problems and stimulate growth. On what base are these prospects and hopes founded? What is special about FDI in comparison to other types of capital inflows like, for example, portfolio investment and foreign aid?

In this chapter, we elaborate important aspects of the FDI phenomenon. The definition of FDI in Section 2.2 is a proper starting point to elaborate what is special (different) with FDI. This step is unavoidable since the term itself is the source of a widespread misunderstanding. Contrary to what it suggests, foreign direct investment is not investment, neither in financial accounting nor in national accounting terms. Furthermore, FDI does not necessary involve flows of financial capital as might be suggested by the fact that balance-of-payments statistics are the main source of FDI data. These distinctions are discussed in Section 2.3. This section also helps properly interpret empirical data on the scope of international production which will be given in Section 2.4. Section 2.5 describes the FDI inflows into transition countries in Central and Eastern Europe in comparison to general developments. The final Section 2.6 concludes.

2.2 What is and what is not FDI?

The most general theoretical concept of FDI is reflected in a definition stemming from Graham (1992):

> *'Foreign Direct Investment (FDI) occurs when citizens of one nation (the 'home' country) acquire managerial control of economic activities in some other nation (the 'host' country).' (p. 148)*

As with all types of investment activities, the objective of the investor is the acquisition of claims to future income, but in the case of FDI the income in question is generated by activities abroad. This, however, is not the constituting characteristic of FDI since this also applies to international portfolio investment.

The unique and distinguishing feature of FDI transactions is the fact that a foreign investor is interested in exercising control over the process of income generation.

But, what does 'control' mean and how could the acquirement of control be identified? Taken from the viewpoint of decision theory, a 'managerial control' over an enterprise in a host country would mean that key decisions on executive personnel, new products, capital investment, research and development, and dividend policy are at least co-ordinated by foreigners.

However, since managerial control is not measurable in a cardinal sense, a proxy variable must be relied upon in order to identify its degree. When looking for a good proxy, one may argue that managerial control implies the existence of a long-term relationship between the foreign direct investor and the enterprise. Ownership is such a relationship. The size of ownership can serve as a measure of power and control upon an enterprise. In this case, 'control of economic activities' would mean an ownership of a stake of equity capital which is high enough to ensure control.[1]

How big this stake should be is not a question which can be answered generally. In practice, two approaches are possible: Firstly, FDI projects should be judged subjectively case by case. Alternatively, an arbitrary choice of threshold ownership is done. The second approach seems preferable when this concept should serve as an operational FDI definition allowing for international comparisons.

The IMF (1993) and OECD (1992) in unison recommend relying on ownership as the objective criterion to identify FDI. The equity participation of 10 per cent is applied as a threshold distinguishing FDI and portfolio investment.[2]

The initial FDI transaction, be it a purchase of shares of an ongoing resident firm or an establishment of a new firm, results in a creation of a *foreign direct enterprise (foreign affiliates* according to the UNCTAD (1995) terminology). These are enterprises in which the foreign direct investor owns at least the

---

[1] However, there is a widely held opinion that a majority of large firms are controlled by professional managers, and that the proportion of large firms controlled by ownership interests is declining (the so-called 'divorce between ownership and control') (Nyman/ Silberstone, 1978). The second argument against the legal concept of control based on ownership reads that in some cases management decisions may be enforced even without legal ownership. Among non-equity forms of FDI, subcontracting, management contracts, turnkey arrangements, franchising, licensing and product sharing are the most common. However, a non-equity FDI represents a negligible small amount of total FDI. Therefore, most investors achieve control by owning a big enough stake of equity capital.

[2] Strictly speaking, §363 of the BoP-Manual (IMF, 1993) allows national classifications of FDI based on the effective-voice-in-management criterion (judged nationally case by case), but only additionally to a classification based on the ownership criterion.

threshold level of ordinary shares or voting power. According to the actual size of an equity capital stake owned by the investor, branches, associates, and subsidiaries may be identified.[3]

These are some examples of different types of FDI transactions:[4]

(i) equity FDI

- a foreign investor acquires (by purchase, donation or inheritance) an ongoing firm (or shares) in a host country;
- a foreign investor finances (wholly or partly) an emerging new firm (greenfield investment) in the host country;
- a foreign investor acquires land or real estate;[5]
- a parent MNC reinvests (part of) its local earnings in the subsidiary in the host country;
- a parent MNC provides funds (loans, both short- and long-term) to the subsidiary in the host country;

(ii) non-equity FDI

- subcontracting, management contracts, turnkey arrangements, franchising, licensing and product sharing.

In practice, most foreign direct enterprises are affiliates of *multinational corporations (MNCs)*, i.e. enterprises which control and manage production establishments located in at least two countries (Caves, 1996). The foreign investors are the parent organisations of these firms. Thus, FDI mainly represents the global expansion of activities of MNCs (UNCTAD, 1995). It explains why the two phenomena: emerging and growth of MNCs and FDI are examined simultaneously in the literature.

Having discussed the FDI definitions, we are now ready to clarify a widespread misunderstanding putting an 'equal' sign between FDI and additional investment (gross fixed capital formation) in the host economy. Whether FDI is related to investment is an important issue especially for less-developed market economies which are frequently characterised by poorly developed financial markets and low savings rates. This constraints their investment expenditures in

---

[3] According to the terminology recommended by the IMF, a 'subsidiary' is defined as a foreign direct enterprise in which a non-resident investor owns more than 50 per cent of the ordinary shares or voting power (for an incorporated enterprise) or the equivalent (for an unincorporated enterprise), 'associate' if an investor owns 50 per cent or less, and 'branches' if these are wholly or jointly owned unicorporated enterprises (IMF, 1993).

[4] We ignore changes in the book value of assets and liabilities due to valuation changes which go back to exchange rates and price changes.

[5] Balance of Payments (BoP) statistics consider purchases of residential real estate by individuals (even holiday and other residences owned by non-residents for personal use) and real estate holdings by investment trusts as direct investment. However, such non-business transactions should not be counted as FDI according to its definition.

aggregate since, without any capital from abroad, domestic investment equals national savings. On the other hand, these countries usually need high real capital formation in order to enhance or modernise production and stimulate growth in the short run.

Take the perspective of a firm in the host country. What is registered as a FDI inflow associated with this firm does not need to be used within this firm, or it may be used for other purposes than investment. Consider some examples: if an ongoing firm becomes a foreign affiliate, then the price paid by the foreign investor is counted as FDI. When it is a private firm, the former owner may or may not use the receipts to purchase new capital goods. Even if he does, the investment may take place in another firm. Expenditures for real capital formation may be even smaller than sale revenues. In case of a state firm, a general government is free about the use of these funds within the domestic economy. It may use it partly or fully for financing investment in this or other state firms, but it may also distribute it among the population via different channels, e.g. through a pension system.[6]

From a national income perspective, FDI is also only a possible source of investment. FDI data record financial flows which may or may not correspond to changes in gross fixed capital formation. The part of FDI flows which consists of mergers and acquisitions and purchase of land is not investment at all. The impact on investment depends on (i) the extent to which FDI substitute for other types of financial flows and (ii) the extent FDI crowds out domestically financed investment.

From the above remarks it arises immediately that, contrary to its name, *foreign direct investment is not investment in the strict economic sense*. FDI may provide foreign capital to finance investment, but the relationship between FDI and investment in the host country is not an accounting identity. It is an empirical relationship which may vary between different countries and periods.[7]

2.3 Measuring the scope of FDI inflows and stocks

Like any economic transaction between residents and non-residents of an economy, FDI flows are registered in the balance of payments (BoP). In

---

[6] In transition countries, privatisation revenues predominantly served to relieve social problems caused by economic transformation, like sectorally and regionally concentrated unemployment. The newest example is the decision of the Polish Parliament from 23.09.99 to allocate the 1999 privatisation revenue to the state pension system, which became insolvent due to arrears in contribution payments by firms.

[7] Fry *et al.* (1995), Nyatepe-Coo (1998) and Borensztein *et al.* (1998) find a positive impact of FDI inflows from industrial countries on domestic investment in a panel of developing countries. Time-series analyses for Mexico and Chile (Corsepius/Schweickert, 1991) as well as a panel analysis by Fry (1994) detect a negative impact of FDI on domestic investment.

accordance with the IMF standards, the BoP-statistics on FDI should include transactions that create or dissolve investments as well as those that serve to maintain, expand, or reduce investments. In general, there are 3 types of such transactions: (i) acquiring (or selling) of equity shares, (ii) investing of the direct investor's share of earnings, (iii) borrowing or lending of funds (including debt securities and suppliers' credits) between direct investors and foreign direct enterprises (IMF, 1993). They are booked separately in the financial account under the item 'direct investment'.

The most reliable and comprehensive annual FDI data for international comparisons are collected by IMF and published in the BOP Yearbook. They are derived from the BOP statistics of national central banks. For making FDI data internationally comparable, FDI values are usually expressed in US dollars. Additional sources for national data are industrial surveys and national statistical offices which provide statistics in sectoral and regional breakdown.

Although FDI by definition is a *flow* variable, one can be also interested in the total net worth of (real, productive) assets under the control of foreign investors. Measuring this stock is a quite difficult task because of differing concepts of value, especially the difference between the book value and market value. Although market values built upon expected future profits would give a more accurate picture of the total stock of assets controlled by foreign investors, these data are difficult to compute. In most countries, balance sheets of enterprises are the only source of value of assets and liabilities. Unfortunately, they are not regularly revalued to current market value in practice.

FDI *stock* data are published together with BoP-data since 1995. The stock-oriented international investment position provides a measure of the net worth (at the end of period) of this part of an economy which is attributable to, or derived from, its relationship with the rest of the world. Whereas FDI flows in the BoP go back only to transactions between residents and non-resident investors, FDI stocks change also due to various kinds of adjustments, valuation, reclassification and others. As with FDI flows, FDI stocks are based on book value or historical costs and reflect prices at the time when the investment was made, unless revaluation took place.

Despite the fact that data on FDI can be taken from the BoP statistics, the scope of FDI is not equal to the international capital transfer registered. For example, FDI inflows can take place even without capital transfer, as is the case when a multinational firm acquires stakes of an ongoing firm and finances this transaction by issuing debt in the host country. However, this point seems to be of a minor importance for less-developed countries which usually suffer under underdeveloped capital markets and insufficient savings.

Unfortunately for international comparisons, the FDI definitions used by IMF member states and their collection methods still vary in several aspects from IMF recommendations.[8] Moreover, national methodologies are often in flow, and modifications are not always clearly defined. The following list summarises the most important problems with FDI data:

- Some countries judge FDI subjectively while applying a criterion of 'the effective voice in management' (e.g. Netherlands, Switzerland).
- For many countries including Germany and UK, a minimum ownership threshold which apply to a direct investment is fixed at 20 per cent, whereas e.g. Japan requires no threshold at all.
- Not all countries record every component of FDI flows (equity investment, reinvested earnings, intra-company loans). Other started reporting on a full set of FDI with a delay. Some countries register only cash but not in-kind investment. Some countries do not include some components of FDI in the geographical breakdown. Gaps exist even when earnings are recorded, since in many cases companies tend to minimise tax payments by reporting lower earnings for their subsidiaries.
- Countries for which reports of resident commercial banks are the source of FDI data exclude in-kind foreign investment.
- Data referring to FDI stocks are cumulated inflows, but the conversion into US dollars is practised in different ways: besides the method recommended by the IMF (end-of-period exchange rate), a cumulating of yearly inflows in US dollars (converted with the prevailing market exchange rate) is widely practised. Contrary to the first method, the second one results always in an increase of stocks. Thus, international comparison of stocks between such countries is only of limited sense.
- Non-equity forms of direct investment are not included in the direct investment account. However, these statistics are reported in the service account (a part of a current account of BOP) under 'royalties and licence fees'.
- Discrepancies may also arise from errors in data reported to statistical agencies (by banks or enterprises) and from systematic overestimation of FDI inflows by some countries.
- Not all countries provide a detailed geographical breakdown. The methodology for compiling FDI data in geographical and sectoral breakdown is not standardised internationally; comparisons should be made with caution.

This long list of shortcomings may falsely suggest that FDI data are unreliable and that we know almost nothing about the phenomenon. This is not true for

[8] Detailed descriptions of national methodologies, compilation practices and data sources are published yearly by the IMF in BOP Statistics Yearbook Part 3. Hunya/Stankovsky (1997) compares the quality of FDI data for Central and Eastern European countries.

several reasons. First, FDI data coming from the biggest investor countries are characterised by a reasonably good quality. Second, even if international comparisons are somehow flawed, time series analyses for a given country give a right picture of the FDI development. Last but not least, the problems with FDI data are not bigger than with entirely all economic variables, starting with so widely accepted ones as GDP or international trade flows. The list above is only to remind that caution when interpreting statistical data is always a necessary virtue.

2.4 Main characteristics of FDI in the global economy

Global direct investment expanded rapidly in the second half of the 1980s with average annual growth rates of about 24 per cent (Table 2.1 and Figure 2.1).[9] It was twice as high as the growth rate of world output at factor costs (12.1 per cent) and almost twice the growth rate of world exports of goods (14.6 per cent). In the first half of the 1990s the growth of world-wide FDI inflows continued by 20.1 per cent yearly. Even the Asian financial crisis could not brake the upwards trend: in 1997 world-wide FDI inflows increased by 19 per cent. In the same time FDI stocks grew by 10 per cent per annum, exceeding the dynamics of world output and exports.

Table 2.1:
Selected Indicators of FDI and International Production, 1981-1997

	Value at current prices (Billion USD)	Average growth rate (in %)			
	1997	1981-85	1986-90	1991-95	1997
FDI inflows	400	n.a.	23.6	20.1	18.6
FDI outflows	424	0.8	27.1	15.1	27.1
FDI inward stock	3456	n.a.	18.2	9.7	12.7
FDI outward stock	3541	5.4	21.0	10.3	13.7
Cross-border M&As	236	n.a.	21.0	30.2	45.2
Sales of foreign affiliates	9500	1.3	16.3	13.4	7.3
Gross product of foreign affiliates	2100	n.a.	16.6	6.2	7.7
Total assets of foreign affiliates	12606	n.a.	18.3	24.4	13.0
Memorandum:					
GDP at factor cost	30551	2.1	12.1	5.5	6.0
Gross fixed capital formation	5393	0.7	12.5	2.6	5.0
Royalties and fees receipts	61	-0.7	21.9	12.4	15.0
Exports of goods and non-factor services	6432	-0.1	14.6	8.9	3.0

Source: UNCTAD (1998), Table I.1, UNCTAD (1995), Table I.1, n.a. – data not available

[9] For global FDI, a development in waves could be registered. After a long boom from the late 1950s until 1967, followed by a relative stagnation in the 1970s, a new upsurge of 1985-1992 took place (Graham, 1996).

By 1997, international production of MNCs - now some 53,000 parent firms and some 450,000 foreign affiliates - dominates international commercial transactions. Global sales of foreign affiliates of multinational firms were higher than world-wide exports of goods and (non-factor) services (USD9.5 trillion against 6.4 trillion USD). UNCTAD (1998) estimates for the global economy that foreign affiliate exports are one-third of world exports. In case of the United States, arm's length transactions in international trade are as little as one-fifth of all trade bills. It means, that 80 per cent of exports by American firms are actually earned from goods and services produced by their foreign affiliates or sold to them.

Figure 2.1:
The Degree of Internalisation through FDI 1980-96 (Percentage of GDP)

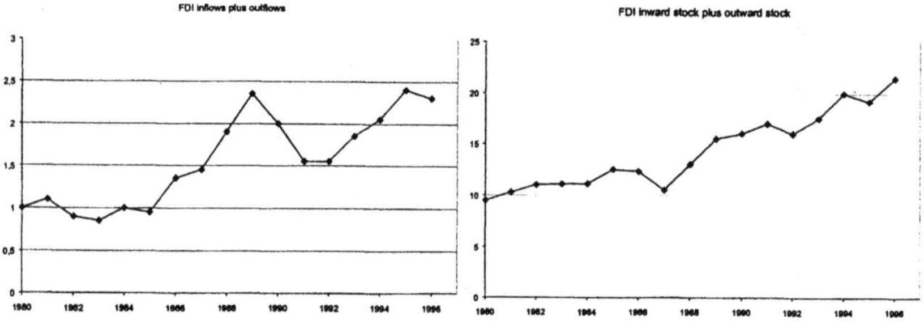

Source: UNCTAD (1998), Figure I.7

Despite impressive FDI dynamics, the vast majority of production in today's world is still undertaken by national producers within their own border. GDP attributed to foreign affiliates accounts for only 7 per cent of global GDP, and the share stayed quite stable over the 1990s.[10] However, the real importance of MNC for the world production is better measured by share of the total output of all MNCs – parent firms and affiliates in host countries – in the world's output. According to estimates by Lipsey *et al.* (1995), MNCs accounted for about 22% of world output during the 80s with a growing tendency in the last years.

The regional pattern of FDI

FDI developments vary considerably across and within regions. Most FDI stocks originate from and are concentrated in developed countries (Table 2.2). In 1997 this group accounted for 90 per cent of global outward FDI stock and about two-thirds of the global inward FDI stock. The stocks are accumulated

[10] One explanation of this seeming discrepancy between FDI flows and production stocks may be the substantial time lag between investment and production.

heavily among the members of the Triad (the United States, Japan and the European Union), with the European Union having the largest share with 35 and 45 per cent of inward and outward FDI stocks, respectively. Over the 1990s, the share of developed countries in global FDI inflows was around 60 per cent, and the share in global outflows still higher with about 85 per cent (Table 2.3). Hence, global FDI is characterised by a 'two-way foreign investment', meaning that a great deal of direct investment occurs between pairs of developed countries.

Table 2.2:
Regional Distribution of Inward and Outward FDI Stock , 1985, 1990, 1995 and 1997

	Inward FDI stock				Outward FDI stock			
Region/Country	1985	1990	1995	1997	1985	1990	1995	1997
Developed countries	**72.3**	**79.3**	**70.6**	**68.0**	**95.7**	**95.6**	**91.5**	**90.2**
Western Europe	33.6	44.1	39.1	36.9	44.4	50.8	51.1	50.4
European Union	31.2	41.5	36.3	34.6	40.6	46.3	45.1	45.1
Other Western Europe	2.3	2.7	2.8	2.3	3.8	4.5	5.9	5.3
United States	24.4	22.7	20.5	20.9	36.4	25.5	25.6	25.6
Japan	0.6	0.6	1.2	1.0	6.4	11.8	8.5	8.0
Developing Countries	**27.7**	**20.6**	**28.1**	**30.2**	**4.3**	**4.4**	**8.4**	**9.7**
Africa	3.1	2.2	2.1	1.9	0.9	0.7	0.5	0.5
Latin America and the Caribbean	10.1	7.1	10.2	10.9	1.1	0.7	0.9	1.0
Developing Europe	0.1	0.1	0.1	0.1	-	-	-	-
Asia	14.3	11.1	15.6	17.2	2.3	2.9	6.9	8.2
West Asia	5.7	2.8	2.1	1.7	0.3	0.4	0.3	0.3
Central Asia	-	-	0.1	0.2	-	-	-	-
South, East and South-East Asia	8.6	8.3	13.4	15.3	2.0	2.6	6.4	7.9
The Pacific	0.2	0.1	0.1	0.1	-	-	-	-
Central and Eastern Europe	**-**	**0.1**	**1.3**	**1.8**	**-**	**-**	**0.1**	**0.2**
World	**100**	**100**	**100**	**100**	**100**	**100**	**100**	**100**

Source: UNCTAD (1998), table I.3.

Since 1986, there is some evidence that the position of developing countries both in their traditional role as host countries as well as home countries gains in importance. The share of FDI flows attracted by developing countries increased from 17 per cent in the 1980s to almost 39 per cent in 1996. In some developing countries, above all in China and some other newly industrialised countries in Southeast Asia, FDI flows yearly grew more than fourfold.[11] A qualitatively new phenomenon is the doubling of the position of developing countries in global outward FDI stock over the 1985-1997 period. Although the top MNCs from developing countries cannot be found on the top of the world's biggest

[11] This upsurge is mostly evaluated as being temporary. The rapid emergence of China as a host country, and FDI due to privatisation programmes in many developing countries are of unique nature.

multinationals, the firms like Daewoo Corporation and Samsung Electronics are well-known as foreign investors in the developed countries.

Table 2.3:
Regional Distribution of FDI Inflows and Outflows, 1985-1997

Region/Country	Inflows				Outflows			
	1985-90 (Annual Average)	1995	1996	1997	1985-90 (Annual Average)	1995	1996	1997
Developed countries	**82.2**	**63.9**	**57.9**	**58.2**	**93.2**	**86.9**	**85.1**	**84.8**
Western Europe	39.2	37.1	29.6	28.7	55.7	49.4	50.6	46.2
European Union	37.1	35.3	27.4	27.0	51.6	45.2	45.3	42.4
Other Western Europe	2.1	1.8	2.2	1.7	4.1	4.3	5.3	3.7
United States	34.3	17.7	22.6	22.7	13.9	26.1	22.5	27.0
Japan	-	-	0.1	0.8	17.9	6.4	7.0	6.1
Developing Countries	**17.4**	**31.9**	**38.5**	**37.2**	**6.8**	**12.9**	**14.8**	**14.4**
Africa	2.0	1.6	1.4	1.2	0.7	0.2	0.1	0.3
Latin America and the Caribbean	5.7	9.6	13.0	14.0	0.9	0.7	0.7	2.1
Developing Europe	-	0.1	0.3	0.2	-	-	-	0.1
Asia	9.5	20.3	23.7	21.7	5.2	12.1	14.0	12 0
West Asia	0.8	-0.2	0.1	0.5	0.5	0.2	-0.3	0.1
Central Asia	-	0.5	0.6	0.7	-	-	-	-
South, East and South-East Asia	8.7	20.1	23.0	20.6	4.7	11.9	14.2	11.8
The Pacific	0.1	0.2	0.1	0.1	-	-	-	-
Central and Eastern Europe	**0.3**	**4.3**	**3.7**	**4.6**	-	**0.1**	**0.2**	**0.8**
World	**100**	**100**	**100**	**100**	**100**	**100**	**100**	**100**

Source: UNCTAD (1998), Table I.8; UNCTAD (1997), Annex Tables B1-B2; own calculations

The sectoral pattern of FDI

Multinational firms conducting FDI are concentrated in a relatively small set of sectors. Within the primary sector, investment in the area of energy and mining dominates, especially in petroleum exploration and refining. In the manufacturing sector, MNCs favour (see Dunning, 1992):

- the most technologically advanced, research-intensive and capital-intensive industries (e.g. computers, chemicals and pharmaceuticals);
- industries supplying products with an above average income elasticity of demand and a high degree of product differentiation (e.g. electronics and electrical equipment, automotive);
- industries where there are substantial economies of scale or scope to be gained from plant specialisation and from a geographical diversification of activities like food and beverages.[12]

[12] The list of empirical studies confirming this generalisation includes Caves (1996), Morck/Yeung (1992) and Brainard (1993a, 1993b).

In the service sector, accounting for more than 40 per cent of FDI outward stocks of major home countries (the United States, Japan, the United Kingdom, Germany, France, Canada, Italy), the overwhelming share of MNCs activities is concentrated in trade, telecommunications, financial services and construction.

Vertical and horizontal FDI

A firm's expansion in production facilities abroad can take the form of horizontal extension or vertical integration. *Horizontal FDI* means that foreign affiliates manufacture the same products or services as their parent firms. This type of foreign investment concerns hotel, restaurants and transportation sectors, as well as banking, insurance, advertising and management consulting. It is also typical for FDI in the pharmaceutical industry, electronics, computers and scientific instruments.

Vertical FDI means that some stages of firm's activities are located in foreign branches. Multinationals can be integrated *backward, i.e.* into the production of raw materials and intermediate products, and *forward, i.e.* into the establishment of own sales agencies, both wholesaling and retailing.

There is no strict empirical evidence which type of foreign production dominates at the global level. Caves (1996) interprets the indirect empirical evidence as supporting the prevalence of horizontal foreign investment. The importance of international merger and acquisitions (M&As), the major driver of FDI flows for developed countries, can constitute another argument for the thesis. Valued at USD236 billion, M&As represented nearly 60 per cent of global FDI inflows in 1997, increasing for the 7th year in turn. Since the liberalisation of financial services after the WTO's agreement in 1997 and deregulation (e.g. in telecommunications), MNCs have followed a strategy aiming at divesting non-core activities and strengthening competitive advantages through acquisitions in core fields. However, most MNCs are integrated both vertically, trading intermediate goods, and horizontally, producing slightly differentiated final products in various locations (UNCTAD, 1995).

2.5 FDI in Central and Eastern Europe

The majority of the countries in Central and Eastern Europe opened up to inward FDI only after the initiation of economic transformation in the early 1990s. However, at the early stage of transition, FDI inflows into most of these countries were legally restricted to minority-owned joint ventures with local companies and to limited participation (minority shares) in privatisation of state enterprises.[13] Some countries have applied sectoral restrictions or barriers to

[13] For a comprehensive survey of FDI in Eastern Europe in the early 1990s, see Dunning/ Rojec (1993).

foreign access (most commonly in the area of defence, public order and infrastructure, financial institutions, energy). Often, government approval in the form of a permit was necessary. On the other hand, many CEE countries tried to encourage FDI in certain priority sectors or regions through various incentives: tax allowances up to tax holidays, exemptions from certain import duties, foundation of free economic zones etc. In course of transition, the disappointing experience with many short-term, profit-seeking ventures that have been of little lasting benefit to the country led to a wider opening to foreign privatisation, reduction or elimination of incentives, adoption of bilateral investment treaties for the protection of FDI and revision of intellectual property framework.[14]

Despite this turnaround and the tendency to grow, the share of the region in global FDI inflows is still low with 4.6 per cent in 1997 (the region's share in FDI outflows is less than 1 per cent) (Table 2.3). The region's share in the world-wide inward FDI stock is low with 1.8 per cent, and it stagnated in the last years.[15] This is not only the result of fairly recently opening of FDI, but also of the problems related to the transition process and their perception by the MNCs.[16]

The distribution of FDI inflows has been determined by the pace of privatisation, especially of large, capital intensive public utilities such as telecommunications and electric power, and by the openness of that privatisation to foreign investors. Until 1995, Hungary was the primary recipient of FDI in the region, Poland and the Czech Republic came in a distant second and third (Table 2.4). At the end of 1995, Hungary accounted to one-third of the FDI inward stock of the region. High and stable growth, acceleration of privatisation and the reestablishment of international creditworthiness helped Poland become the leading recipient in the 1996-1998 period.[17] Together, Poland, Hungary and the Czech Republic are host to nearly 70 per cent of FDI stocks in the region. Recently, FDI unconnected to privatisation is growing in response to the perspective of the EU accession.[18]

---

[14] See OECD (1995) for more about the experience of transition countries with tax incentives for FDI.

[15] The region's inward FDI stock in 1997 was lower than that of Indonesia, Malaysia or Singapur taken separately.

[16] Risk and search costs associated with starting bussiness in an unfamiliar enviroment can explain why 'wait and watch'-approach dominated on the side of MNCs in the early transition phase. For those who engaged, usually small projects were typical. For theoretical arguments in favour of this investment pattern, see Thimann/Thum (1998) or Rauch/Watson (1999).

[17] The fact that privatisation in Hungary and the Czech Republic is quite advanced was important as well.

[18] Lansbury *et al.* (1996) found a significant effect of privatisation programmes, labour costs and research intensity, and existing trade links on the scope of FDI inflows to the CEE. Further empirical studies on the determinants of the FDI inflows into CEECs include

Relating the scope of the FDI inflows to the size of the host country shows that small transition countries like Estonia, Hungary and Latvia have attracted over-proportionally much FDI. However, even for the leaders the scope of FDI inflows was low as compared with some other host countries which are considered to be instructive examples of the positive FDI impact on domestic growth (e.g. Ireland, Spain and Mexico).[19]

Table 2.4:
FDI inflows into Central and Eastern Europe (mn USD), 1989-1998

Country	1990	1991	1992	1993	1994	1995	1996	1997	1998	Stock 1998 (%)	Flows in % GFCF[b]	Flows in % GDP[c]
Bulgaria	-	56	42	55	105	90	109	497	270	1.5	3.2	1.6
CR[a]	207	600	1103	654	878	2568	1428	1301	1400	9.8	11.2	2.9
Estonia	-	-	82	162	215	202	138	130	565	1.9	32.8	6.4
Hungary		1462	1479	2350	1144	4519	1982	2085	1150	22.2	29.5	5.0
Latvia	-	-	29	45	214	180	292	418	200	1.7	-	4.6
Lithuania	-	-	10	30	31	73	152	355	950	2.0	-	2.7
Poland	89	291	678	1715	1875	3659	4498	5000	7500	32.0	10.0	2.8
Romania	-	40	77	94	341	419	265	1224	884	4.5	3.9	1.4
Russia	-	-	700	700	637	2017	1800	6241	1100	16.1	0.9	0.6
Slovakia	-	-	-	199	203	183	150	50	350	1.4	6.2	1.1
Slovenia	-	-	111	113	128	176	186	321	301	1.6	6.6	1.1
Ukraine	-	-	200	200	100	400	521	623	700	3.2	-	1.4
CEE	367	2448	4444	6287	5882	14317	13074	19114	16500	100	11.1	-
Ireland	192[d]	1062	1438	1113	934	2317	1455	4152	n.a.		18.0	19.2
Greece	711	1135	1144	977	981	1053	1058	1500	n.a.		5.0	17.4
Portugal	1041	2448	1873	1534	1270	685	708	1713	n.a.		5.0	6.2
Spain	6570[d]	12493	13276	8144	9359	6118	6396	5556	n.a.		9.8	9.8
Mexico	2618[d]	4762	4393	4389	10972	9526	8169	12101	n.a.		10.3	13.3

Source: UNCTAD (1997, 1998); for 1998 – BCE (1999); [a] – 1989-1992 Czechoslovakia (former), [b]- GFCF (gross fixed capital formation), average over 1991-96, [c] – average over 1992-1998 (for transition countries) and average from 1980, 1985, 1990, 1995 values (for memorandum countries), [d]- average over 1985-90.

Measured against the domestic gross fixed capital formation, FDI inflows into Estonia, Hungary (30 per cent) and the Czech Republic (10 per cent) are high and even higher than in Ireland or Spain. But, only FDI inflows less acquisition outlays are part of gross fixed capital formation: green-field investment, restructuring investment following acquisition, increase of capital stock. Taking

Wang/Swain (1995), Altomonte (1997, 1998), Brunetti *et al.* (1997) and Brenton *et al.* (1998).

[19] Although there is no a simple linear relationship between the scope of FDI inflows and subsequent economic growth, in the context of transition low FDI usually bring low privatisation revenues for the state budget. Since privatisation revenues could play an important role in temporary financing of restructuring in a transition economy, their low availability restricts these programmes or necessitates relying on domestic and foreign credits or tougher taxation. Through these channels, low FDI inflows might reduce the potential for growth in the host transition country.

into account that FDI through foreign acquisition, which dominated in these countries, do not directly contribute to gross investment, the direct impact of FDI is much smaller. Hunya (1998) has estimated that in 1993-1996 the direct contribution of FDI to gross fixed capital formation amounted to 10-16 per cent in Hungary, 2-3 per cent in the Czech Republic and Slovenia, and 1 per cent in Slovakia. These very low numbers show that, except for Hungary, FDI almost negligibly enhance customarily low indigenous savings in most of the transition countries.

The large share of FDI has been in manufacturing: it accounted for around 40 per cent of the FDI stock in Hungary and in the Czech Republic and around 60 per cent in Poland (see Table 2.5). Food and consumer goods, electronics, motor vehicles, and telecommunications have been the most popular industries for foreign investment. The common branch with above-average foreign penetration is the manufacturing of motor vehicles. The new or rapidly modernising car industry was attracted by unsatisfied domestic demand and favourable conditions for low-cost production. The tobacco industry is almost totally foreign owned in the Czech Republic, Hungary, Slovenia and Poland. FDI inflows into wholesale and retail trade, services (in particular financial and business services) and infra-structure (transport, utilities and telecommunications) are high and still growing.

Three different types of foreign investors are engaged in transition countries. The first group consists of large multinational companies, mainly from the OECD countries. The second one are medium-size companies form nearby countries, predominantly Germany and Austria. A separate category constitute one-man ventures, founded by individuals with personal ties to the host country, mainly native eastern Europeans. The last category dominated, as measured both by the number of enterprises with foreign capital and the amount of capital engaged, in the early stage of transition (Hunya, 1996). In the most advanced economies in Central Europe, multinationals in the course of time became the most important foreign investors as measured by their share in foreign capital stock and output, although the vast majority of foreign investors are still small and medium companies not belonging to any of the multinationals.[20]

The ownership structure in foreign affiliates changed from the predominance of minority owned firms to those majority or wholly foreign owned. In Hungary, for example, in 1990 only 4 per cent of all foreign enterprises are wholly foreign-owned. The paid-in capital of these firms amounted to only 2 per cent of

[20] If small and medium investors can be defined as those who engaged less than 1 million US$, then their share in Poland is now 12 per cent of all foreign capital engaged, in contrast to their share of 94 per cent of the number of firms with foreign capital (GUS, 1998a). In 1996, about one quarter of Polish firms with foreign capital were affiliates of a MNC (Zagozdzinska, 1998).

all foreign capital invested in the country, which shows that these were smaller than average ventures. The share of wholly owned foreign firms increased rapidly and reached above 40 per cent in 1996 independently of the indicator used (HCSO, 1997). In Poland, about 50 per cent of all firms with foreign capital in 1997 were wholly foreign-owned. Above 50 per cent of all FDI inflows has been invested in those firms (GUS, 1998a).

Table 2.5:
Sectoral and Industrial Distribution of Inward FDI Stock in Selected Transition Countries, 1997 (in %)

Sector/Industry	CR	Hungary	Poland	Romania	Russia	Slovenia[a]
Primary sector		**2**	**2**	**6**	**16**	
Secondary sector	**38**	**39**	**62**	**53**	**23**	**30**
Food, beverages & tobacco	16[b)]	9	21	14	9	2
Textiles, leather & clothing		2	3[c)]	4[c)]		
Wood, paper, publishing & printing		3	5	2	4	7
Chemicals, chemical products & coke & petroleum products	8	8	6	5	3	6
Non-metallic mineral products (cement & building materials)		3	6	6		2
Basic metals & metal products		2	1	1	3	
Machinery & equipment		12[d)]		14	4[e)]	5
Electrical machinery & apparatus	1			3		
Automotive	13		14	3		
Unspecified secondary		0	3			7
Tertiary sector	**45**	**59**	**36**	**35**	**51**	**55**
Construction	1	4	3	1		
Wholesale trade & distributive trade	9	12	8	16	11	11
Finance (& banking & insurance)	9	9	18	5	32	17
Unspecified	**17**			**6**	**10**	**15**

Source: UNCTAD (1998), table IX.2, for Poland – PAIZ (1999). [a]- End 1996; [b] - Includes „consumer goods“; [c] - Includes other light industries; [d] - Includes electrical machinery & automotive industries; [e] - Includes basic metals & metal products.

In the early transition period, the short-term and risk-free maximisation of profits, mostly in trade projects, played a weighty role for investments in Eastern Europe. Later on, various empirical studies and surveys of FDI investors have shown that their main motive for investing in the most advanced transition countries is widening of the market for products.[21] Firms are either expanding into new markets or preparing the ground for future expansion through establishing of sales agencies. Cheap labour and the existing scope for lowering

[21] An early survey of (private) western European investors operating in Eastern Europe conducted on commission of EBRD is Genco *et al* (1993). A comprehensive discussion of motives for FDI in CEE as identified by empirical literature is provided by Schmidt (1995).

production costs are important, but usually of relatively minor significance. Worthy to note, financial and tax incentives are regarded by investors as subordinate factor to attract inward FDI (UNCTAD, 1998).

2.6 Conclusions

Foreign direct investment is the major channel through which international production by multinational companies (MNCs) expands. Unlike with portfolio investment, FDI is aimed at acquiring income abroad but under managerial control of the investing foreign company. OECD countries are the biggest source of MNCs and the largest destination of FDI. The acceleration of FDI which started in the second half of the 1980s led to the emergence of developing countries, especially in South-East Asia, China and, more recently, Mexico as important host countries.

The sectoral pattern of FDI differs for projects in developed and developing countries. In the first group of countries, FDI is concentrated in the most technologically advanced, research-intensive and capital-intensive industries (e.g. computers, chemicals and pharmaceuticals, machinery), as well as in banking and financial services. In developing countries, FDI is directed into the primary extraction and agricultural industries (food, beverages and tobacco).

FDI inflows into transition countries in Central and Eastern Europe rose from negligible levels in the first years of the transition to 16.5 billion USD in 1998. The region has now the share of about 4.6 per cent in global FDI inflows. Still, measured against the size of the economy and investment, inward FDI has been moderate for most of the transition countries, with the exception of Hungary and Estonia. The uneven distribution of FDI among the CEECs suggests that only a few of them may count on a substantial contribution of foreign capital to economic growth and restructuring. Other countries will have to make progress in macroeconomic stabilisation, privatisation and institutions building before they will be able to attract significant amounts of FDI.

Since the direct positive impact of FDI is not expected to be considerable in most of the transition countries, it is of major importance how the emergence of foreign firms impacts the behaviour of the locally-owned enterprises. If FDI did enforce market behavior of the enterprises, induces restructuring process by implementing advanced technology and know-how to companies dominated by obsolete equipment and inefficient management, then the positive indirect effect on the host economy could go far behind the direct one. Whether FDI is associated with such productivity spillovers and positive linkages to local firms is the central question that will be investigated in the following chapters.

Chapter 3:
FDI as a mode of international technology transfer

3.1 Introduction

In the past two decades, there has been a general movement in the attitudes of national governments towards inflows of FDI. Many countries turn to FDI because local savings are simply too low to finance increased investment needs. However, what makes FDI more attractive than other sorts of capital inflows, like portfolio investment or foreign aid, results from the fact that FDI serves as a mode of transfer for capital, technology, research, management etc. within the network of a multinational company.

As foreign affiliates of MNCs in less developed countries posses more efficient technology than local firms, it explains a potentially positive impact of FDI on the productivity of domestic industry as a whole and on industrial growth in the host country.[22] Indeed, there is strong empirical evidence referring to less developed countries that FDI inflows increase total capital accumulation and growth rates of the host economy.[23]

In the present chapter, we interpret and describe FDI as a mode of international technology transfer in both its manifestations mentioned above. In doing so, we adopt the viewpoint of FDI as the activity of (fully or partly) foreign-owned enterprises within the host country. In consequence, we widely neglect another important aspect of FDI, namely a potential inflow of foreign capital. We do that for two reasons. First, we want to concentrate on effects which are special for FDI, and that do not occur when pure international capital transfer, *i.e.* portfolio investment, takes place. Second, for international capital flows an ample economic literature already exists. [24]

In Section 3.2, the definition and characteristics of technology as well as technology transfer between firms are discussed in more detail. Section 3.3

---

[22] Usually, foreign firms need some time for the new technology to be implemented, if necessary, adjusted to local conditions of factors' supply and local demand conditions. Only after that time one can reasonably assume a higher productivity of their technology.

[23] There is a vast empirical literature testing macroeconomic impact of foreign capital inflows on productivity growth in the recipient countries within a growth accounting framework (for a well-written survey, see De Mello, 1999). According to these studies, the FDI impact is positive. However, its scope depends on openness, human capital endowment and technological level of the host country.

[24] Plum (1995) reviews static effects of international capital transfers in foreign trade and macroeconomic models. See Zukowska-Gagelmann (1997) for a summary of theoretical models analysing FDI impact in less developed countries under different trade regimes. IMF (1991) and Gács *et al.* (1999) are examples of empirical studies assessing macroeconomic consequences of FDI inflows.

summarises empirical evidence on the role that multinational companies play in technology creation and its world-wide dispersion. Section 3.4 deals with the intentional transfer of MNC technology to its foreign affiliate. We argue that FDI represents an international transfer of a technological ownership asset possessing by a parent firm to production facilities controlled abroad in order to internalise gains from its use. Section 3.5 argues that FDI has the potential to trigger technological spillovers, *i.e.* unintended technological transfer from foreign affiliates to local firms In Section 3.6, we summarise conclusions that can be derived from the microeconomic theory of technology transfer through FDI.

3.2 The nature of technology and technology transfer

According to a conventional definition, 'technology' is a form of industrial knowledge, possessed by an individual firm, industry or country, which refers to the way of production of goods and services from inputs (Patel/Pavitt, 1995). This knowledge comprises ideas and information at three different levels: (i) about materials and compounds; (ii) about ways of arranging or using them, and (iii) about ways of designing new goods and services.

The above-given definition is wide enough to comprise two types of technological knowledge: codifiable and non-codifiable technology.

Codifiable technology consists of knowledge which can be identified, collated and transmitted between different users, either in form of manuals or in form of physical tangible assets. Manuals include the so-called 'tangible knowledge' referring to products or to production processes. It consists of blueprints for products and descriptions of manufacturing techniques. Further, manuals may comprise description of intermediate inputs and services for production. Some manuals take the specific form of a patented process, design or a trademark. Tangible assets have the form of machinery and physical equipment for production.

Non-codifiable technology consists primarily of intangible (or tacit) knowledge such as product and process design, management or marketing techniques shared by the employees. This kind of knowledge is being accumulated through previous experience in the development of products and processes, experience in production activities, and through on-the-job training. Since it is mainly embodied in persons and/or institutions, it cannot be easily sold or rented.

As economic good, technology, independently of the type, possesses mixed features: it is, to some degree, a public good, and to some degree a private one (Romer, 1990). Like all public goods, it is non-rival in the sense that many firms may use the same technology, even simultaneously. Unlike pure public goods, firms can be excluded from the access to new pieces of technology developed by others. This constitutes an incentive for private innovators to engage in research and development. Since the improvement of technology is costly, an innovator must be given a guarantee of an (at least temporary) exclusive use of the fruits of his innovation effort. With a legal system offering effective protection of intellectual property rights, a relatively high level of excludability of technological innovation may be achieved. Consequently, the benefits from technological improvements may be largely reaped by the innovators. However, the degree of excludability depends not only on legal institutions, but on the nature of this piece of new knowledge itself. Romer (1990) gives examples of innovations with a high degree of excludability due to the nature of product (independent of the property rights protection) and innovations characterised by low degree of excludability even with strong protection of intellectual property rights.

At any point in time, an individual firm or a community is characterised by a certain state of industrial knowledge. Through improvements of the products and production processes, of materials and intermediate inputs used in the production processes (codifiable technology), as well as through changes in management methods, e.g. in marketing know-how (non-codifiable technology), technological progress occurs (Stoneman, 1995).

Own research and development (R&D)[25] or engaging in R&D joint ventures with other innovating institutions is one source of technological change for a firm. Additionally, every firm may acquire industrial knowledge from outside, *e.g.* universities, research agencies, other firms or individuals. Within the group of other firms, knowledge may either stem from direct competitors, or from firms producing completely different products, but with relevant technologies.

A firm may get assess to codifiable technology through market transactions. New capital goods and intermediates can be purchased at home or imported. Technical information such as designs, descriptions, plans can be acquired in form of a patent or a license. Another possibility of learning about a new piece of a codifiable technology is through scientific exchange and trade journals. This does not rely on any commercial transactions.

Reverse engineering of products successfully marketed by rivals is a popular form of acquiring codifiable technology. In the opinion of more than 600 industrial R&D directors in large US firms, reverse engineering and independent R&D are far more important as means of learning about competitors' product innovations than licensing or patent disclosures (Nelson, 1990).

---

[25] 'Research' activities comprise the developing, testing and refining scientific laws and models, whereas 'development' is designing, building and testing prototypes and pilot plants. On average, business firms spend at least 3 times more on development than on research (Patel/Pavitt, 1995).

Since non-codifiable knowledge is person-embodied, the mobility of employees from innovating firms is a necessary condition for its transfer. In case of licensing, the personnel of the licensor frequently helps install and debug the technology or train the licensee's operators. These services are regulated on the basis of market transactions between firms engaged. Another channel for person-embodied knowledge transfer between firms is the hiring of persons, mainly researches and managers, previously employed by competitors. Through the adjustment of their technological knowledge to the purposes and environment of the other firm, the process of further differentiation and technological improvement takes place. It creates proprietary assets which can be further subject to transfer along different channels.

3.3 The dominant position of MNCs in technology creation and transfer

This section examines available data on technology creation and transfer, and shows that both of them are dominated by multinational firms.

Technology creation

In today's world economy, a great bulk of research and development (R&D) of technology, technological capabilities and skills is concentrated in MNCs. According to estimates by Dunning (1992), about 75 to 80 per cent of all world (civilian) expenditures for R&D are spent within the system of MNCs.[26] This magnitude is confirmed by UNCTAD (1997) which estimates from US and German data that some 80 percent of global payments of fees and royalties for technology take place between parent firms and their foreign affiliates. If patents are considered to be an alternative measure for research activities, the 700 largest industrial firms (most of which are MNCs) account for a half of the world's commercial inventions (Cantwell, 1991). In the United States, the global leader in R&D, about 90 percent of all private R&D expenditures are undertaken by 400 largest corporations, most of which are MNCs (Scherer, 1991).[27]

[26] The two most common measures of technological activity are R&D expenditure and the share of the labour force engaged in R&D activities. There are numerous limitations of such R&D statistics: they measure input and not output of innovation processes, they capture only very imperfectly the development of technology in small firms, they underestimate the creation of non-codified technology (mostly: skills and capabilities of management and employees). Statistics about patenting activities measure technological activities from the output side. However, like R&D, they do not measure satisfactorily advances in non-codified technology and intangible knowledge.

[27] According to the long accepted so-called 'Schumpeterian hypothesis', enterprises with a larger market power are better endowed to generate innovative activities. While R&D expenditures as a measure of innovative activities confirm this hypothesis, studies of patent activity do not support this view (see Audretsch, 1994).

Within the system of a multinational company, a great bulk of innovative activities is usually performed in the home country. According to patent data, on average, only 11 percent of all patents applicated over the period 1985-90 by 569 large MNCs were registered outside their home country (Patel/Pavitt, 1995).

As a consequence of the concentration of R&D in industrial countries which are the home countries of MNCs, almost all world R&D activity takes places in OECD economies. According to US patenting data on private R&D in OECD countries, more than 95 per cent of the world's technological activities are concentrated in 11 countries (Belgium, Canada; France, Germany, Italy, Japan, Netherlands, Sweden, Switzerland, UK and USA). Seven out of these countries, namely the USA, the UK, Germany, France, Japan, Italy and Canada, accounted for 92 percent of world R&D-capital stock in 1991 (Coe *et al.*, 1997).

Technology transfer

Since most countries in the world invest relatively little in R&D activities, they must search abroad for access to new technologies. Technological innovations may be (formally) transferred between firms in different countries through the following channels:

- Sale of licenses and patents, as well as trade with other intellectual property rights and technical know-how,
- Sale of machinery and equipment, including transport equipment, or supply of turn-key plants,
- FDI by establishing foreign subsidiaries or joint ventures with local partners.

It is not easy to distinguish the most important channel of intra-firm technology transfer because there are no comprehensive and actual data available, and because the technology content of different transactions is difficult to compare. As being measured by royalties for the use of patents and licences fees, international trade in technology has intensified dramatically during the 1980s and 1990s. As compared to 1983, global payments of fees and royalties for technology have increased 5 times till 1997 and reached 61 billion USD (UNCTAD, 1998). Global export of intermediate and capital goods with embodied technology doubled every 10 years and amounted to 2016 billion USD in 1996.[28] The FDI inflows grew over the same period with an average growth rate of 20 per cent and reached the value of 400 billion USD in 1997.

The regional pattern of technology transactions is similar to the pattern of foreign investment – about 70 per cent of total FDI stock is in industrial countries and over ¾ of technology transactions are within industrial countries. Technology trade is concentrated among a few developed countries – the USA,

[28] The numbers refer to the export of machinery and transport equipment (Section 7 according to the Standard International Trade Classification) and are taken from UN (1997).

Germany, France, the UK and the Netherlands. The USA account for 56 per cent of global receipts – her role as a technological leader has strengthened during the last two decades.

Technology flows between parent companies and their foreign affiliates dominate global technology trade. Royalties (patents and licence fees) and fee receipts for technology and technical services take place largely on an intra-firm basis, i.e. within the multinational company. According to data for USA and Germany - the two global leaders in technology creation – in 1995 some 60 per cent of these payments are on intra-firm basis.

Technology payments between associated firms are most pronounced in research-intensive industries, in which multinational firms are important. The predominant way how multinational companies exploit their technological inventions, particularly in research-intensive industries, is FDI. This explains the fact that technology transactions take place largely between associated firms linked by equity holdings. These payments are usually to cover parent expenditures for R&D, organisation, administration and provision of business services.[29]

Most affiliates, especially in developing countries, are involved only in production operations. They acquire technology from their parents in the form of patents and licences as well as by importing machinery, intermediate products as well as services. If R&D is conducted in local affiliates, its main function is to adjust products or production processes to local conditions. Research-intensive industries - often called 'high technology industries' (electrical and electronics, office machinery including computers, measuring and controlling instruments, pharmaceutical and aerospace) - are involved in a significant share of international technology transactions. But, technology trade is also important in traditional industries dominated by multinational firms, like the food, drink, tobacco industries and rubber products industries.

Technology licensing between independent firms is predominant in traditional industries, such as textiles and metal-working, or industries with very small firms, since such firms are more likely to buy and sell technology with unrelated firms. This is especially the case when the relevant piece of technology does not require adaptation to foreign conditions and is not research-intensive.

The scattered empirical evidence discussed in this section documents close relationship between FDI and technology flows between firms and countries. This gave rise to a thesis of a strong proprietary asset base of FDI. The existence

[29] However, payments between related firms may be biased upwards through considerations of profit distribution, exchange rate fluctuations and taxation law (transfer pricing).

of such assets as a precondition for direct investment is the core of theoretical treatment of FDI over the last 40 years.[30]

3.4 Intentional technology transfer along with FDI

The phenomenon of international production – its emergence and development as summarised by the stylised facts in Chapter 2 - has been intensively addressed by theoretical economists since the beginning of the 1970s. The complexity of the issue resulted in a multitude of partial contributions trying to explain many different aspects of FDI.[31]

Theories of international production have drawn on six separate branches of economic theory (Cantwell, 1991): the theories of international capital movements, international trade, location, industrial organisation, innovation and the firm. Whereas approaches characterised by the microeconomic perspective relied on the theory of the firm, those at the macro-economic level built on the economic theory of international capital flows and trade.

The dissatisfaction with the existing, only partial explanations of international production and the distinction between the theories of MNCs and of FDI led to a search for generalisation. Starting in the 1970s, Dunning (1973, 1992) proposed an eclectic approach which draws upon and integrates some existing strands of economic theory to explain why and under which modus an enterprise enters foreign markets. This approach combines the industrial organisation theory and the theory of the firm (Hymer, 1976; Kindleberger, 1969) with an internalisation theory (Buckley/Casson, 1976) which emphasises the role of transaction costs for the development strategy of the firm. The eclectic theory of international production is also called the OLI-paradigm since it argues with the existence of three types of advantages: **O**wnership, **L**ocation and **I**nternalisation, which a firm must possess to become a multinational.

Dunning (1992) states that a firm will engage in FDI if **four conditions** are satisfied:[32]

---

[30] The seminal theoretical paper is Hymer's doctoral thesis from 1959 which was first published in 1976.

[31] One strand analysed international production at the microeconomic level, addressing the questions 'why' and 'how' as well as 'where' and 'when' a firm will expand abroad. The second strand takes the mesoeconomic perspective and looks at the competitive interaction between firms in international industries. The third strand concentrates on the macroeconomic level and tries to explain the international distribution of FDI flows and its changes over time.

[32] The eclectic paradigm has evolved over the years, and the number of conditions changed from 3 to 4. More importantly, Dunning (1997) recognises that technological changes in the 1990s and the emergence of co-operative intra-firm agreements show that the eclectic framework needs to be modified. Especially, the role of innovation in sustaining and upgrading the competitive advantages of firms (and countries) should be better recognised.

1. The firm possess sustainable **ownership-specific advantages** over the competing firms in the markets it serves. These ownership advantages commonly take the form of the possession of intangible assets, which are exclusive or specific to the firm.[33] The following list contains some examples: technological capacity (property rights protected by patents over a product or technological process), organisational and human skills shared among employees of the firm like production management, marketing system, research and development capacity, exclusive or favoured access to inputs or product markets. Some of these advantages, like the ability to take advantage of international differences in factor prices or ability to diversify risk, arise as a result of the pre-existing multinationality, *i.e.* common governance of activities in many locations.
2. Assuming condition (1) is satisfied, it must be more efficient for the firm to retain control of O-advantages through hierarchies (**market internalisation advantages**) than through arm's length contracts like leasing or licensing them to the local firms. The efficiency gains arise because licensing leads to search and negotiating costs, costs of moral hazard and adverse selection, and costs of broken contracts.[34] On the other hand, internalisation allows a better protection of reputation and quality of products. Additionally, internalisation enables avoidance or exploitation of government interventions (protection, tax differences, tax incentives) and allows for practices like transfer pricing.[35]
3. Assuming condition (1) and (2) are satisfied, it must be more profitable for the firm to utilise these advantages in a foreign location than to serve foreign markets entirely by exports. **Location-specific variables** favour some foreign locations over the domestic one and over any others. This may result from uneven spatial distribution of resource endowments (inputs) and consumers (markets), transport and communication costs, cross-countries differences in economic, political and cultural systems.
4. Given conditions (1)-(3), FDI must be consistent with the long-term management strategy of the firm.

If the four conditions are not satisfied, FDI does not arise and foreign markets are served entirely by domestic production. Dunning assumes that the configuration of OLI advantages across countries, industries and enterprises is uneven. At any given moment of time, the more a country's enterprises - relative

---

This would give further support to the view of FDI as a way a international technology transfer.

[33] 'Intangible assets', 'firm-specific assets', 'proprietary assets' and 'monopolistic advantages' are used interchangeably in the literature.

[34] See Dunning (1992) for a list of seven categories of transaction costs which can be minimised or avoided through internalisation.

[35] See Markusen (1995) for a full discussion of arguments for superiority of foreign investment over licensing.

to those of another - possesses O advantages, the greater are their incentives to internalise them; the more attractive foreign locations, the more enterprises are likely to engage in FDI. Changing OLI configurations may lead to changes in the strategy of firms concerning the modes of economic integration, making exports or licensing more likely.

The eclectic paradigm can explain different types of FDI (Hennart, 1991). FDI through horizontal integration arises because of the public nature of technology or reputation as the proprietary asset of the firm.[36] FDI through vertical backward integration of downstream activities will be chosen when markets for raw materials and intermediate inputs are characterised by high transaction costs. FDI through vertical forward integration takes place when quality control of distribution services supplied by independent distributors is too costly in comparison to operating company-owned distribution facilities.

The eclectic paradigm of international production still dominates as the theory of the emergence and rise of MNC. It postulates the existence of competitive ownership advantages resulting from some kind of technological assets as prerequisite for FDI. FDI motivated by internalisation serves as a vehicle through which technology crosses boundaries and is adopted by foreign affiliates in the host countries. This way, multinationals directly contribute to international technology transfer. Therefore, FDI has the potential to be an important channel through which industries in less developed countries gain access to more efficient technologies, helping them improve productivity and upgrade their production structure.

In reality, the type of direct investment, the precise scope of investment and the type of technology transferred are crucial concerning the role of FDI as a source of technology for host countries. What are their determinants? Which country characteristics favour international technology transfer through FDI? We return to these questions in Chapter 4, summing up the evidence and experience with FDI.

3.5 Technology transfer through productivity spillovers

In the previous section, we concluded that FDI represents an act of intentional transfer of technology to the foreign affiliate. However, the role of MNC in this process goes further. Among other channels, technological spillovers on local firms in the host country attracted much interest in the literature and political practice. Spillovers are particularly important if the technologies used by foreign affiliates are not available in a country, or cannot be obtained through market

[36] On the public nature of technology and its consequences for the existence of spillovers, see Section 3.3.

transactions like licensing. Then, positive productivity spillovers are hoped to be the principle way of gaining access to advanced technology.

The potential of FDI to initiate (unintended) technology transfer to local firms through productivity spillovers may be derived from the semi-public nature of technology and the way how it is disseminated between firms. As already pointed out in the previous section, technology, despite the possibility of legal protection of intellectual property rights, is characterised by incomplete excludability.

The conceptual framework of knowledge spillovers was introduced by Griliches (1979).[37] He distinguishes two kinds of externalities: pecuniary (rent) and technological.

Pecuniary knowledge spillovers are a by-product of a market transaction. They can be detected when firms purchase R&D-intensive inputs from other firms at less then their full 'quality' price. Rent spillovers are probable, for example, with capital equipment prices which do not reflect fully the improvements in their quality. Such undervaluation of official prices for capital equipment is being observed in industries under intensive competitive pressure like the computer industry. The more competitive an industry and the higher the price elasticity of demand, the smaller the extent to which price increase offsets the quality increases.

Technological spillovers occur whenever (i) firms acquire access to technological innovations without paying for that information in a market transaction, and (ii) the innovator (or current owners of patents) does not have an effective recourse, under prevailing laws on protection of intellectual property rights, when other firms make productive use of her innovation.

Technological spillovers may benefit production and/or research abilities of other firms (Park, 1995). Through spillovers into production, technological innovations directly affect production possibilities of the rival. Through spillovers into research, successful innovation by the rivals becomes more likely or less costly.

Whereas rent spillovers are related to trade flows among supplying and using industries and the market structure in the technology-producing industries, technological spillovers stem from the non-rival and (partially) non-excludable character of technology. They do not need the existence of any market transactions. It is even not clear that this kind of borrowing of ideas is related to input purchases. To give an example, Griliches (1979) points out that the photographic equipment industry and the scientific instruments industry may not

[37] His contribution was to apply the concept of externalities by Scitovsky (1954) on the effects of R&D on individual firms.

buy much from each other but may work on similar things and benefits from each other's research.

The first, indirect support for the emergence of technology spillovers between foreign and local firms in host countries was provided by an ample empirical literature on R&D spillovers. These studies tested the magnitudes of the benefits from R&D undertaken by other firms. The difference between social and private rates of return to R&D would indicate an externality of R&D investment.[38] Similarly, estimating positive elasticities of productivity of a firm (industry or country) with respect to R&D undertaken by others confirms external effects created by innovative activities.

Cameron (1996) summarises previous estimates of private vs. social rates of return on R&D at the firm and industry level.[39] In most studies, social rates of return to R&D capital were significantly greater than the private returns to R&D capital. Hence, the evidence points sizeable R&D spillovers effects in both intra- and inter-industrial context. These studies were limited to developed countries: the USA, Canada, the UK and Japan.

Further research concentrated on international R&D spillovers. Coe/Helpman (1995) estimates positive elasticities of total factor productivity with respect to the foreign R&D capital stock in a group of 22 industrialised countries during the period 1970-90 with country-level data. The effects are largest in the G7 group. The estimated rates of return to national R&D stock are substantially higher at the world as compared to the national level. About one quarter of the benefits of R&D investment in each of the most advanced industrialised countries (G7) occurs to her trade partners. Furthermore, the effect of foreign R&D on domestic productivity is stronger for those countries which are more open to trade. Nadiri/Kim (1996), Lichtenberg /van Pottelsberghe de la Potterie (1996), Engelbrecht (1997) (among others) re-examine the question of international R&D spillovers – in each case, the data confirm the existence of positive productivity spillovers from foreign R&D.

[38] A variety of data may be used to measure the innovative output of an industry. Most researchers take R&D spending for reasons of data availability, but patenting and technological balance of payments have also been applied. The domestic R&D capital stock for 22 developed countries was computed by Coe/Helpman (1995) and is extensively used in other studies.

[39] The estimated rates of return to R&D investment vary considerably depending on the type of data used (cross-section or time-series), the country, the method of estimation, and whether the unit of analysis is the firm, the industry, or a country. On average, net rates of return on own R&D are about 20 to 30 per cent. In most studies, social rates of return to R&D vary from 20 to over 100 per cent in various industries, with an average somewhere close to 50 per cent.

Positive effects of R&D conducted in the industrial countries could also be detected in developing countries. Coe *et al.* (1997) finds that the elasticities of total factor productivity (TFP) with respect to foreign R&D differ substantially across countries – both for 77 developing countries and 22 industrial countries. The USA as the country with the largest domestic R&D stock has the largest impact on TFP in developing countries. Among developing countries, those which are more open to foreign trade derive higher marginal TFP growth from foreign R&D. Moreover, developing countries with trade more biased towards industrial countries with higher R&D gain higher marginal TFP growth from increasing imports.

This evidence suggests that MNC affiliates may trigger substantial positive spillovers on local firms in host countries.

3.6 Conclusions

In these times, MNCs have a dominant position in creating, controlling and transferring advanced technology. A great bulk of the multinationals trade in technology is intra-firm, *i.e.* between foreign affiliates in different countries. FDI itself is a mode of technology transfer since it aims at internalising the benefits from technological proprietary assets possessed by a parent firm. The internalisation theory, an integral part of the eclectic paradigm of FDI, holds that such intangible assets have some characteristics of public goods.

The fact that technology is to some extent a non-excludable good leads to external effects associated with its implementation. This is the reason why the emergence of foreign affiliates of multinationals in the host country is believed to generate technological spillovers on locally-owned firms.

Chapter 4:
FDI impact on productivity of local firms: the evidence

4.1 Introduction

The previous chapter argued, mostly on theoretical ground, that FDI, especially from industrialised countries, might have a positive impact on locally-owned firms through the generation of productivity spillovers. Such spillovers contribute to the spread of technology within the host country: best-practice industrial know-how, as well as organisational and managerial knowledge voluntary transferred to foreign affiliates may leak to and be adopted by firms without any foreign participation. This chapter summarises the empirical evidence.

In Section 4.2, we present various linkages between foreign and local firms in the host economy, and show how they serve as channels for the diffusion of productivity spillovers. Backed by an ample case-study literature on MNCs in less developed host countries, we underline the factors determining the emergence of linkages as a precondition for spillovers.

In general, one can classify relationships between a foreign firm and its local partners on the base of market transactions. Upstream relationships with suppliers of raw materials and intermediate products as well as downstream relations to the local customers constitute the so-called *direct linkages* (Lall, 1978). Relations with competitors are usually not characterised by arms-length transactions. We call them *indirect linkages*. Evidence supports the view that direct linkages cannot be reduced to pure market transactions in goods and services. Similar to indirect linkages, they are a precondition for a set of technological, marketing or entrepreneurial impulses provided by a foreign firm to which the local firms will response. These impulses are technological externalities (spillovers) in the sense given by Scitovsky and Grilliches (see Section 3.5).

Section 4.3 reviews the existing econometric research on the existence and scope of spillovers from FDI in less developed countries. We first discuss the analytical framework for detecting spillovers, before presenting and comparing results of various country studies. Conclusions from this survey helps choosing the most appropriate analytical framework and tools for dealing with the presence of foreign firms in Poland – an analysis to be conducted in Chapter 6 of the present work.

4.2 Channels for productivity spillovers of FDI: case-study evidence

There are various transmission mechanisms for the spread of technological spillovers. Not all of them are related to FDI. In some cases, simple inspection of the product or a reverse engineering process may be applied to detect a new technological information embodied in innovations. In other cases, successful researchers publicly disclose technological innovations (journals, conferences) – either because it is not covered by intellectual property rights protection, or because their enforcement is very weak.[40]

However, reverse engineering and studying of professional literature serve as a diffusion channel for only one part of industrial knowledge, namely codifiable technology embodied in physical capital, goods and production manuals. Non-codifiable knowledge – skills and abilities of people who were engaged in innovation, production or marketing – cannot be copied in the way described above. Non-codifiable knowledge may be transferred between firms only through personal contacts of researchers, workers or managers. Here, the presence of foreign affiliates might be a precondition for knowledge diffusion.

At a time when most less developed countries viewed FDI in a rather hostile way, Caves (1974) recognised the potential benefit of FDI through its indirect impact on local firms. He divided potential benefits into three classes:

- *Improvement of allocative efficiency under monopolistic distortions:* Where barriers to entry by new firms are high, the entrance of a foreign firm raises the productivity of the host-country's resources by improving their allocation.
- *Higher technical (or X-efficiency) within local firms*: In case of competing firms, higher competitive pressure would possibly enforce a search for more efficient use of existing resources. In case of local firms connected with the foreign subsidiary through backward or forward linkages, competition for contracts between them would enhance their efficiency.
- *Increasing rates of technology transfer:* The foreign firm may speed the transfer of technology and innovations to local firms which compete with it or through backward or forwards linkages. If this channel of technology transfer to local firms is swifter or less costly than alternative modes like the free flow of public knowledge between countries, licensing of patents and know-how, import of capital goods and equipment, then the host country may derive net benefits from the activity of the foreign subsidiary.

In the present section, we elaborate from existing case studies how and under what conditions linkages may serve as a channel for spreading these benefits. A large number of existing case studies examines various aspects of FDI impact on host countries, directly or indirectly suggesting the existence of spillovers.

---

[40] Grossman/Helpman (1991) discusses empirical evidence on different practices of innovating firms.

4.2.1 Vertical linkages with local firms

The potential of direct linkages for creating positive effects on local firms is long known and justified the so-called local content provisions with which many developing countries pushed firms into buying large proportions of their inputs from local sources. This section collects the case-study literature and presents main findings.

Backwards linkages

Backwards (upstream) linkages arise from relationships of a foreign firm with its local suppliers of raw material and components. When a foreign affiliate decides to purchase intermediates from local firms, this might positively affect domestic employment and output. However, this beneficial direct effect must be judged against possible indirect demand-reducing effects. Whenever foreign firms crowd local competitors out of the market, only the net impact on suppliers is important. It is positive only when a foreign firm buys locally more then its vanished competitors. Empirical literature on this issue suggests that foreign firms do not generally buy more (or less) than local firms (Dunning, 1992). The scope of local sourcing is product-specific and depends positively on the level of indigenous technology, the sophistication of local subcontracting infrastructure, and the skill of the local labour force (Halbach, 1988). There is a tendency for the share of local inputs purchased by a foreign firm to increase over time, which might coincide with economic and industrial growth in the host country, obscuring the casual relationship between growth and the scope of linkages.

Foreign firms producing for a domestic market purchase more from local subcontractors than export-oriented firms (Lall, 1978). One reason might be that foreign firms producing for local consumers in less developed countries may produce goods of lower quality and sophistication than goods which are sold in developed countries. MNCs affiliates which protect their technology from imitation by local firms might be unwilling to order by local subcontractors because of fear of imitation and technology leakage.

Government import restrictions and local performance requirements can effectively enhance the percentage of local subcontracting as well. In the past, governments in developing countries usually imposed local content provisions, pushing foreign firms, especially in import-competing sectors, to buy large proportions of their inputs from local sources. Consequently, foreign affiliates developed extensive relationships with local enterprises. Governments that pursue export-generating policies usually impose fewer local content requirements on foreign firms. However, this co-operation was not free from problems raised by the high cost, poor quality, and unreliability of local suppliers. This inefficient practice results in higher costs and lower quality of products.

A higher degree of local subcontracting is also believed to improve the quality of locally produced inputs (Blomström/Kokko, 1997). This effect stems from the fact that foreign affiliates are supposed to possess not only more efficient manufacturing techniques, but also better intermediates, better technology for producing them and more information about efficient sourcing. Empirical findings support the view that the presence of foreign-owned firms has forced local suppliers to meet higher standards of quality, reliability, and speed of delivery, while providing them with more generous assistance and advice then indigenous firms usually do (UNCTAD, 1995).

Foreign firms influence the productivity of their subcontractors through a number of channels. From a great number of empirical studies, eight of them were identified (Dunning, 1992):

- *Technical assistance*: It implies adjustment of produced inputs to the requirements of the ordering foreign firm. Usually, foreign firms provide designs, drawings and specifications for components. Often, they get involved even deeper in the production process of their suppliers: through the training of staff, sharpening of quality control, inventory management, machine maintenance, even factory layout and so on. Sometimes, provision of used machinery is also included.
- *Financial assistance:* This may consist of loans and grants, pre-financing of machinery and tools and special price agreements.
- *Managerial and organisational assistance:* Help is given on a range of financial, accounting and general managerial control procedures.
- *Pricing assistance:* This includes help in calculating prices, as well as help in bargaining prices with sub-contractors.
- *Information exchange:* Information is provided concerning market characteristics and trends, government regulations, foreign suppliers of capital equipment, raw materials and intermediates, as well as on potential joint-ventures partners for suppliers.
- *Procurement assistance:* This covers help in obtaining capital equipment, raw materials and other intermediate products at competitive prices (other than in (5)).
- *Location advice:* Information given to potential suppliers on the sitting of a planned foreign plant which should influence their own location decision.
- *Other assistance:* This covers advice on market access to markets which are familiar to the multinational, dealing with foreign suppliers, advice on diversification strategy and so on.

The existence of all eight types of relationships (usually a few of them simultaneously) and the resulting productivity effects on local suppliers have been detected in a number of studies (for a discussion, see Blomström/Kokko, 1997).

None of these empirical studies investigated whether a foreign affiliate is able to extract the full value of the resulting productivity increases by suppliers, i.e. whether it generates spillovers. But, the examples of relationships given suggest that the majority of them supply information, knowledge and access to goods and markets, for which competitive markets do not exist. This suggests externalities and provides support for the hypothesis that productivity spillovers from FDI are at work.

Forwards linkages

Forwards linkages exist when local firms (i) act as secondary processors of raw materials extracted by a foreign affiliate, as in oil refining, metal processing or agricultural business; (ii) provide product packaging, delivery, marketing and sale; and (iii) buy technically complicated products and equipment from foreign affiliates for industrial use.

Concerning the first group of customers, there is scattered empirical evidence that foreign-owned firms may engage in, or promote local processing through training of local labour, setting-up loans or other types of assistance similar to assistance given to their suppliers (Dunning, 1992). The amount of secondary processing undertaken by local firms is highly product- and country-specific; in host countries with a high political risk and in those which lack internal transport facilities and technological competence, multinationals usually do not invest in secondary processing. Whether the local sector does, depends on its technological competence. If costs of promotion and setting-up local secondary processors are viewed by a multinational as too high, these activities will be undertaken abroad, and the potential for linkages vanishes.

For local firms implementing foreign machinery, multinationals may provide expertise, offer functional guidance about the technical aspects and the usage of the products being sold and about servicing requirements. Even if a MNC did not invest directly in manufacturing locally, own information and sales centres are common in countries which are prospective hosts to multinationals.

Although there is a potential for positive externalities in line with forward relationships, there has been little research work on this phenomenon. Empirical analyses are rare, often incomparable and difficult to generalise. In one of the few, Aitken/Harrison (1994) detects forward linkages in case of Venezuela – an important oil exporter and politically a high-risk country. However, other case studies do not confirm the existence of forward linkages[41]. No evidence of relative importance of backwards and forwards linkages as two possible channels of externalities on local firms has been given so far.

4.2.2 Horizontal linkages with competitors

The entry of foreign-owned firms into a particular manufacturing sector in a host country will obviously affect existing producers. In case of FDI in less developed countries, the fact that most foreign affiliates have their parents in industrialised countries implies they are likely to utilise technological innovations – be they product- or process-related. This knowledge is not directly available to local competitors, since it is protected by patents. Moreover, foreign firms typically have better marketing capabilities, more efficient managerial and organisational practices and easier access to financial resources than indigenous firms. This implies relatively higher productivity of foreign affiliates.[42] Competition introduced by such firms in the form of new or better products or services is forcing local producers and service providers to enhance their own performance.[43]

For this reason, local firms does not benefit directly when the foreign subsidiaries are more productive. On the contrary, their market share comes under massive pressure and the possibility of crowding-out of local firms becomes high. The resulting transformation of the domestic industry might be positive for the consumers, but the impact on local firms and their employees is hardly positive from their point of view.

Local firms may rather gain if productivity spillovers are at work which occur when the multinational corporation cannot capture all quasi-rents due to its productive activities, or to the removal of distortions by the subsidiary's

[41] See Reuber *et al.* (1973) or McAleese/McDonald (1978).

[42] Possessing ownership advantages does not necessarily mean higher productivity. First, foreign firms face comparative disadvantages since they are unfamiliar (at entry) with the local market Second, local productivity or profitability is not a yardstick for a FDE - its performance is often judged by a parent according to its contribution to achieve the global strategic goals of the MNC, not according to higher than local productivity. Third, due to accounting and transfer pricing practices of multinationals, productivity and profitability of an individual foreign project may not reflect its actual performance. However, most empirical studies confirm that total factor productivity (and labour productivity controlled for the capital/labour ratio) of foreign-owned firms is higher than of local firms. See Jenkins (1990) for an empirical survey on this issue.

[43] In case of foreign affiliates producing for local markets, the increased competitive pressure on local rivals is the decisive factor for adjustment. In case of export-oriented foreign firms, the induced upwards impact on local wages may harm local firms (operating in the same local labour market, not necessary in the same sector). That multinationals pay higher wages than local firms in less developed countries is documented in a survey by Jenkins (1990).

competitive pressure. There are two channels for the diffusion of positive spillovers on local rivals: (i) a *demonstration* effect; and (ii) a *competition* effect. The demonstration effect arises when a local firm learns from a multinational about a new technology or a product. Learning by watching reduces costs due to uncertainty about the market and encourages the local firm to adopt the innovation. The very presence of foreign affiliates is often sufficient as a catalyst for adopting new management techniques. This is clearly documented by the widespread adoption of quality control practices in developing countries.

Competition effects comprise all responses of local firms to the entry of foreign-owned firms. In the short-run, when the primary goal is the immediate survival of the enterprise, this strategy includes one or a combination of the following measures:

- reduction of own mark-ups over costs;
- reduction of costs through improving X-efficiency of production within a firm, stricter or more cost-conscious management, better motivated employees or reduction of over-employment at the firm level, and higher utilisation of capacity;
- search for new markets - domestic or foreign - for low-quality products with less competitive pressure.

In the medium run, local firms may follow various strategies to adjust to the enhanced competitive pressure.[44] They may try to:

- install more efficient productive equipment: for less developed countries, enhanced imports of machinery and capital equipment is likely to be the main channel of market access to modern productive facilities;
- Acquire more efficient technologies: licensing agreements with other foreign firms or purchase and application of patents are possible solutions; Implementing better managerial techniques and skills, better marketing techniques, better quality of intermediates are the others;
- Upgrade product quality, diversify a range of products supplied, further differentiation of existing products: This requires successful own R&D effort and/or purchase of licences or patents.

In practice, it is difficult to register pure demonstration effects. In case of adjustment strategies which are based on imitation or adoption of new technologies, it is difficult to distinguish between demonstration and competition effects. Sectoral evidence from less developed countries suggests that improving X-efficiency in the short run has a strong potential of enhancing

[44] Grosfeld/Roland (1995) calls the short-term strategies 'defensive restructuring' and the medium-term ones 'strategic restructuring'.

productivity of local firms due to its initial slack.[45] In addition, the costs are small relative to costs of acquiring new technologies. It is especially important for local firms in countries with a poorly developed financial sector.

Whenever a local firm has already used its potential for raising productivity, the ongoing competitive pressure of FDI ultimately leads to crowding-out of the market. This might be a case, for example, when improving management or shedding labour is not possible, and when (further) financing of access to better technologies is not guaranteed.

4.2.3 Linkages due to labour mobility

Foreign-owned firms employ not only extern managers and technicians, but also local personnel. From the point of view of a foreign firm, local personnel possesses initially superior knowledge about the market, and is cheaper than exogenous managers and technicians, which usually require an almost prohibitive compensation for their mobility. The share of local personnel usually rises over time.

Apart from on-the-job training, a foreign firm offers a wide scope of other programmes for newly employed, starting from training abroad (mostly in-house training within the corporation) and management centres to general schooling (*i.e.* MBA programmes) and after-work classes (*i.e.* foreign languages), depending on the skills needed.[46] While working for a foreign firm, this staff - workers, professionals and managers – learns about the production technology, management and business organisation, about the market features and unexploited market opportunities. The acquired knowledge usually spills over to the local sector when previous employees of multinationals move to existing enterprises or set up their own firms. Labour turnover of this kind causes externalities, since institutions which recruits workers trained at the cost of foreign affiliates do not bear the full costs of his training – in most cases, such a move takes place without any compensation between firms engaged.

As a channel for technology diffusion, labour turnover might be important not only for local competitors of foreign firms, but also for local down- and upstream firms. The first may be able to imitate foreign technologies, but they are still exposed to competition from the foreign rival. Local suppliers may develop without any fear of competitive pressure from a foreign firm, and additionally benefit from its assistance in the sense described in Section 4.2.2.

---

[45] For a survey of evidence, see Blomström/Kokko (1997).

[46] At the onset of transition, the majority of local managers lacked the basic corporate skills required to run business in a market economy. Multinationals played an important role in providing local staff with managerial skills and practice, as documented in UNCTAD (1995).

Empirical studies on spillovers from the training of local employees in foreign owned firms are still rare, mainly limited to developing countries, and to transfer of organisational and managerial practices (see references in Blomström/Kokko, 1997). In fact, most studies report training in foreign affiliates to be generally more intensive than in local firms. However, this constitutes a direct positive effect of foreign firms, not an indirect one due to externalities. Others indicate cases of set-ups of subcontracting firms by former foreign employees and a high proportion of managers of local firms in some countries who have been trained by foreign affiliates (Behrman/Wallender, 1976; Gerschenberg, 1987; Katz, 1987).

4.2.4 Determinants of linkages

As sketched in the previous sections, the activity of foreign-owned firms which have access to superior but patented technology, more efficient management, access to export markets and financial resources from the MNC system has the potential of enhancing productivity of local firms due to externalities which may come in work. However, the effective impact in practice is not clear. There is ample empirical evidence that the change in performance of local firms depends on the coincidence of various conditions (Dunning, 1992). They refer to the characteristics of local as well as foreign firms, to the features of the industry and the product itself, and also to economic and political conditions of a host country. Although this evidence has a case study feature and generalisations are not possible, it is useful to study this literature to understand the source of successes and failures observed in the past.

It is not entirely clear from a theoretical perspective what the relation between the level of technology used by foreign firms and local firms facilitates technology transfer. There are two opposite arguments given by the literature. The first one has been summarised under the so-called *technology gap hypothesis*, namely that productivity spillovers increase with the technological gap between local and foreign firms (Findlay, 1978). This view may be justified by the argument that technology diffusion to local firms occurs mostly through imitation of products and processes applied by multinationals. Since many developing countries have not signed international treaties concerning protection of intellectual property rights (or since they are not respected in practice), the abuse of property rights is tolerated and even supported by the country's authorities.[47]

Imitation might be an interesting alternative to innovation for firms from less developed countries since it is usually cheaper. Mansfield *et al.* (1981) find in a study of innovations in the drug, chemical, electronics and machinery industries

[47] In the last decade, China was the most active imitator of high tech products, for the home market and export.

that the cost of imitation average 65 percent of the costs of innovation. Multinational firms are found to be more intensively targeted by local competitors in the host country than foreign firms active abroad. Evidently, imitation costs are lower and the prospects for successful competition better than in case of goods produced abroad. The potential of FDI for facilitating imitation by local firms is usually explained by two factors: first, there is a demonstration effect. No matter how hard a foreign affiliate tries to keep its technology secret, it definitely wants to demonstrate how it works. This spreads the information about the existence of this technology and about preferences of the consumers through revealing demand conditions for this good. This information is valuable for imitators since it serves as a pre-selection of attractive products: it helps avoid costs of testing the market, avoid investing in flops and helps target goods with high growth potential. The higher the technological gap, the easier (less costly) it is to pick out a readily applicable technology and achieve productivity gains. Second, mobility of R&D personnel from foreign affiliates to research departments of local firms together with mobility of experienced engineers and workers facilitates diffusion of non-codifiable knowledge necessary to conduct reengineering.

For imitating firms successful reengineering is only a prerequisite of a successful competition against the original supplier. In order to capture the market local firms must possess relative advantages in manufacturing process. Indeed, relative to foreign firms from developed market economies, local rivals often have substantial cost advantages due to lower wages.

Other authors challenged the technology gap hypothesis and argued that high technological gaps may rather be an obstacle for technology transfer through FDI. The argument is based on the fact that considerable preparation and technical effort in adaptation, education and training, and developing on-the-job experience must accompany all technological transfer (Teece, 1977; Patel/Pavitt, 1995). Even if the firm purchases legally protected intellectual rights (patents, trade marks), these expenditures are only a small fraction of the total cost of adoption. A long list of empirical studies provides clear evidence for complementarity between domestic R&D and purchased technology.[48] Audretsch (1995) concludes from numerous case studies presenting evidence of firms' limits with regards to adopting external technology that R&D helps a firm expand its 'absorptive capacity', *i.e.* the ability to adopt new technologies. Hence, there might be a minimum level of technological capability which local firms must possess in order to absorb technological spillovers. In less-developed countries, weak local firms may be unable to conduct and finance research and investment, especially if their access to capital markets is poor.

[48] The list includes Katrak (1989), Braga/Wilmore (1991) and Bertschek (1995).

In addition, while mobility of employees seems to constitute an important channel for the transmission of technology and managerial skills outside the system of a MNC, its role is limited in practice due to the low movement of labour from foreign to locally-owned firms. Evidence from host countries reveals that labour mobility to local firms is higher in more developed host economies (Gerschenberg, 1987; Pack, 1997). In less developed countries, opportunities of switching to existing local firms are missing or financially unattractive, since foreign firms usually pay higher wages than local ones. [49] Setting up local firms is limited, among others, by an underdeveloped financial sector hampering provision of venture capital.

Hence, small or moderate technology gaps seem to identify cases where foreign technologies are useful to local firms, and where the local firms possess the skills needed to apply innovations. Large gaps, on the other hand, may signal that foreign technology is not relevant, that local firms have nothing to learn from the foreign firms, or that local technological capability is so weak that foreign technologies can not be used in local firms. This all together constitutes an argument against the technology gap hypothesis.

Another important empirical issue is related to the *competition* effect of FDI. In particular, a question arises when the competitive pressure from FDI triggers positive adjustment by local rivals, and when it affects their productivity adversely, causing crowding-out and market concentration. Unfortunately, the few studies that exist for less developed countries have not elucidated these problems (Lall, 1978). On the one hand, FDI, particularly in small and medium enterprises, has helped to de-monopolise markets and stimulate competitive behaviour. On the other hand, scattered data available for individual countries in Latin America and South Asia suggest that in less developed countries, the entry of multinationals does speed up the natural process of concentration, and that the weakness of local competitors enables them to achieve a much higher degree of market dominance than would be the case in developed economies. The only exception are enterprises owned, financed and fostered by the state. Foreign investors' participation in privatisation of large public enterprises has often led to reduced competition by foreclosing market entry, fixing prices and engaging in anti-competitive mergers (Fingleton *et al*, 1997). This phenomenon is partly due to government policies. The host countries often use trade incentives like exclusive market supply rights for extended periods, in order to attract FDI.

The level of competition prior to the entry of multinationals might be also important for the scope of technology transfer to local firms through imitation and labour turnover. Theoretical arguments for the beneficial role of competition for growth-stimulating knowledge spillovers between firms can be found in

---

[49] For empirical evidence, see Aitken *et al* (1996).

Porter (1990). He points out that local competition accelerates imitation and improvement of the innovator's ideas. Although such competition reduces the returns to innovators, it also increases pressure to innovate. Ruthless competition between local competitors leads to rapid adoption and improvement of the innovations of the others, and so generates industry growth. Contrary to Porter, in the Marshall-Arrow-Romer-type models of externalities, innovators realise that some of their ideas will be imitated or improved on by their neighbours without compensation. If innovators had a monopoly on their ideas, or at least if they had fewer neighbours who imitated them immediately, the pace of innovation and growth would rise. Local concentration is good for growth because innovators can internalise the externalities.

To summarise briefly Section 4.2: the existence of linkages between foreign affiliates and locally-owned firms is well supported by the business-oriented literature based on case studies. They show that a multitude of factors related to the FDI project, local firms and the host country, interact and determine the ability of local firms to absorb potential productivity spillovers of FDI. However, given the fact that most of these studies focus only some of the linkages and that the results are conditional on specific constellations of the characteristics of a FDI project and those of the local industry, only very cautious qualitative generalisations could be drawn. They may be used as hypotheses that can be submitted to econometric testing. We report on these tests in the rest of this chapter.

4.3 Productivity spillovers of FDI: econometric evidence

In principle, any econometric study focusing on the existence and scope of productivity spillovers of FDI, should be based on detailed data for individual domestic firms, both local and foreign. The data set should include annual accounts - both balance sheet and profit and loss statement - in a very detailed qualitative breakdown. In order to work out the precise importance of different channels for productivity spillovers at the firm level, quantitative data on the scope of linkages between foreign and local firms, including suppliers'-buyers relations and labour turnover, would be necessary. Tracing the development of technology and productivity requires that a study must cover a longer period. With data stretching over several years, a search for spillovers occurring with a time-lag could be performed. Furthermore, testing the existence of inter-industrial spillovers requires micro data for a large number industries. Only this kind of information allows a comprehensive empirical analysis of the scope and determinants of spillovers. However, the extreme data requirement is an obstacle to conduct such a study. This section shows that there exist only a few empirical analyses which pursue this data-intensive approach.

When (panel) data for a large number of individual firms are not available, aggregate industry-specific data might be the alternative. Then, econometric tests on the relationship between the activity of foreign enterprises and productivity (or productivity change) in the locally-owned part of the industry may be conducted. This approach examines intra- as well as inter-industrial spillovers. Moreover, it provides a tool for testing whether and how other industry characteristics affect the scope of spillovers.

In Section 4.3.1, we present a theoretical framework generally used for identifying productivity spillovers on local firms. Results are reviewed in Section 4.3.2. Section 4.3.3 discusses the usefulness and shortcomings of the applied econometric approach.

4.3.1 Econometric framework

To quantify the economic performance of local firms, various indicators can be taken into consideration. Measures of profitability and loss, of export performance or of average variable costs are occasionally applied in empirical studies, but the most commonly used ones are labour productivity and total factor productivity (TFP).[50] Nearly all econometric studies testing the existence and determinants of productivity spillovers from FDI relied on one of these measures when calculating the performance of local firms.

The standard econometric approach is derived from a production-function framework. The underlying assumption is that the *j*th locally-owned firm in industry *i* produces (real) output in a given period *t*, according to a standard neoclassical Cobb-Douglas production function:

$$Y_{jit} = A_{jit} L_{jit}^{\alpha} K_{jit}^{1-\alpha} \qquad j=1,...,m \qquad i=1,...,n \qquad t=1,...,T \qquad 1>\alpha>0 \qquad (4.1)$$

where L_{jit} is total labour input and K_{jit} is total capital input of the firm. A_{jit} gives the firm -specific technological level at time *t*, the total factor productivity *(TFP)*.[51] It represents all factors affecting output other than tangible ones: in the first place, technological change and organisational capital like management practices and labour organisation. The specification obviously implies a Hicks-

[50] An example of a study using unconventional measures of the economic performance of firms' is Pohl *et al.* (1997). Benacek *et al.* (1998) measures firms' technical efficiency (TFP relative to the best practice within the industry) and allocative efficiency (deviation of the factor mix applied by a firm from the cost-minimising factor mix). Clerides *et al.* (1998) applies average variable costs.

[51] Real output should be measured by real value added of the firm. Alternatively, Basu/Fernald (1995) postulates a production function for gross output with labour (L), capital (K) and intermediates (M) in the following form:

$$Y_{jit} = A_{jit} K_{jit}^{s_1} L_{jit}^{s_2} M_{jit}^{1-s_1-s_2} \qquad j=1,...,m \qquad i=1,...,n \qquad t=1,...,T \quad s_1, s_2 \in (0,1).$$

neutral (output augmenting) technological progress and imposes a unit elasticity of substitution.[52]

The production function can be expressed in log-linear form as

$$y_{jit} = a_{jit} + \alpha\, l_{jit} + (1-\alpha)\, k_{jit} \tag{4.2}$$

where lowercase letters denote logs of the corresponding uppercase symbols. After taking first differences of the production function in its log version, output growth is given by

$$\Delta y_{jit} = \Delta a_{jit} + \alpha \Delta k_{jit} + (1-\alpha)\Delta l_{jit} \tag{4.3}$$

where $\Delta var_{jit} \equiv ln(Var_{ij,t} / Var_{ij,t-1})$ and $Var = Y, A, K, L$, respectively. The first term on the right side of Eq. (4.3) gives the change of technological level of the firm j in industry i within the period t.

The main hypothesis tested in the above framework is the so called *contagion hypothesis* (Findlay, 1978). It says that productivity spillovers from the activity of foreign firms on local part of an industry are increasing with higher foreign presence within the domestic industry. The foreign presence within an industry i in the host country, given by the *FDI*-variable, is measured either as the share of employment, or assets, or value added (sales) of foreign firms in the total performance of each industry (see Table 4.1).[53] The share of foreign firms in output of the ith industry is most commonly used since it is expected to affect productivity of local rivals positively through the demonstration and competition effect. Moreover, the positive backward-forward linkage effects on local suppliers and customers are expected to be higher.[54] Consequently, a higher foreign presence implies a higher likelihood of contacts between foreign and local firms, a higher probability of technology diffusion to the latter and a higher average productivity growth for the industry.[55] The alternative measures of the foreign presence are typically highly correlated with the foreign share of output. Since, on average, foreign firms have higher labour productivity and capital-labour ratio than local firms, the estimated coefficients for the foreign share of employment are higher and for the foreign share of assets lower than those for the foreign share in the output market

52 More general formulation of technological progress are discussed below.

53 Some authors take the *FDI*-variable in its log version which implies from Eq. (4.1) that the productivity level, A, contains the term FDI^{β} (instead of $e^{\beta FDI}$).

54 There is no reason to expect that linkages for an individual foreign firm should be higher if the foreign output share is higher. But, if more foreign firms are engaged, it is more likely that some of them establish suppliers or customers relations with the local firms.

55 This view is the fundament of the so called 'epidemic' model of technology diffusion among firms. For an excellent survey of models of technology diffusion, see Geroski (1999).

The existing literature investigates the existence of productivity spillovers in a static sense as well as in a dynamic one. In a static sense, spillovers from foreign firms should impact on the productivity *level* of local firms in the same industry (intra-industrial spillovers) or in some other industries (inter-industrial spillovers). In a dynamic sense, spillovers should affect productivity *growth* in locally-owned firms. For a static analysis, the index of the present firm-specific technological level, A_{jit}, is assumed to depend on a mixture of firm and industry characteristics as well as indicators of the presence of foreign firms. The investigated question is whether a higher foreign presence in a sector leads to a higher productivity of local firms in the same sector (intra-industrial spillovers). The econometric specification can be derived from Eq. (4.2):

$$y_{ji} = \beta_0 + \beta_1 FDI_i + \beta_2 k_{ji} + \beta_3 l_{ji} + \beta_4 X + \varepsilon_{ji} \qquad j = 1,...,m \qquad i = 1,...,n \qquad (4.4)$$

where FDI_i is an indicator of the activity of foreign firms within the industry, X is a vector of other determinants of productivity, and ε_{ji} is an idiosyncratic disturbance to productivity of the *j*th firms in industry *i;* ε_{ji} is $NID(0,\delta_1^2)$.[56]

For a dynamic investigation, the econometric model is derived from Eq. (4.3) and it reads

$$\Delta y_{ji} = \gamma_0 + \gamma_1 FDI_i + \gamma_2 \Delta k_{ji} + \gamma_3 \Delta l_{ji} + \gamma_4 X + \varepsilon_{ji} \qquad (4.5)$$

where X is a vector of other firm- and industry-specific determinants of the productivity growth and ε_{ji} is an idiosyncratic disturbance to productivity growth of the *j*th firms in industry *i;* ε_{ji} is $NID(0,\delta_2^2)$.

In both cases, a positive and significant coefficient of the *FDI*-variable is interpreted as the existence of positive productivity spillovers from FDI on local firms. Negative and significant coefficients on FDI are interpreted as supporting the existence of negative productivity spillovers. The value of the coefficient gives the magnitude of productivity spillovers from the activity of foreign affiliates.

4.3.2 Results

Positive impact of FDI on macroeconomic growth in the host economy has been detected in panel- and time-series studies for developing countries (De Mello, 1997). This result has been often explained with the idea that FDI acts as a catalyst for output growth. However, empirical testing of this hypothesis has long been neglected.

[56] We omitted the time index, since in a cross-firm analysis all data refer to the same period. With a panel of firm-level data, firm-specific constant can be included.

The first econometric analyses of productivity spillovers date back to the 1970s and examine intra-industry spillovers for Australia (Caves, 1974), for Canada (Globerman, 1979), and for Mexico (Blomström/Persson, 1983). At that time, all three countries were not themselves home of multinational firms. On the other hand, the domestic industry was supposed to be mature enough in order not to be crowded-out entirely from the domestic markets. In fact, all three studies came to the conclusion that a higher foreign presence in terms of foreign share in employment (value added) in an industry has a positive impact on labour productivity in local firms.

Concerning less developed countries, the existing empirical studies on the extent of spillovers relates to only few of them. The reason lies in the non-availability of comprehensive data. Only Mexico, Morocco, Venezuela and Indonesia provide detailed firm-level data for local firms, which allow testing for determinants of productivity growth. Industrial panels over a sub-sample of local firms were the source of data for China (Kinoshita, 1998) and the Czech Republic (Djankov/Hoekman, 1999). In other cases, industry-level data aggregated over firms with the same ownership status, provide an alternative (see Kokko, 1994 and Blomström/Wolff, 1994). In these studies, it was impossible to control for firm-specific features supposed to influence productivity (changes). Instead, the average productivity (productivity change) in local firms was related to foreign presence and average characteristics of all local firms within a industry.

In all studies, the foreign presence is measured for a narrowly defined industry (at least at the 3-digit level of ISIC). The detected spillovers are intra-industrial in kind and refer to local competitors of foreign firms. Sjöholm (1998) is the only test on inter-industrial spillovers.

The evidence of productivity spillovers according to the contagion hypothesis (see Section 4.2) is mixed (Table 4.1). Positive static spillovers were detected in Mexico and Indonesia, negative in Venezuela (Aitken/Harrison, 1993). No statistical relationship exists between a higher presence of FDI and the productivity of locally-owned manufacturing plants in Uruguay. Aitken *et al.* (1996) found negative spillovers from FDI on average wages in local firms in Venezuela and insignificant spillovers in Mexico. While there is evidence of positive dynamic spillovers in Mexico and Indonesia, negative dynamic spillovers have been detected in Morocco, and in transition countries - China and the Czech Republic.

Most studies tested additionally the *technology gap* hypothesis (see Section 4.2.4). The 'technology gap' is measured as the (relative) productivity differential between a local firm and the average, or the best one, of its foreign-owned rivals. Obviously, observed differences in labour productivity may result from different sources which are not necessary linked to technology. For example, foreign and local firms may work with different capital/labour ratios (quite likely since local and foreign firms face different relative factor prices) or produce on a different scale (important if returns to scale are not constant). Sjöholm (1997) is the only study which tries to correct for this bias. Kokko (1994) applies alternative measures of relative technological levels, like patent fees or investment ratios. However, they seem to be less appropriate since they give differences in technology only under additional restrictive assumptions discussed by the author.

Technology gap is an important determinant of the extent of productivity spillovers. A larger technology gap seems to enhance productivity spillovers only in one of the studies surveyed (Blomström/Wolff, 1994). All other cases contradict the technology gap hypothesis: spillovers are higher for lower technology gap.

Only one study (Sjöholm, 1997) dealt with the role of competition for the extent of productivity spillovers. He has found positive spillovers from FDI in Indonesia only when a higher foreign presence coincides with a high competition level within the industry. Tougher competition may be good for spillovers since it strengthens adjustment pressure for local enterprises, and is usually associated with more innovating activity.

It has been argued in the literature, that majority-owned foreign firms have higher incentives to invest in technology than minority-owned joint ventures (Ramachandran, 1993). However, wholly-owned foreign affiliates may have fewer links to local firms in host countries, reducing the channels for technology transfer as compared with joint ventures. Where there is strong commitment to hiring local staff, especially local executives, and to training and integrating them into the organisation, the transfer of know-how to other enterprises is more likely, since local employees may move to indigenous enterprises. This could explain higher spillovers from minority-owned foreign firms. Ramachandran/Shah (1998) finds in three African countries (Zimbabwe, Ghana, Kenya) positive impact of a higher FDI on the productivity of the whole domestic industry only for majority-owned foreign affiliates. However, the Indonesian study by Blomström/Sjöholm (1998) does not confirm the view that spillovers from majority owned foreign firms are higher.

The picture of FDI-related productivity spillovers emerging from the above survey is quite uneven since the studies are country- and period-specific. The results support the findings of industrial case-studies. However, there is insufficient econometric testing of productivity spillovers. Time-series studies which allow to control for changes in the industrial, trade and FDI policy, as well as in short- and long-time behaviour are missing. Cross-country panels for different industries are absent as well.

Table 4.1:
Studies on Productivity Spillovers from FDI on Local Manufacturing Firms in Less Developed Host Countries

Study, host country, period, data	Measure of foreign presence	Measure of firms' performance	Existence of spillovers	Determinants of the scope of spillovers	Additional results
Static externalities					
Aitken/Harrison (1993), Venezuela			Negative		
Kokko (1994) Mexico, 1970, industry level data	Share of employment in foreign-owned firms in total 4-digit industry employment	Labour productivity	Positive for a cross section of 4-digit industries	Technology gap between foreign and local firms (spillovers higher for smaller technology gaps)	In industries with a high presence of foreign firms applying technology substantially different from that used by local firms (high technology gaps) spillovers are less likely or may be even deterring
Kokko *et al.* (1996) Uruguay, 1990 firm-level data	Share of total output in foreign-owned firms in total 4-digit industry output	Value added per worker	Positive but insignificant for a cross section of firms	Technology gap – spillovers positive for industries with small technology gap, negative but insignificant for industries with high technology gap	
Aitken *et al.* (1996) Venezuela, 1977-89 Mexico, 1984-90, plant- and industry-level data	Share of employment in foreign owned firms in total 4-digit industry employment	Average annual wage	Negative (Venezuela) Negative but insignificant (Mexico)	Skills of local workers are insignificant	
Sjöholm (1997) Indonesia, 1980 and 1991 firm-level data	Share of total output in foreign-owned firms in total 5-digit industry output	Value added per worker	Positive (1980 and 1991) and higher in 1991 for a cross section of firms	Technology gap (in 1980 – spillovers higher for smaller technology gaps, in 1991 – higher for larger technology gaps) Competition (in 1980 – spillovers higher for higher competition, in 1991 – higher for lower competition)	
Blomström/Sjöholm (1998) Indonesia, 1991 firm-level data	Share of output in foreign-owned firms in total 5-digit industry output	Value added per worker	Positive in a cross section of firms	Independent of the share of industry output produced by majority owned foreign firms	Labour productivity in foreign firms is significantly higher than in local firms (controlled for capital intensity, skills, capital utilisation and scale) independently of the size of foreign ownership. Productivity spillovers are restricted to non-exporting local firms

Dynamic externalities					
Haddad/Harrison (1993) Morocco, 1985-89, firm-level panel	Share of foreign assets in total assets of a 3-digit industry the firm belongs to	Value added growth	Negative but insignificant	No difference between: - high and low technology firms, - protected and open sectors, - sectors with small versus high technology gap	TFP in foreign firms is, on average, higher than in local firms in the same sector TFP growth in foreign firms is not higher than in local firms in the same sector Smaller deviation from maximum productivity level for local firms in sectors with a higher foreign presence
Blomström/Wolff (1994) Mexico, 1970-75, industry level data	Share of employment in foreign-owned firms in total 2-digit industry employment	Gross output growth	Positive in a cross section of industries	Technology gap – spillovers higher for industries with bigger initial technology gap	Positive impact of a higher foreign presence on productivity convergence between foreign and local firms in a sector Positive impact of a higher foreign presence on productivity convergence between local and US firms
Sjöholm (1997) Indonesia, 1980-91, firm level panel	Share of output in foreign-owned firms in total 5-digit industry output	Value added growth	Positive in a sample of all firms and industries	Technology gap – spillovers insignificant in industries with a high initial technology gap Competition – spillovers insignificant in industries with a low level of competition Concentration – spillovers insignificant in industries with a high level of concentration	
Sjöholm (1998) Indonesia, 1980-91 firm level panel	Share of output in foreign-owned firms in total 5-digit industry output within the region Share of total output in foreign owned firms in all other industries within the region	Value added growth	Positive intra-industrial spillovers on the national level; Negative intra-industrial spillovers on regional levels Positive inter-industrial spillovers on regional levels		Intra-industrial spillovers are not regionally concentrated, but inter-industrial spillovers are
Kinoshita (1998) China, 1990-92, firm-level panel	Share of employment in foreign owned firms in total 2-digit industry employment	TFP growth	Negative but insignificant		
Djankov/Hoekman (1999), CR, 1992-96, firm-level panel	Share of assets in foreign firms in total assets of all firms in 2-digit industry	Sales growth	Negative		

Notes: Productivity spillovers are defined to be positive when the regression coefficient on the *FDI*-variable is positive, and negative – otherwise.

4.3.3 Theoretical problems with measuring productivity spillovers

While the production-function framework generally applied for testing various hypotheses about productivity spillovers is a standard tool in the empirical growth literature, it is not free from shortcomings. We list them and discuss their importance for the purpose of detecting spillovers.

Productivity growth and technological progress

The main criticism is that the part of output growth not attributed to the growth of inputs, the so-called Solow residual given by Δa_{jit} in Eq. (4.2), captures not only technological progress. In fact, it measures a net effect of many different factors: capital deepening (Rodrik, 1997), a change in factor utilisation (Burnside *et al.* 1995), a change in quality of inputs and materials used (Denison, 1967), changes in mark-ups (Harrison, 1994), and changes in the X-efficiency within the firm, in addition to pure technological changes. All terms are supposed to be firm- or sector-specific.

For testing productivity spillovers, this debate is not crucial since it is not the absolute extent of productivity growth, but only the link to FDI that is of interest. With our broad definition of technology (see Section 3.2), improvements in the quality of intermediates, workers' skills and equipment, in management and organisation, as well as in implementing of new industrial knowledge might all serve as a channel for productivity spillovers. However, since the method fails to distinguish the technological transfer component attributable to spillovers from other factors such as the increase in competition, pressure from export markets and technology import, complementary research on these issues is necessary.

Another problem with the sketched approach for measuring dynamic spillovers arises from the fact that the growth of capital input may in fact be driven by technological progress (and FDI). The method, however, treats capital growth as independent. Consequently, productivity spillovers are underestimated.[57] This might especially be an issue when the nature of technological progress differs between sectors.[58] Then, conclusions from cross-industrial data might be misleading.

[57] For example, assuming labour augmenting technological progress, the measured rate of TFP growth and technology growth is $(1-\alpha)$ times less than the true one.

[58] In a recent papers, Rodrik (1997) argues that standard measures of total factor productivity growth in countries where the capital-labour ratio has risen rapidly will understate true productivity growth if the elasticity of substitution is less than one and there is labour augmenting technological progress.

The problem of reverse causality

The static investigation evidently suffers from a causality problem: if positive coefficients for the *FDI*-variable are detected, does it mean that foreign investment really exhibits a positive impact on local productivity, or do foreign firms simply engage in sectors with higher productivity? We know from Chapter 2 that, indeed, FDI is a highly sector-specific phenomenon, particularly characteristic for high-tech sectors. If these sectors are more productive than the others, regressions might be spurious and the opposite causation may be valid. To the best knowledge of the author, statistical tests of the direction of causation between foreign investment and productivity of local firms cannot be found in the literature.[59] The most probable reason is the lack of comprehensive data for longer periods necessary to run the Granger causality test.[60]

In a dynamic investigation, the causality can run in both directions, as well. For instance, FDI may take place in industries and markets because of their growth prospects. As a result, larger foreign presence and productivity growth of local firms within the industry may coincide without any productivity spillovers from FDI.

Industry-level data

When firm-level data are not available, analysing productivity of the whole locally-owned part of the industry might be considered an alternative. In practice, two processes may stimulate aggregate productivity growth: (i) incumbent firms become more productive, (ii) more productive incumbent firms expand and/or new high productive firms enter the market, displacing less productive exiting establishments, but incumbent firms' productivity is constant (Levinsohn/Petrin, 1999).

FDI may support both processes. Exit of firms with below average productivity might be accelerated in the presence of FDI due to the competition effect, but this effect is per se not FDI-specific. Rather, it is an immediate implication of Ricardo's theory of comparative advantages and specialisation. In contrast, the emergence of new local firms with higher than average productivity might be due to the demonstration effect of foreign affiliates. Moreover, all of the channels through which spillovers propagate - linkages, imitation and labour turnover - can reduce barriers to entry. Whenever a higher foreign presence

---

[59] The usual solution to this problem is using lagged instead of current values of the *FDI*-variable as an exogenous term in the cross-firm or cross-industry regression. This is obviously not a correct remedial if high firm and industry productivity is autocorrelated over time.

[60] Causality between foreign investment and labour productivity in the whole domestic industry (foreign and local firms) was investigated by Kholdy (1995). He found no support for the existence of spillovers in Mexico, Brazil, Chile, Singapore and Zambia for the period of 1970-90.

accelerates the speed of entry, this is the manifestation of productivity spillovers, even if the incumbent firms do not increase their productivity.

Industrial productivity growth through exit is detrimental to the less competitive firms with all economic and social consequences of structural adjustment. Besides, it is a temporary process. When technology transfer is at work, then it might be a perpetual process in which local firms learn along with FDI. Foreign firms are then forced to upgrade their technology, initiating the second round of learning in local firms. Productivity spillovers which lead to the increase in the productivity of incumbent firms – the art of spillovers analysed with firm-level data – are more attractive from the viewpoint of the host country.

One can only distinguish the kind of process underlying industrial productivity growth with plant- or firm-level data. Consequently, analyses using industry-level data have drawbacks – they tell us less about productivity spillovers than studies using firm-level panels.

4.4 Conclusions

The present chapter provided an overview, as well as a critical analysis, of the existing empirical work exploring productivity spillovers. We have considered two types of complementing evidence: industrial case-studies and econometric research.

Case-studies of individual FDI projects in developing countries are quite numerous since they have been conducted for many years. They reveal that the emergence of foreign affiliates may change the nature and evolution of concentration, they may affect the profitability and growth of indigenous firms, they may alter financing, marketing, technological, or managerial practices of the sectors that they enter; they may, by predatory conduct, drive domestic firms out of business, and so on. In general, both positive and negative externalities from the activity of foreign affiliates for the host country possibly arise.

The main contribution of this literature consists in identifying channels through which emerging foreign affiliates impacts the performance of local firms. Direct linkages to local suppliers and customers of foreign affiliates, indirect linkages to local competitors in output markets as well as mobility of workers from foreign to local firms constitute potentially powerful relations for stimulating industrial growth in the host country. Table 4.2 shows for each type of local firms the potential channels for transmission of productivity spillovers.

The case-study evidence reveals that a potential for productivity spillovers which arises with the emergence of FDI is conditional. Similar, the scope of spillovers may differ substantially. The type of FDI: motives, the entry mode, strategic goals of the parent company and the technology implemented, matters a lot. The local conditions: relative technological level of local firms, the strength of competition, industrial and trade policy related to FDI, build the second pole of factors which impact the market behaviour of foreign firms and the ability of local enterprises to absorb the potential for the productivity enhancing spillovers.

Table 4.2:
Transmission Channels for Spillovers from FDI on Local Firms in Host Countries

Local Firms:	Access to technology[1] and markets
Suppliers	Backwards linkages, Labour turnover
Customers	Forward linkages, Labour turnover
Competitors	Competition effect, Demonstration effect, Labour turnover

Note: [1]- including organisational and managerial practices, labour skills and physical capital

The econometric analyses testing hypotheses on the scope of productivity spillovers, derived from case-studies literature, are rare. The major obstacle is that only for a few countries (Morocco, Mexico, Indonesia), the necessary data are available. Within a standard production-function framework, these studies are capable to detect intra-industrial productivity spillovers at the side of local competitors of foreign affiliates. Positive (or negative) spillovers emerging by local suppliers and customers cannot be detected separately, but they may contribute to the productivity growth of local rivals of foreign direct enterprises.

The conclusions derived from these analyses are not unique. As formulated in the contagion hypothesis, the scope of intra-industrial foreign presence seems to be a principal factor determining the extent of spillovers: both positive and negative. Proportionality between foreign presence and productivity growth (or fall) on the part of local firms have been detected.

Productivity spillovers seem to depend on the relative technological level of local firms. Three out of four studies testing the relationship detected that technologically more advanced firms benefit more in terms of productivity growth from a higher intra-industrial foreign presence. This contradicts the standard technology gap hypothesis.

There is only one study testing the impact of the structure of local industry on the scope of spillovers. It confirms the hypothesis of the beneficial role of higher competition for the emergence of spillovers.

In the following Chapter 5, we would analyse theoretical models of productivity spillovers of FDI. Hereby, the empirical findings summarised in the present chapter allow us to structure the existing theoretical literature according to the type of local firms and channels for technology transfer it focuses on.

Chapter 5:
FDI impact on local firms: the theory

5.1 Introduction

The theoretical literature on the role of FDI in recipient countries is very ample. Early analyses were conducted within a neo-classical two-commodity two-factor model of international trade. Foreign investment was rendered as an inflow of foreign capital augmenting domestic capital endowment. As a production factor, capital was assumed to be homogenous regardless of its origin, and perfectly mobile between the foreign- and the locally-owned sector. Consequently, producing with foreign capital is as much efficient as with domestic capital.

In this model world, opening to FDI inflows cannot serve as a vehicle for transfer of superior technology from abroad. The only advantage of capital inflows was a fall in its rental price and expansion of a capital-intensive sector. The welfare effects of capital inflows depend on the structure of protection: Brecher/Diaz-Alejandro (1977) showed that tariff-induced inflows of foreign capital with full repatriation of its earnings may lower national welfare. Neary (1988) compared welfare effects of capital imports under different protective measures in a common framework and found out that capital mobility raises the welfare costs of tariff protection and it reduces them by means of quantitative restrictions.

Theoretical attempts to incorporate some characteristics of less developed countries into economic modelling relied on the Harris-Todaro (1970) framework. The main stream of this literature still regarded the only role of FDI as augmenting domestic manufacturing capital stock.[1] Only very recently, in some theoretical works foreign investment is modelled as the emergence and expansion of multinationals.[2] Foreign subsidiaries were assumed to produce different goods than domestic firms (as viewed by consumers) or to posses superior technology. However, the only link with the host economy was established on factor markets: foreign firms employed domestic labour and capital (sometimes additional to capital imported from abroad). With exception of Gupta (1998), technological spillovers have been excluded.

This literature has concentrated on four dimensions of changes in a local economy which may be enforced by the expansion of foreign capital inflows: the behaviour of the unemployment (absolute level and rate), the size of locally-owned sectors, aggregate national welfare and national income. There is not a universal insight about the consequences of foreign capital inflows: they depend on the structure of the host economy and the type of prevailing market

[1] The list includes Khan (1982), Grinols (1991) and Lal (1995), among others.
[2] See Khawar (1997) or Gupta (1998).

distortions. This literature has also supported very uneven distribution of gains from capital flows within the domestic economy which has been identified by empirical studies.

Despite empirical interest on technological spillovers from FDI, theoretical literature widely neglected this aspect while studying the interaction between multinationals and the host economy. Only quite recently, some authors focused on spillovers - their emergence and scope – in a more theoretically founded way. In doing so, one strand of the literature has assumed that the level of spillovers is exogenous: Local firms benefit automatically from the emergence of multinationals to the extent which increases with the degree of industrial foreign presence (*contagion hypothesis*) and with technological lead of multinationals relative to local firms (*technology gap hypothesis*). With these *ad hoc* hypotheses on spillovers, theoretical models of FDI impact on growth in the host country has been elaborated.

However, exogenous spillovers are at odds with empirical facts. As Chapter 4 pointed out, the evidence of productivity spillovers according to the both hypotheses is quite mixed – positive impact of a higher FDI is not necessary beneficial. Hence, analytical convenience of the black-box approach may obscure important determinants of the emergence and scope of positive externalities from FDI.

Another group of authors has analysed spillovers without imposing any *a priori* hypotheses. In doing so, they studied different channels through which multinationals may impact productivity of the local industry in the host country. In Section 4.2 we identified three such mechanisms: linkages with local suppliers and customers, labour movement, and linkages to competitors. At present, the literature on endogenous spillovers is only emerging, and only a few papers belong to this category.

The purpose of this chapter is to review the theoretical literature dealing with productivity spillovers from FDI. In Section 5.2, we first introduce formally the contagion and the technology gap hypotheses and then study how FDI impact growth in the host country when such 'black box' type of spillovers occur. In the rest of the present chapter, we analyse the conditions for the emergence of spillovers. In doing so, we check whether the current literature on endogenous spillovers gives theoretical support for both 'ad hoc' hypotheses. Section 5.3 studies productivity spillovers due to the existence of vertical linkages to local firms. Section 5.4 examines labour mobility between multinational and local firms as a transmission mechanism for technology. Section 5.5 deals with spillovers facilitating technology creation and adaptation in local firms. A short summary and conclusions are given in Section 5.6.

5.2 Technology diffusion in the presence of spillovers from FDI

5.2.1 Local technology gap and FDI spillovers

Technology diffusion, *i.e.* transmission of a piece of technological information from one firm to another firm, shows a typical pattern: diffusion rates first rise and then fall over time, leading to a period of relatively rapid adoption sandwiched between an early period of slow take-up and a late period of slow approach to satiation.

Probably the most popular explanation of this S-curve is an 'epidemic' model of information diffusion which builds on the premise that what limits the speed of usage is the lack of information available about the new technology, how to use it and what it does. The model is associated with the work of Mansfield (1961, 1968). He showed empirically that the rate at which an innovation is adopted in an industry is an increasing function of the proportion of firms within the industry that have already adopted the innovation. He explains it by assuming that technological innovations are most effectively copied when there is personal contact between the prospective imitators and those who already have the knowledge of the innovation. Evidently, the chance for such a contact arises with the higher proportion of firms with the new technology adopted. Due to the analogy with the spread of a contagious disease, the idea of Mansfield is labelled the 'contagion hypothesis'.

The second important hypothesis on the speed of technology diffusion between countries borrows from ideas articulated by Veblen (1915) and reformulated by Gerschenkron (1962). The Veblen-Gerschenkron effect implies that the rate at which a less developed country can catch-up (in terms of development level) with the already industrialised part of the world is positively related to the backwardness of the country at the outset of industrialisation process. The argument reads that the greater the pool of available opportunities for the developing country, which is assumed to rise with the development differential to the developed countries, the greater is the pressure for change and the higher the speed at which the development process occurs. The above hypothesis is usually labelled the 'backwardness' or the 'technology gap' hypothesis.

In their original formulation, neither the 'technology gap' nor the 'contagion' hypothesis referred to the technological impact of FDI on the host country. Findlay (1978) was the first to combine both arguments and to propose an explicit analytical model of technological change in the host country along with FDI. In Findlay model, technological growth is measured by the rise of the index of the overall technical efficiency. Let $A_S(t)$ denote the level of technical efficiency at time t in the backward country which is host to FDI (S for South), whereas $A_N(t)$ gives the technological level of the more advanced home country

(N for North) in the same period. The technology gap of the host country is measured by $GAP(t)$

$$GAP(t) \equiv \frac{A_N(t)}{A_S(t)}. \tag{5.1}$$

The extent of foreign presence in the South is measured by the ratio of the capital stock in foreign-owned (multinational) firms, $K_m(t)$, to the capital stock of locally-owned firms, $K_l(t)$:

$$FDI(t) \equiv \frac{K_m(t)}{K_l(t)}. \tag{5.2}$$

Then, the speed of technological growth in the South, $\dot{A}_S / A_S$, is postulated to be

$$\frac{\dot{A}_S}{A_S} = f(GAP, FDI) \tag{5.3}$$

where the dot denotes a derivative with respect to time and

$\partial f / \partial FDI > 0$ in accordance with the 'contagion' hypothesis;

$\partial f / \partial GAP > 0$ in accordance with the 'technology gap' hypothesis.

Wang (1990) is a good example how the Findlay's technological transfer function given by Eq. (5.3) can be incorporated into a dynamic, two-country growth model with FDI.[3] The model is based on the following assumptions.

(W.1) There are two countries: South and North, denoted by S and N respectively, each producing one final good. The production function for output, X, is of Cobb-Douglas type with constant returns to scale in physical capital, K, and labour, L: $X_i = A_i L_i^{\beta} K_i^{1-\beta}$ with A_i an index of technology level of an economy i, $i = S, N$ where $1 > \beta > 0$. The actual technological level in the production of output, A_i, depends positively on the average human capital of the country's labour force, h_i. More specifically, let $A_i = h_i^{\beta}$. South is initially a backwards country in the meaning that $A_S < A_N$ and $K_S < K_N$. For simplicity, let us assume that the labour force is constant and identical in both countries, $L \equiv L_S = L_N$. The per-capita output in country i depends positively on the capital-labour

[3] The literature on technology transfer through externalities related to foreign investment contains also Koizumi/Kopecky (1977), Das (1987), and, within the Harris-Todaro framework, Gupta (1998). In these models, host country productivity growth is postulated to be an increasing function of the presence of foreign capital in accordance with the contagion hypothesis.

ratio, k_i, and the actual technological level: $x_i = X_i / L = h_i^{\beta} k_i^{1-\beta}$ with $k_i \equiv K_i / L$.

(W.2) The two countries are linked in an international capital market. Let K_m denote the amount of foreign capital located in the South by multinationals with headquarters in the North. In per-capita terms, the output in each country equals

$$x_N = h_N{}^{\beta} (k_N - k_m)^{1-\beta} \tag{5.4a}$$

$$x_S = h_S{}^{\beta} (k_S + k_m)^{1-\beta} \qquad \text{where } k_m \equiv K_m / L. \tag{5.4b}$$

With perfect capital mobility, the marginal productivity of physical capital in the output production is the same in both countries, $r \equiv r_S = r_N$, at every instant of time

$$r = h_S{}^{\beta-1} \beta (k_S + k_m)^{-\beta} = h_N{}^{\beta-1} \beta (k_N - k_m)^{-\beta} \tag{5.5}$$

(W.3) The earnings of the multinationals in the South are fully repatriated to the North. Then, the national income of each country in per-capita terms equals its output adjusted for the foreign investment earnings:

$$y_N = h_N{}^{\beta} (k_N - k_m)^{1-\beta} + r k_m \tag{5.6a}$$

$$y_S = h_S{}^{\beta} (k_S + k_m)^{1-\beta} - r k_m \tag{5.6b}$$

(W.4) In each country, accumulation of physical capital is financed by savings out of national income. The country-specific saving rates, s_i, and the common depreciation rate, v, are exogenously given and constant. The accumulation equations for capital read

$$\dot{k}_i = s_i y_i - v k_i \qquad \text{for country } i = S, N \tag{5.7a, 5.7b}$$

(W.5) In the North, technological progress through accumulation of human capital proceeds at an exogenous and constant rate

$$\dot{h}_N = \gamma_N h_N \tag{5.8a}$$

(W.6) With the inflows of foreign capital into the South, advanced technology and managerial skills are transmitted to the local part of the economy through the presence of multinational firms. The Southern technological progress is assumed to be positively affected by the presence of multinational firms, measured by the ratio of the foreign to the domestically owned capital, $FDI \equiv K_m / K_S$, and by the technology gap, measured by $GAP \equiv h_N / h_S$

$$\dot{h}_S = \gamma_S f(FDI, GAP) h_S \qquad \text{for } FDI \geq 0 \text{ and } GAP \geq 1 \tag{5.8b}$$

with $f(0,1)=1$, $\partial f/\partial FDI>0$ due to the contagion hypothesis, and $\partial f/\partial GAP>0$ due to the technology gap hypothesis.

The meaning of the constant γ_S is twofold. In autarky ($FDI=0$), it stays for the exogenous rate of human capital formation in the South. With foreign investment ($FDI>0$), it can be interpreted as the rate of technological diffusion of the Northern technology to the South or as the *adaptive efficiency* of the South.

The direction of FDI inflows and the amount of capital invested are endogenously determined by the relative factor endowment of the countries. From its definition, $FDI=K_m/K_S=k_m/k_S$. Using Eq. (5.5), we obtain

$$FDI=(k^{-1}-GAP)/(1+GAP) \qquad (5.9)$$

Since $\partial FDI/\partial k<0$ and $\partial FDI/\partial GAP<0$, the FDI stock is higher when country S is relatively worse endowed with physical capital, ($k\equiv K_S/K_N$ is lower), and when South has a better relative human capital endowment ($GAP\equiv h_N/h_S$ is lower). Intuitively, a higher k (a higher GAP) lowers the relative marginal productivity of physical capital in the South and its relative rate of return. It reduces incentives for foreign investment in the South. For further analysis, we assume that the relative factor endowment always ensures that $FDI>0$, i.e. there is foreign capital inflow from the North to the South.

Combing equations (5.9) and (5.8b) shows that relative backwardness of the Southern economy affects the growth rate of Southern human capital through two different channels. From (5.9), a higher *GAP* induces lower inflows of foreign investment to the South and thus a lower pace of human capital accumulation. But from (5.8b), the productivity spillovers from foreign investment specified by the function *f* are higher. It is assumed that the second effect dominates the first one. Hence, the more backward the technological level of the South, the higher is the rate of technological progress following Southern opening to the foreign investment.

Wang (1990) proves that under assumptions (5.4)-(5.9) there exists a unique and stable steady state for the world economy with positive FDI in the South. In the dynamic equilibrium, relative endowments of the South with human capital and with physical capital, measured by *GAP* and *k,* as well as the ratio of human to physical capital stay constant. It follows that Northern and Southern physical and human capital all grow with the same rate γ_N. On the balanced growth path, the measure of foreign presence in the South, *FDI*, becomes a constant (see Eq. (5.9)). Then, Eq. (5.5) implies that the equilibrium rate of return to physical capital does not change. Finally, Eqs. (5.6a-5.6b) state that the per-capita national income in each country grows with the same rate as physical capital which is equal to γ_N.

In the autarkic steady state with $FDI = 0$, Southern physical and human capital both grow with the rate γ_S (see Eqs. (5.7b) and (5.6b)). This is also the pace at which the per-capita output and national income in the South continuously increase. Intuitively, the technological progress enhancing labour productivity with the rate γ_S exactly offsets the effects of diminishing returns associated with physical capital accumulation. The Southern output grows due to a permanent accumulation of human and physical capital. Since in the North the national income as well as both types of capital grow with the rate γ_N, Northern and Southern income levels diverge at the rate γ_N-γ_S. As long as $\gamma_N > \gamma_S$, the relative income of the backward country permanently worsens. Comparison of the steady state in autarky and the one under perfect capital mobility yields the following proposition:

Proposition 5.1:

(i) ***Whenever $\gamma_N > \gamma_S$, FDI inflows raise the steady state growth rate of national income in the host country from γ_S to γ_N. The growth rate of Northern national income stays unchanged.***

(ii) ***In the autarkic steady state the ratio of Southern to Northern per-capita income falls with the rate γ_N-γ_S. Opening to foreign investment prevents this ratio from falling, and the relative Southern per capita income becomes a constant in the steady state.***

The relative steady-state income in the South is determined by exogenous parameters of the model: technological parameters γ_S and γ_N as well as the saving rates s_N and s_S. Liberalising FDI might lead to narrowing the income gap between South and North, but it is not for sure. Moreover, the Southern income ratio may even deteriorate. But, the beneficial impact of the FDI is the higher rate of technological progress and stabilising the income gap in the long-run. If the steady-state relative income with FDI is smaller than the one before the South opened to international investment, the average growth rate of the South during the transition process is higher than the average growth in the North. Figure 5.1 shows the time-path of the Southern economy in transition to the steady-state with FDI. It is drawn for $s_N = 0.15$; $s_S = 0.10; \gamma_N = 0.050$; $\gamma_S = 0.026; \beta = 0.667; v = 0.10$ and $f = (1 + FDI)GAP$.

How does the Southern technological adaptive efficiency, γ_S, affects the scope of the FDI impact on the economy? A higher γ_S improves the rate of technological adoption and the relative rental rate of capital. This attracts additional FDI. Wang shows that in the long-run, a higher capital-labour ratio and higher level of human capital relative to the North results. In the new steady state, the Southern income ratio is higher and the magnitude of foreign presence, *FDI*, smaller.

A higher rate of technological progress prior to FDI, γ_S, does not implicate a higher growth rate with FDI, but only a higher relative income. The above result can explain the interpretation of γ_S as an absorptive efficiency of the host country – higher absorptive efficiency leads to a higher productivity change in the reaction to FDI. Within the model, the catching-up of the income with the technological leader depends on whether the host country has a high enough absorptive efficiency. Hence, ex-post income ratio change is not the strongest in countries that are technologically most backward, but a high absorptive efficiency may allow a less backward country narrow or close the income gap most.[4]

Figure 5.1:
The impact of FDI on the South

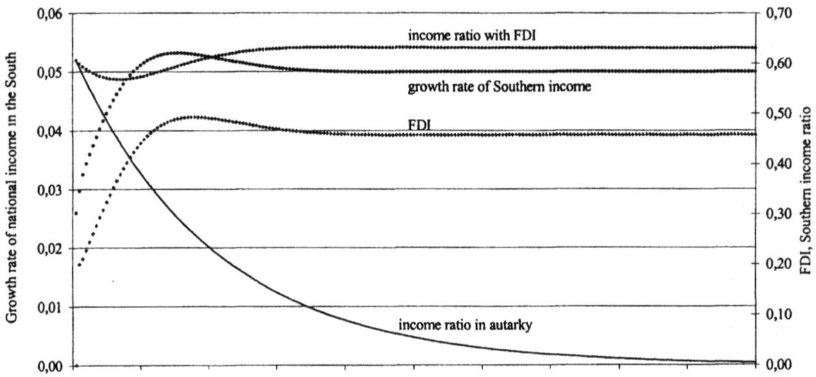

[4] This result is similar to the point made by Keller (1996) who argued that a sufficiently high human capital accumulation is a necessary condition for a country importing technology embodied in goods to increase its growth rate.

5.2.2 Concluding remarks

If FDI leads to technological externalities in accordance with the contagion and the technology gap hypothesis, liberalising FDI has a beneficial impact on a backward host country: the steady-state rate of income growth would increase and the income gap between it and the technological leader could be prevented from falling down. However, the host country does not necessarily catch-up with the foreign income level. The scope of reducing the income gap depends positively on the absorptive efficiency of the advanced technology by firms in the host country. One conclusion from the model presented here is that if countries want to benefit more from FDI, they should concentrate on supporting their domestic firms in accumulation of human capital.

In the rest of this chapter we investigate whether the *a priori* hypotheses on the scope of spillovers can be derived from the present theoretical literature.

5.3 Spillovers through linkages with local firms

The substantial body of empirical evidence presented in Chapter 4 indicates that most common linkages of foreign affiliates to local firms take the form of direct relationships with local suppliers of intermediate goods or producer services. The purpose of this section is to show how *creation of linkages to local suppliers of inputs* serves as a channel through which the emergence of multinational firms may benefit the domestic economy. We present two supplemental theoretical models which allow us to identify the effects in work and their determinants.

The models abstract from direct 'vertical' technology transfer to local suppliers – the fact well-documented in numerous case studies as discussed in Section 4.2.1. Until very recently, theoretical analysis of 'vertical' technology transfer were missing. The only paper dealing with this process is Pack/Saggi (1999). It makes the point that intentional technology transfer to a local supplier may initiate its uncontrolled diffusion to other firms producing intermediates in the host country through labour movement or the informal interchange of knowledge between managers and workers. Technological progress in the upstream industry may in turn benefit local firms in the downstream industry. But this is exactly the effect analysed in detail within the two models we discuss in this section.

The present section is organised as follows: Section 5.3.1 introduces the standard approach to modelling backwards linkages. Section 5.3.2 presents a simplified version of a Markusen/Venables (1999) model of the FDI impact on local firms through creation of linkages. Despite its partial equilibrium nature, it is very useful in working out various effects associated with the entry of multinationals. But, because of its partial equilibrium nature, it cannot distinguish and quantify factors determining the strength of these effects. This has been done by Rodríguez-Clare (1996). In Section 5.3.3, we present and discuss his approach. Section 5.3.4 concludes on the support given by the discussed models to the *a priori* hypotheses on spillovers.

5.3.1 Economic modelling of linkages

A formalisation of the concept of linkages as a channel through which multinationals impact local firms in the host country was elaborated only recently. Rivera-Batiz/Rivera-Batiz (1991) were the first who applied this idea, but modelled FDI as a capital inflow increasing homogenous capital stock in the host country. Rodríguez-Clare (1996) and Markusen/Venables (1999) go the same way when modelling linkages, but view FDI as the emergence of multinational firms in the host country. The three papers rely on similar assumptions concerning the creation of linkages:

(1) Productivity in the consumer goods' sector, which is a host to multinational firms, increases by the use of a wider variety of specialised, differentiated intermediates (physical goods or business services).

(2) Specialised inputs are internationally non-tradable. However, firms may obtain access to inputs produced abroad by becoming multinational, *i.e.* by locating their headquarters and production plants in different countries.

(3) The local supply and the degree of product differentiation in the intermediate goods is limited by the size of the market, *i.e.* the demand of the consumer goods' industry for inputs.[5]

Formally, linkages with the above characteristics can be incorporated in a model of product differentiation in a Dixit/Stiglitz (1977) manner. Let the consumption good C be produced with a composite intermediate input I which is assembled from a set of differentiated intermediate goods. The production functions for the final good C reads:[6]

$$X_c = \left(\int_0^n x_j^{\alpha} dj \right)^{1/\alpha} \qquad 0 < \alpha < 1$$

where x_j denotes the quantity of the jth variety of the intermediate input employed. The set of varieties available to the producers of good C is given by the interval $[0, n]$. We refer to n as the 'number' of available varieties.

All differentiated inputs enter the production function for C symmetrically. Since the marginal productivity of intermediate input j is independent of the

---

[5] This idea reflects Adam Smith's theory of the division of labour and growth (see also Romer, 1987)

[6] Dixit/Stiglitz (1977) proposed this functional form for a utility function. Ethier (1982) applied this specification to the production theory.

employed quantity of another variety *i*, they are neither direct substitutes nor direct complements. The elasticity of substitution between any two intermediate inputs, ε, is defined as $\varepsilon := -\frac{\partial \ln(x_i / x_j)}{\partial \ln(X_c^i / X_c^j)}$, where X_c^i is the partial derivative of the production function for C with respect to the *i*th variety. The elasticity of substitution, ε, equals approximately (for large n) $1/(1-\alpha)$, so that $\varepsilon > 1$. It is constant and identical for any two varieties of the differentiated input. A higher ε means that different varieties are better substitutes in the production of the final good. In other words, a high ε reflects a low degree of product differentiation in the i-industry as viewed by the producers of the final good, with ε tending to infinity for perfect substitutes.

In Appendix 5.A we argue that because of diminishing returns to each individual input, a firm producing good C has clear incentives to use all n available varieties of inputs. Proposition (5.A.1) states that the total factor productivity in the production of good C rises when the employed number of varieties of intermediate input increases.

With this principle result, the way how a liberalisation of FDI may impact the productivity of local firms is quite evident. Consider multinationals which relocate their productive activities into a foreign country. In doing so, they win access to locally produced inputs (see assumption 2) which rises their productivity and lowers costs (assumption 1). Whenever the entry of multinationals results in additional demand for intermediates in the host country, the intermediate goods industry grows by offering a richer variety of inputs (assumption 3). This benefits both multinationals and local firms in the consumer's good sector of the host country since their productivity increases.

However, the above effect relies heavily upon whether the appearance of multinationals really cause a higher demand for locally produced intermediates. This might not be the case because two simultaneous effects working in opposite directions must be considered. The first one – the *backward linkage* effect – is the one already presented. But, multinationals and local producers of the consumption good are competitors in product and factor markets. Due to the *competition effect* on local producers, their profits may shrink and some local firms may be crowded out of the market. Obviously, it reduces *ceteris paribus* the domestic demand for intermediates. The net effect of multinationals entry on the demand for intermediate goods depends on the relative scope of both effects. The following sections study how these effects emerge, and they focus on the determinants of the net positive impact of multinationals on productivity of locally-owned firms.

5.3.2 Enhancing productivity of local firms through creation of linkages

The interplay between the competition and the backward linkage effect can be conveniently traced within the theoretical framework developed very recently by Markusen/Venables (1999). Here, we present a simplified version of their basic model which assumes that some foreign firms have an incentive to become multinationals.[7]

Consider a country *S* which liberalises FDI. Local firms are engaged either in producing of a final consumption good *C* (c-industry) or in manufacturing of an intermediate input *I* (i-industry) for the c-industry.[8] Multinationals in country *S* have their headquarters in country *N* and are active in the host country's consumer good industry.

The main assumptions of the model read:

(M.1) There is monopolistic competition in the i-industry. The produced input *I* comes in a number of differentiated varieties. Labour is the only production factor for the i-industry. All producers of the intermediate goods face identical cost functions.

(M.2) There is monopolistic competition in the c-industry. Varieties of the differentiated consumption good *C* may be supplied by local firms, exporters from the country *N* and by multinationals. The number of exporters and multinationals is exogenously given with n_e and n_m, respectively.

(M.3) The good *C* is produced using labour, *L*, and a composite input, assembled from varieties of the differentiated intermediate good, *I*. Labour is internationally immobile. Varieties of the differentiated input are internationally non-tradable, so only varieties produced in the country may serve as an input for the domestic c-industry. Inputs requirements may different for local and multinational firms in the c-industry.

(M.4) The firms face a perfectly elastic supply of labour (from elsewhere in the economy) at a wage equal to one (by normalisation).

The firms simultaneously and non-cooperatively choose prices in order to maximise profits in the presence of fixed costs, ignoring its own impact on the price choice of other competitors. The firms simultaneously and non-cooperatively choose prices in order to maximise profits in the presence of fixed costs, ignoring its own impact on the price choice of other competitors. The standard model of product differentiation in a monopolistically competitive

[7] The authors explore a more general case in which they endogenise a decision of a foreign firm to become a multinational. This extension turns out to produce similar results. Despite our simplification, the model is still rich enough to outline the main interactions between different types of firms.

[8] There exists a single, representative consumer who derives utility from the consumption of all varieties of the differentiated good *C*.

industry is presented in detail in Appendix 5.A. Here, the main characteristics of the equilibrium in a monopolistically competitive market will be pointed out:

Proposition 5.2:

(i) Each variety of the differentiated good is produced by a single firm. Each firm produces one and only one variety of the differentiated good.

(ii) In symmetric Nash equilibrium each firm charges the same, fixed mark-up over marginal costs.

(iii) In symmetric Nash equilibrium each variety of the differentiated good is priced and demanded equally.

(iv) In symmetric Nash equilibrium each firm makes zero profits.

Since for each firm representing a given type (local firms, multinationals, exporters from the *N* country) costs, prices and output sold are identical, we apply the following notation for different types of firms active in the host country:

Type of the firm	Number of firms	Price	Output of each firm
Local firms in the i-industry	n	p	x
Local firms in the c-industry	n_l	p_l	x_l
Multinational firms in the c-industry	n_m	p_m	x_m
Foreign exporters in the c-industry	n_e	p_e	x_e

Demand for intermediate goods:

Each of the n firms in the i-industry faces a demand coming from domestic producers of the differentiated good *C* (local firms and multinationals) given by Eq. (A.9)[9]

$$x = p^{-\varepsilon} q_i^{\varepsilon} E^r \tag{5.10}$$

where q_i is the price index of the composite input *I* and E^r is the total real income (in prices of labour) spent by the domestic c-industry on all intermediate goods. The elasticity of substitution between any two varieties of the intermediate input in the production of good *C* is ε, $\varepsilon > 1$. The price index for the basket of intermediates, q_i, is decreasing in the number of available varieties as given by Eq. (A.7)

$$q_i = pn^{1/(1-\varepsilon)} \quad \text{and} \quad \partial q_i / \partial n < 0 \tag{5.11}$$

Hence, from Eq. (5.10) each firm in the i-industry faces a demand for its output equal to

[9] Equations numbered with a letter are derived in appendices.

$$x = n^{\varepsilon/(1-\varepsilon)} E^r \qquad \text{and} \qquad \partial x / \partial n < 0 \qquad (5.12)$$

The demand faced by a single firm is inversely related to the number of active firms in the i-industry. It is independent on the individual price, since prices for all varieties are identical.

The total demand for intermediates, E^r can be derived as follows. Let us assume that each of the n_l locally-owned firms has a total input requirement of $(F_l + x_l)$ in units of labour for producing x_l units of good *C*. F_l is a fixed total input requirement, and for each additional unit of output, inputs equal to one unit of labour must be employed. Similarly, let the total input requirement of each of the n_m multinationals necessary to produce x_m units of good *C* be $(F_m + x_m)$. Local firms spend for labour a fraction $(1 - \mu_l)$ of the total amount of inputs, whereas μ_l is for a composite intermediate good priced q_i. Multinationals spend a fraction equal to μ_m for a basket of intermediates. Both μ_l and μ_m are assumed to be exogenously given; for example, $\mu_m < \mu_l$ means that multinationals are less intensive users of domestically produced inputs than the local firms are.

With the above specifications of the production technology for different firms in the c-industry, the total demand for intermediates (in units of labour) is

$$E^r = n_l \mu_l (F_l + x_l) + n_m \mu_m (F_m + x_m) \qquad (5.13)$$

which is split equally between all produced varieties of differentiated intermediates (compare to Eq. (5.12)).

Supply of intermediate goods

Each of the *n* firms in the i-industry needs a fixed amount of *F* units of labour to start production and one additional unit of labour for each additional unit of output. Each firm maximises profit given by

$$\pi = px - (F + x) \qquad (5.14)$$

by charging a fixed mark-up over marginal costs and selling its variety at price, *p*

$$p = \frac{\varepsilon}{\varepsilon - 1} \qquad (5.15)$$

The output and the profits of each firm producing intermediate goods decreases with n (see Eq. (5.12)). Assuming free entry and exit of firms in the i-industry, the number of competing firms immediately adjusts until profits are zero in equilibrium. Using Eqs. (5.14)-(5.15), the zero-profit condition in the intermediate goods industry is

$$\pi = 0 \quad \Leftrightarrow \quad x = (\varepsilon - 1)F \qquad (5.16)$$

Choosing units in which to measure output of the intermediate good, we can normalise the equilibrium output of each firm in the i-industry to one. This normalisation allows writing the equilibrium condition for a firm in the intermediate goods industry, namely, demand from Eq. (5.12) equals supply from Eq. (5.16), in the following way:

$$\pi = 0 \quad \Leftrightarrow \quad n_l \mu_l (F_l + x_l) + n_m \mu_m (F_m + x_m) = n^{\varepsilon/(\varepsilon-1)} \tag{5.17}$$

With the number of multinationals exogenously given, there is a positive relationship between the number of local firms in c-industry, n_l, and the number of local firms in the i-industry, n. With a higher number of local firms, the total demand for intermediates (the left hand side of Eq. (5.17)) and demand for each single variety of the intermediate good (Eq. (5.12)) increases. Positive profits for the incumbent producers result (Eq. (5.14)). This attracts new entrants into the i-sector. The number of firms and locally-produced varieties of good I increases which drives down the profits of a single firm in the i-industry, until in equilibrium all profits are zero.

Demand for consumer goods

In accordance with assumption (M.2), utility from consumption of good C has a Dixit-Stiglitz form $U = U(Y, n_l^{\theta/(\theta-1)} x_l + n_m^{\theta/(\theta-1)} x_m + n_e^{\theta/(\theta-1)} x_e)$ where Y is a vector containing quantities of other consumer goods and $\theta > 1$. The price index for a composite consumption good C can be derived from Eq. (A.7):

$$q_c = \left(n_l p_l^{1-\theta} + n_m p_m^{1-\theta} + n_e p_e^{1-\theta}\right)^{1/(1-\theta)} \tag{5.18}$$

where θ denotes elasticity of substitution between any two varieties of good C.

Since the model is of partial equilibrium type, the authors just assume that the total demand for a basket containing all available varieties of good C equals $K_1 q_c^{-\eta}$ where K_1 is a positive constant and η is the price elasticity of demand, $0 < \eta < \theta$.[10] For the following presentation, I assume that foreign and multinational firms supply at equal prices determined outside the host country, $p_e = p_m$.[11] This simplification leaves the main results unchanged.

[10] Modelling the number of imported varieties of good C would imply modelling the intermediate goods sector in the rest of the world.

[11] For a global multinational, its decision about entry and price in a given host country does not necessary reflect profit maximisation in this market. Strategic considerations and expectations about future profit opportunities may, among others, cause that the number of active multinationals and the prices charged are exogenous in view of the host country. If multinationals also export to the host country, prices for foreign and domestically produced goods of multinationals may be equal.

The demand function for each variety of the consumption good is given by Eq. (A.9)

$$x_l = K_1 p_l^{-\theta} q_c^{\theta-\eta} \quad \text{for locally owned firms} \quad (5.19)$$

$$x_m = x_e = K_1 p_m^{-\theta} q_c^{\theta-\eta} \quad \text{for multinationals and exporters} \quad (5.20)$$

Supply of consumer goods

Multinationals and local firms supply the demanded quantity of good *C* at a fixed price p_m. Locally-owned firms in the c-industry set prices so as to maximise profits. With input requirement specified in the previous section, local firms reap profits

$$\pi_l = p_l x_l - \left[\mu_l (F_l + x_l) q_i + (1-\mu_l)(F_l + x_l)\right] \quad (5.21)$$

They maximise profits by charging a fixed mark-up over marginal costs (see Eq. (A.11))

$$p_l = \frac{\theta}{\theta-1}\left(\mu_l q_i + 1 - \mu_l\right) \qquad \partial p_l / \partial q_i > 0 \quad \text{and} \quad \partial p_l / \partial n < 0 \quad (5.22)$$

The price of good *C* produced by local firms decreases when more varieties of the intermediate good are available for its production. In equilibrium, the zero-profit condition $\pi_l = 0$ specifies supply of a single variety of the differentiated good *C*

$$x_l = (\theta - 1) F_l \quad (5.23)$$

Outside equilibrium, the number of local firms changes, adjusting the demand viewed by a single firm (Eq. 5.10) to the equilibrium level given by Eq. (5.14). We choose units for output of the good *C* so that $x_l = 1$ results in an equilibrium with zero profits. Substituting for the price index of consumption goods, we obtain the following equilibrium condition for local firm in the c-industry

$$n_l = max\left\{0, (K_1 p_l^{-\eta})^{(\theta-1)/(\theta-\eta)} - (n_m + n_e)(p_m / p_l)^{1-\theta}\right\} \quad (5.24)$$

With n_m, n_e, and p_m being exogenous and p_l being a function of *n* (via Eqs. 5.22, 5.11 and 5.15), the zero profit condition for local firms implies a relation between the number of local firms, n_l, and the number of firms producing intermediates *n*. With a higher number of firms in the i-industry, the price index for intermediates, q_i, and the price for consumer goods produced by local firms, p_l, are lower. This raises profits for the producers of the consumer good and new firms commence. Hence, there is a positive relation between the number of local firms producing intermediates and locally owned firms in the c-industry: $\partial n_l / \partial p_l < 0$ and $\partial n_l / \partial n > 0$.

If the number of firms in the intermediate goods industry is too small, the shadow price for the differentiated input, q_i, is so high, that any local firm would make losses (see Eq. (5.21)). Hence, there are no local firms in the c-industry, i.e. $n_l = 0$, and all demand is met by exporters and multinational firms.

Equilibria in the South without multinationals

In a simultaneous equilibrium, the number of local firms in each industry is such that each of the n firms in the i-industry and each of the n_l local firms in the c-industry has zero profits.

The relationship between n and n_l which ensures that there are zero profits for local firms in the c-industry is given by Eq. (5.24). There are zero profits for local firms in the i-industry when (see Eq. (5.17))

$$n_l \mu_l (F_l + x_l(n, n_l)) + n_m \mu_m (F_m + x_m(n, n_l)) = n^{\varepsilon/(\varepsilon-1)} \tag{5.25}$$

Note that the sales of local firms, x_l, are *via* Eqs. (5.19), (5.22) and (5.18) a function of the number of local firms in both industries. By Eqs. (5.20) and (5.18), the same is true for the sales of multinationals, x_m.

The relationship between n and n_l given by Eqs. (5.24) and (5.25) is illustrated in Figure 5.2 which has n on its horizontal axis and n_l on its vertical one.[12] The curve $\pi_l = 0$ is upward sloping. There are too many firms in the i-industry below this curve and room for entry above it. For $n < \bar{n}$, there are no local firms in the c-industry. The curve $\pi = 0$ is upward sloping as well. Right to this curve, there is exit of i-industry firms, while left to it there is room for entry. The curve goes through the origin only if there are no multinationals, since only then the total demand for intermediates is zero.

The cross-section of both curves gives combinations of n and n_l at which there are simultaneously zero profits for locally-owned firms in each industry. For different parameter values, up to three equilibria exist. The arrows in different regions of the $n - n_l$-space created by the cross-section of both curves reveal how the number of local firms would adjust to restore zero profits whenever the initial number of firms would be represented by a point (n, n_l) lying in the region. In Figure 5.2 which is drawn for $n_m = 0$, there are 3 equilibria. At point (0,0) there is no local production of intermediates and local firms in the c-industry do not commence. The consumption good is supplied by foreign exporters. Equilibria with local production are represented by points U and E.

[12] The figures 5.2 and 5.3 are derived for the following parameter values: $\mu_l = \mu_m = 0.667$; $\varepsilon = \theta = 5$; $F_m = 3$; $F_l = 0.25$; $n_e = 0.1$; $K_1 = 3$; $\zeta = 0.41$.

The number of firms in both industries, is higher in equilibrium E than in equilibrium U. The analysis of the arrows reveals that the equilibria O and E are stable, whereas the one at point U is unstable.[13], [14]

Figure 5.2:
Equilibria with no multinationals in the Markusen-Venables model

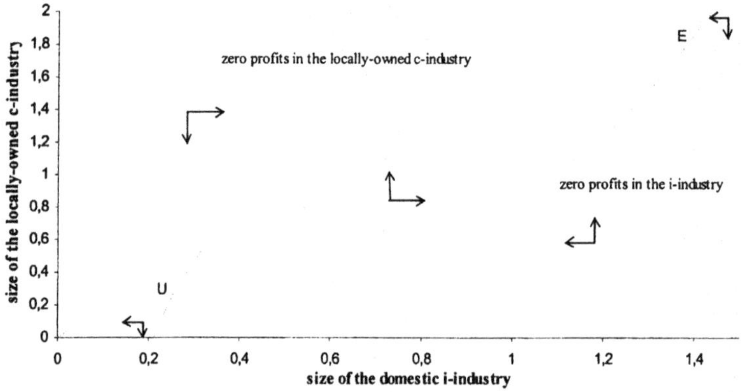

In what follows, we assume that without multinationals the level of local production is given by n and n_l at point E. We ask how the entry of multinationals into the c-industry affects the local firms in different industries. Especially, we are interested in the question whether the entry of multinationals may change productivity of local firms in the c-industry. We know that it is the case when the entry of multinationals leads to an increase in the number of firms in the intermediate goods industry. Hence, our purpose is to establish conditions under which $\left.\frac{dn}{dn_m}\right|_E > 0$.

Impact of multinationals entry on local firms

The entry of multinationals changes profits of local firms in both industries. Consider the c-industry first. The direct impact on local competitors in the c-industry is negative: for any given *n*, the enhanced competition reduces sales and profits of the existing firms. Exit of some incumbent producers is needed in

---

[13] If we assume that entry and exit of firms follow in reaction to instantaneous profit levels, directions of motion can be easily derived for each part of the space $n - n_l$.

[14] If there are 2 or less equilibria, the only stable one is the one at point 0 with no local production.

order to restore zero-profits for the rest of locally-owned firms in the c-industry. Due to the negative *competition effect*, the $\pi_l = 0$ curve in the Figure 5.3 shifts downwards when n_m increases.[15]

For local firms in the i-industry, two opposite forces are at work. First, for a given n_l, demand for intermediates increases due to the entry of multinationals. This is *the backwards linkage effect:* it is positive and it leads to an entry of new firms in the i-industry.[16] The curve $\pi = 0$ in Figure 5.3 is shifted to the right and labelled *b-l*. Second, because of the competition effect on local firms in the c-industry, the demand for intermediates is affected indirectly as well. The competition effect reduces sales of intermediates to the incumbent firms (given n_l) and the total demand for intermediates. The new curve $\pi = 0$ labelled *comp* is shifted to the left, as there is now only room for less firms producing intermediates than before.

Figure 5.3:
Equilibria with exogenuos multinationals in the Markusen-Venables model

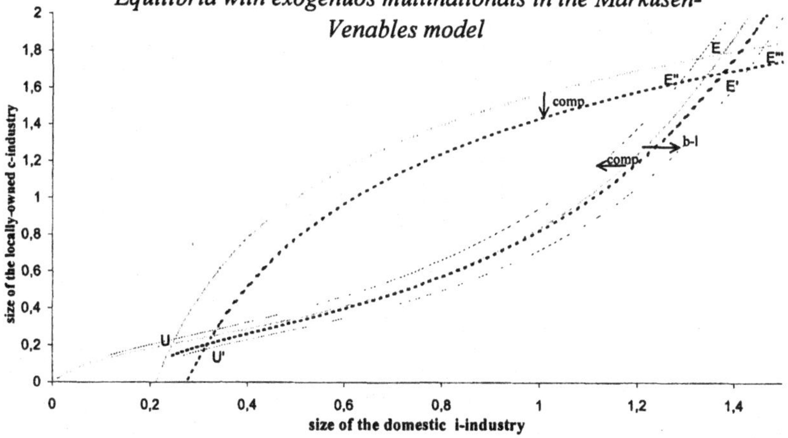

The net shift of the curve $\pi = 0$ which results in a new equilibrium at point *E'* depends on the relative strength of the competition and the backwards linkages effect. Consider two polar cases:

[15] For a given *n*, differentiating the condition $\pi_l = 0$ (Eq. 5.24) leads to

$\partial n_l / \partial n_m \big|_{comp} = -(1-\zeta)(p_m / p_l)^{1-\theta} < 0$ where ζ gives the replacement coefficient of exports through multinationals, $dn_e = -\zeta dn_m$ and $\zeta > 0$.

[16] From the condition $\pi = 0$ (Eq. (5.17)) we get for a given n_l:

$\partial n / \partial n_m \big|_{b-l} = (1 - 1/\varepsilon) n^{1/(1-\varepsilon)} \mu_m (F_m + x_m) > 0$

No competition effect: Imagine a situation when all foreign exporters shift their production activities into the host country. When the production by multinationals fully replace imports ($\zeta = 1$), the entry of multinationals does not change the shadow price of the good *C*.[17] The sales of local firms in the c-industry are not affected, and there is no need for any adjustment in the number of locally owned firms producing good *C* (no direct competition effect). The total demand for intermediates coming from the locally-owned firms stays constant (no indirect competition effect). Additional demand for intermediates comes from multinationals and rises the number of firms in the i-industry due to the *backwards linkage* effect. The now decreasing price index for intermediates lowers prices for the consumer goods and rises sales of locally owned firms. New local firms enter the c-good sector (*forwards linkage*). This hives the demand for intermediates once more. After the adjustment is completed in a stable equilibrium at point E'', both industries are larger. Because of a higher number of available varieties of the differentiated input, the total factor productivity of local firms in the c-industry increases. We obtain the following result:

The entry of multinationals rises the number of local firms in the consumption goods industry and their productivity through backwards and forwards linkages.

This is the most advantageous situation from the point of view of the host country within this model.[18] The analysis also applies to the case when multinationals export all output and do not at all compete with local firms in the host market.

No backwards linkage effect: Imagine that multinationals employ only local labour but do not use local intermediates at all ($\mu_m = 0$). This might be the case when they purchase intermediates abroad and ship them to the host country to take advantage of its cheap labour force. Due to a direct competition effect, the sales and profits of local competitors fall and some of them exit the market. This lowers demand for intermediates from local firms in the c-industry and the number of local firms in the i-industry goes back (indirect competition effect).

[17] The economic behaviour of multinationals and foreign firms is not modelled here. A replacement of imports through production of multinationals is possible when some previous foreign exporters relocate their production facilities abroad (a 100% displacement) and when multinationals (at least partially) engage in production of varieties not sold before.

[18] Since profits are zero and wages constant, the only source of welfare is the increased real supply of the consumer good resulting from a fall of the price index q_c. It can be easily shown that welfare is increasing in both n and n_l. At the new equilibrium E'', the host-country welfare is higher than in the initial equilibrium E.

Again, the lower availability of differentiated inputs lowers profits of the producers of the good C and new exits follow. During the adjustment, the equilibrium shifts from E to E''' with a number of locally owned firms in each industry smaller than before liberalising multinationals entry. We obtain:

The entry of multinationals reduces the number of local firms in the consumption goods industry and their productivity through backwards and forwards linkages.

From the point of view of local firms and consumers, this is the most negative situation which can occur following the entry of multinationals. Moreover, the price index for consumer goods q_c falls, and so the welfare of the host country consumers.[19]

General case: When multinationals do not replace all export firms ($0<\zeta<1$) and also use some local intermediates ($\mu_m > 0$), both competition effect and backwards linkage effect are in work. The productivity change of local firms in the c-industry depends on how the entry of multinationals affects the number of local firms in the i-industry. We show in Appendix 5.B that the marginal impact of multinationals entry on the size of i-industry is given by:

$$\frac{dn}{dn_m} = K_2\left[\frac{\mu_m(F_m + x_m)}{p_m x_m(1-\zeta)} - \frac{\mu_l(F_l + x_l)}{p_l x_l}\right] \tag{5.26}$$

where K_2 is a positive constant, and all endogenous variables are evaluated at a stable equilibrium *E*. Hence, the sign of the multiplier depends on the sign of the expression in brackets. The ratios in brackets represent demand for intermediate goods per unit of additional output (net, *i.e.* including the displacement of foreign exporters) of a given type of firm (multinational and local, respectively) in the c-industry. We conclude with the following proposition.

Proposition 5.3:
When a multinational has a higher relative demand for locally-produced intermediates than a local firm in the c-industry (measured in relation to the full effect of its entry on domestic supply of the consumer good), then an increase in the number of multinationals generates an increase in the number of firms in the intermediate goods industry. This rises the total factor productivity of local competitors of multinationals in the consumer goods industry.

[19] Since both n and n_l fall, at the new equilibrium E''', the host-country welfare is lower than in the initial equilibrium E.

The positive effect on the productivity of local firms is a positive externality resulting from the entry of multinationals. Positive productivity spillovers are more likely when (i) μ_m is higher, *i.e.* when multinationals are relatively more linked to the local economy through purchases of intermediates than through hiring labour; and (ii) μ_l is lower *i.e.* when local firms use labour more intensively than intermediates.

When varieties of the consumer good are bad substitutes for each other (θ is low), the curve $\pi_l = 0$ becomes flatter. Then, the entry of multinationals has *c.p.* a smaller effect on the composite price index for the good *C* and a smaller effect on the number of local competitors in equilibrium, whereas the effect on downstream industries is higher. Hence, multinationals are more beneficial for the host country if they invest in the sectors where they compete less with local firms, since they produce different goods.

For a host country without domestic firms in the c-industry, the model predicts that sufficiently high entry of multinationals may create backwards linkages which not only profit the intermediate goods producers but which are strong enough to cause the development of the local firms producing the c-good from scratch. Imagine that initially the number of intermediates available locally was too small to make local production of the consumer good profitable. However, development of the intermediate goods sector induced by multinationals demand lowers the price index for the composite intermediate good and may rise sales of each variety of good *C* so that the marginal revenue is high enough to cover average fixed costs. The forwards linkages to the c-good industry induce its emergence. Since new developed firms enhance total demand for intermediate inputs in the economy, the i-sector develops further on giving second-round positive impact on the development of the c-sector. The parallel development of both industries settles down in a stable equilibrium, given for example by E'.[20] Hence, within the model multinationals may play a role as catalyst for the development of the local c-industry.

The process described here is usually labelled '*cumulative causation*'. It is initiated at the demand side of the economy (here: due to a higher demand for local intermediates) and proceeds through following supply and demand reactions.[21] The creation of the new local industry is welfare-enhancing since the price index for the consumer good is falling.

---

[20] Notice that the unstable equilibrium U' in Figure 5.3 vanishes for a high enough number of multinationals.

[21] This is known in the literature as 'Verdoorn-Kaldor Law'. Kaldor (1975) presented a view of path-dependent development in the economy in which 'a change becomes progressive and propagates itself in a cumulative way'. The role of FDI in this process is comprehensively discussed in Li (1996).

Markusen/Venables (1999) shows that creation of linkages by multinationals to their suppliers in the host country may also benefit their local rivals. Assuming away employment effects, they concentrate on the potential of multinationals to impact productivity of local firms positively. However, such positive technological spillovers are not for sure. They occur only when the local industry producing intermediates expands due to a higher demand which is the case when additional demand from multinationals more than compensates the possible fall of demand from local firms. The negative competition effect on local producers in the consumer good industry may be so strong that not only some will be crowded out, but also the rest will be negatively affected through lower availability of intermediates, and their productivity will fall.

Positive effects on the productivity are more likely *c.p.* when (i) multinationals are more linked to the host economy through linkages to their suppliers than through labour market, when (ii) their local rivals produce relatively labour intensive, μ_l is smaller, and when (iii) goods produced by multinationals and local firms are worse substitutes for each other in consumption.

The productivity spillovers in the Markusen/Venables model are a once-for-all response of the domestic economy on the entry of multinationals. A steady technological growth due to spillovers is only possible when the number of multinationals grows over time.

5.3.3 Determinants of productivity spillovers

The Markusen/Venables model presented in the previous section is a very helpful analytic tool for understanding how multinationals may affect local firms in different industries connected with each other through input-output relations. Direct negative intra-industrial effects on local competitors in the host country may be offset by positive inter-industrial effects. The net effect depends crucially on the strength of the backwards linkages effect, which is within the model positively related to the share of intermediates in the amount of total input purchased in the host economy by a multinational firm, μ_m.

But what determines this coefficient and its relation to the same coefficient for a domestic firm, μ_l? This question was analysed theoretically by Rodríguez-Clare (1996). His analysis focuses only on the linkages effects between local firms and multinationals in the developing host country and abstracts from direct competition in output markets. However, local firms and multinationals compete in labour market, hence the entry of multinationals crowds out local firms and may reduce local production. For this reason, the overall welfare effect on the host country and the effect on productivity of local rivals must weight both effects.

The assumptions of the Rodriguez-Clare model mimic those of the Markusen/Venables one. Consider a country *S* which opens to multinationals with headquarters in the country *N*.[22] Local firms are engaged either in producing a final good Z for consumption (z-industry) or in manufacturing an intermediate input I (i-industry). Manufacturers in country *N* are engaged either in producing a final good *Y* for consumption (y-industry) or in manufacturing an intermediate input I (i-industry). Multinationals in country *S* produce good Y.

The main assumptions of the model are:

(R.1) There is monopolistic competition in the i-industry. The produced input I comes in a number of differentiated varieties: n_S in the host country and n_N in the home country. Labour is the only production factor for the i-industry. It is internationally immobile. All producers of the intermediate goods face identical cost functions. (like M.1)

(R.2) The z-industry in the host country and the y-industry in the home country of multinationals are perfectly competitive. Good *Z* and *Y* are produced using labour and locally produced varieties of the intermediate good *I*.

(R.3) Varieties of the differentiated input are internationally non-tradable (no arms length transactions), so only varieties produced in the country may serve as an input for the domestic consumer good industry. Firms can gain access to intermediates produced in both countries by becoming multinational, *i.e.* they purchase intermediates in both countries, but produce the consumer good only in the host country.

(R.4) There are n_m multinationals active in the y-industry in the host country *S*.[23]

(R.5) There is full employment in the labour market of the host country *S*.

The production function for the final goods *Z* and *Y* are of Cobb-Douglas type $X_z = \delta_z L_z^{\beta_z} X_i^{1-\beta_z}$ and $X_y = \delta_y L_y^{\beta_y} X_i^{1-\beta_y}$, respectively, where $X_i = \left(\int_0^n x_j^{\alpha} dj \right)^{1/\alpha}$. The parameters are all constants, $0 < \alpha, \beta_z, \beta_y < 1$. The y-good industry uses intermediate goods more intensively than the z-industry, which implies that $\beta_z > \beta_y$. Note that a higher equilibrium variety of intermediate inputs, *n*, leads to an increase in total factor productivity of firms in the consumer goods industry (from Proposition A.1 in Appendix 5.A).

---

[22] The author specifies a condition for which only firms from *N* have an incentive to become multinationals.

[23] Similar to Markusen/Venables (1999), Rodríguez-Clare (1996) analyses also an extended two-country model with endogenous number of multinationals and intermediate goods produced in *N*. We return to this extension at the end of the present section.

Rodríguez-Clare shows that whenever in autarky the consumer good industry in country *S* specialises completely in good *Z* and the one in country *N* in good *Y*, then the equilibrium number of varieties of the differentiated input is higher in country *N*, $n_N > n_S$. The result is quite intuitive since by assumption good *Y* is more intermediates-intensive. The author shows that the wage in country *N* is also higher, and since there are zero profits for firms, the welfare is higher with specialisation in *Y*.

Firms from country *N* have a cost incentive to become multinational: access to a greater variety of inputs lowers the price for a basket of intermediates. Beside it, wages are also lower abroad. However, there is a trade-off between these cost-reducing factors and additional transportation costs for shipping intermediates bought in country *N* to production facilities in country *S*.

When multinationals set-up production of good *Y* in country *S*, additional demand for intermediates changes the zero-profit condition for the intermediate goods sector and the wage level through the full-employment condition. Let the labour demand by various types of firms in country S be given as follows:

- Domestic producers of the final good *Z* require L_z units of labour directly. Indirectly, $n_S v_z L_z$ units of labour must be employed in firms producing intermediates to cover the derived demand for intermediates. Then, v_z is the level of employment generated by producers of the good *Z* in each of the n_S firms in the i-industry per unit of labour hired directly by them.
- Similarly, multinationals hire L_m units of domestic labour directly and create demand for $n_S v_m L_m$ units of labour by the producers of intermediates indirectly. L_m is exogenous. v_m is the level of employment created by multinationals in each firm in the i-industry per unit of labour hired directly.
- There is a fixed requirement of one unit of labour to start production of each variety of intermediates.

Then, the full-employment condition reads

$$L_S = L_z + n_S v_z L_z + L_m + n_S v_m L_m + n_S \,. \tag{5.27}$$

The ratio of employment generated by a firm in the consumer good industry to the labour hired directly by the firm, $n_S v_z$ for a local firm and $n_S v_m$ for a multinational, is called by the author a *linkage coefficient* of the firm.

The full-employment conditions determines the size of the local industry. The total demand for labour by the producers of intermediate goods (out of a fixed labour requirement), denoted L_i, can be derived from Eq. (5.27). It depends on the number of local and multinational firms in the production of consumer goods:

$$L_i(n_S,n_m) := n_S v_z(n_S)L_z + n_S v_m(n_S)L_m(n_m)$$
$$= (L_S - n_S - L_m(n_m))\frac{n_S v_z(n_S)}{1+n_S v_z(n_S)} + L_m(n_m)\frac{n_S v_m(n_S)}{1+n_S v_z(n_S)} \quad (5.28)$$

Due to the symmetry of the producers of the differentiated input and the assumption of marginal costs in the production of intermediates being equal to one unit of labour, each firm has the same output equal to $x(n_S,n_m) = L_i(n_S,n_m)/n_S$. The zero-profit condition for these firms implies that the output of each of them in equilibrium is equal to $\varepsilon - 1$ (from Eq. (A.17)). Hence, given n_m, $L_i(n_S,n_m)/n_S = \varepsilon - 1$ is a condition which specifies the number of firms producing intermediates in the host economy. Rodríguez-Clare shows that $L_i(n_S,n_m)/n_S$ is falling in n_S and rising in n_N, i.e. in a (x,n_S)-space it intersects $\varepsilon - 1$ from above.

How does the entry of multinationals affect the number of local firms in the intermediate goods sector, n_S?[24] Graphically, how does the rise in n_m shift the $x(n_S,n_m)$-curve? For a given n_S, the entry of multinationals changes the demand for each variety of I by $\partial x/\partial n_m = (1/n_S)\partial L_i/\partial n_m$. If this partial derivation evaluated at the initial equilibrium is positive, the sales and profits of the incumbent producers of intermediate goods rise. It means that there is room for entry of new firms into the i-industry until in a new equilibrium the sales of an individual variety equals $\varepsilon - 1$ again. When on the contrary, $\partial x/\partial n_m = (1/n_S)\partial L_i/\partial n_m$ is negative at the initial equilibrium, then the number of firms in the i-industry is negatively affected by the entry of multinationals.

What determinates the change of demand for intermediate goods caused by the entry of multinationals? To determine the sign of $\partial L_i/\partial n_m$, note that from Eq. (5.28) $\frac{\partial L_i}{\partial n_m} = \frac{n_S v_m(n_S) - n_S v_z(n_S)}{1+n_S v_z(n_S)}\frac{\partial L_m}{\partial n_m}$. Since by assumption $\partial L_m/\partial n_m > 0$ (to shift production into the host country foreign firms need to employ local labour), the sign of $\partial x/\partial n_m$ is given by the expression in the numerator. We obtain

$$sign(dn_S/dn_m) = sign(\partial x/\partial n_m)\big|_E = sign(\partial L_i/\partial n_m)\big|_E$$
$$= sign(n_S v_m(n_S) - n_S v_z(n_S))\big|_E \quad (5.29)$$

24 Let us assume for a moment, that there exists a unique equilibrium which is stable. The conditions for stability will be discussed in what follows.

Proposition 5.4:
Whenever the linkage coefficient of multinationals is higher (lower) than the linkage coefficient of local firms, $n_S v_m - n_S v_z > 0 (< 0)$, the entry of multinationals has a positive (negative) effect on the number of local firms in the i-industry. In this situation, multinationals have a positive (negative) linkage effect on the domestic economy.

When the entry of multinationals has a positive linkage effect, it affects the sales and profits of the local incumbents in the intermediate goods sector positively. It stimulates entry of new firms until in equilibrium the sales per firm fall down to $\varepsilon - 1$. This result is very intuitive. Whenever the net effect of the entry of multinationals on the total demand for intermediates is positive, *i.e.* multinationals demand more than domestic firms crowded out of the market previously did, the demand for labour rises which results in higher wages. When multinationals have a lower linkage coefficient than local firms they crowd out from the market. In this case, the number of intermediates produced in the host country decreases, so do the wages.

Due to a positive relationship between the wage level and the locally produced number of varieties of the differentiated input, an increase in the number of firms results in higher wages in the host country. Given that there are zero profits in equilibrium, higher wages with multinationals mean higher welfare for the host country.

Notice that the condition (5.29) is analogous to the condition (5.26) in Section 5.2.2. In both cases the entry of multinationals has a positive impact on the development of the intermediates goods industry and on the productivity of local firms in the final good industry, when multinationals induce higher labour demand in the intermediate goods sector than the crowded-out local firms did. Whereas in the Markusen/Venables model this depends essentially on exogenous constants μ_m and μ_l, the linkage effect of local firms and multinationals in the present model is endogenous. Hence, it is essential to work out the determinants of the linkage effect, *i.e.* the sign of the expression $n_S v_m - n_S v_z$.

Consider first local firms in the z-industry. Recall that from its definition $n_S v_z(n_S) = n_S x / L_z$, the quantity of each variety of I purchased by local producers of good Z per unit of labour hired. In order to maximise profits, firms purchase X_i units of a composite intermediate good, so that $X_i / L_z = \frac{1-\beta_z}{\beta_z} \frac{w}{q_z}$, where w stands for wage in country S, and q_z is the shadow price of the composite intermediate input for local firms in the z-industry. Hence, firms adjust to a higher wage by substituting intermediate goods for labour (the intermediates-labour ratio increases). Expressing X_i and q_S through output and price of a single variety of the intermediate good (see (A.1) and (A.14)), we obtain

$$v_z(n_S) = (1/\beta_z - 1)\alpha / n_S \tag{5.30}$$

Intuitively, when the z-industry uses intermediate goods more intensively (β_z is lower), then the created demand for intermediate goods is higher. When intermediates are better substitutes for each other (α is higher), then the number of firms is smaller and output of each individual variety of good I is higher (see Proposition A.4 in Appendix 5.A) which results in a higher v_z. Note that the total level of employment in the intermediate goods sector induced by the production of local firms per unit of labour hired directly, $n_S v_z(n_S)$, does not depend on the number of firms in the i-industry.

What about the linkage coefficient of a multinational firm? It is defined by

$$n_S v_m = n_S x_m / L_m . \tag{5.31}$$

According to (A.9), multinationals demand for a single variety of the intermediate good produced in the host country equals $x_m = p_S{}^{-\varepsilon} q_m{}^{\varepsilon} X_m$, where p_S is the price of a single variety of the intermediate input in the host country, q_m is the shadow price of the composite intermediate input for multinationals and X_m denotes a total demand of the composite intermediate good induced by multinationals in S.

Recall that multinationals employ n_N imported intermediates from the home country N in addition to n_S intermediates purchased in the host country. q_m is given by (A.7) and depends positively on the price of an individual variety in country N and S, p_N and p_S, respectively

$$q_m = \left[(1-\tau)^{\varepsilon - 1} n_N p_N^{1-\varepsilon} + n_S p_S^{1-\varepsilon} \right]^{1/(1-\varepsilon)} \tag{5.32}$$

τ reflects the existence of 'iceberg' transportation cost of the composite input bought in country N to country S; τ is between 0 (no transportation cost) and 1 (infinite cost). For a given number of firms producing intermediates in country N, n_N, the shadow price index of the intermediate good for multinationals declines as the number of varieties of good I produced in the host country rises.

Profit maximising gives the following rule for X_m relative to the level of the labour input: $\frac{X_m}{L_m} = \varphi_y (p_y / q_m)^{1/\beta_y}$ where $\varphi_y = \delta_y (1-\beta_y)^{1/\beta_y}$, and p_y is a world-market price for good Y.[25] The intermediates-labour ratio increases with a lower shadow price for the composite input. Substituting into Eq. (5.22) gives the linkage coefficient of multinationals as a function of the available number of intermediates produced at home and in the host country

$$n_S v_m(n_S, n_N) = n_S \varphi_y p_y^{1/\beta_y} \left(\frac{w_S(n_S)}{\alpha} \right)^{-\varepsilon} q_m(n_S, n_N)^{\varepsilon - 1/\beta_y} \tag{5.33}$$

where w_S is the nominal wage level in the host country S. It depends positively on the local availability of intermediates.[26]

In a stable equilibrium for which $\varepsilon > 1/\beta_y$ is a sufficient condition, the linkage coefficient of multinationals, $n_S v_m(n_S, n_N)$ is decreasing in n_N and increasing in n_S. The economic reason for this result is the following. Given n_S, an increase in n_N reduces demand for a single variety – including varieties produced in the host country - of the intermediate goods. Given n_N, an increase in n_S lowers the shadow price of a differentiated input for multinationals. When the elasticity of substitution between varieties of the differentiated input (ε) is higher than the price elasticity of demand for the composite input by multinationals $(1/\beta_y)$ (what we assume to hold), multinationals relocate their demand for intermediate goods from the home to the host country in such a way that the linkage coefficient increases.

Now, we are ready to analyse the net effect of multinationals entry on the number of local producers in the i-industry. The sign of the linkage effect is given by the sign of $n_S v_m(n_N, n_S) - n_S v_z(n_S)$. Rodríguez-Clare demonstrates that it is positive if and only if the following condition holds

$$\frac{1/\beta_y - 1}{1/\beta_z - 1} > \left[1 + (1-\tau)^{\varepsilon - 1}\right]^{(\varepsilon - 1/\beta_y)/(\varepsilon - 1)} \tag{5.34}$$

This condition contains entirely the characteristics of goods produced by multinationals and local firms and the level of costs resulting from the separation of headquarters and production facilities. The intuition behind this condition is quite straightforward. Since multinationals produce a more complex good than local firms ($\beta_y < \beta_z$), they demand a higher quantity of intermediate goods per unit of labour hired directly in the final good production. But multinationals purchase intermediate goods in the host country as well as in the

---

[25] The production function for multinationals is $X_y = \delta_y L_m^{\beta_y} X_m^{1-\beta_y}$. Both countries are small in the sense that the prices for consumer goods are exogenous.

[26] Zero-profit conditions for the local producers in the z-industry imply that $w_z(n_S) = p_z \alpha^{1-\beta_z} n_S^{\phi_z}$ where $\phi_z = (1-\beta_z)/(\varepsilon - 1) > 0$.

home country, so their total demand is spread between a higher number of varieties. Because these two effects work in opposite direction, the net effect of multinationals entry on employment in the intermediate goods sector depends on factors determining the size of both effects. A multinational producing more complex goods (operating technologies with a lower β_y), are more likely to create positive linkages effects. With a higher transportation and communication costs between the home and the host country, the multinationals enhance their demand for locally produced inputs. This makes *ceteris paribus* the positive linkage effect more likely.

As in the Markusen/Venables model, multinationals in the present setting may even act as a catalyst for the development of the local industry. When the positive linkage effect is high enough (the number of intermediates n_S is shifted above a threshold level), local producers of consumer goods in country *S* find complete specialisation in good *Y* more profitable and start producing it instead of good *Z*.[27]

Positive linkage effects are also more likely, when the initial development level of the i-industry in country *S* is not too low in comparison to its development in the home country. Otherwise, the linkage coefficient of a multinational can be lower than the one of local firms for all permissible development levels of the i-industry in country *N* (see Eq. (5.33)).[28] Hence, positive linkage effects are more likely when the host i-industry lies above a certain threshold development level. Below this level, the emergence of multinationals lowers the number of available varieties of the differentiated intermediates (despite creation of suppliers linkages), crowds out local producers of the consumer good *Z* and have negative productivity spillovers on the remaining rest of the industry.

Rodríguez-Clare demonstrates in an extended two-country version of the basic model with endogenous numbers of multinationals and firms in country *N* that the positive linkage effect of multinationals is less likely since additional conditions have to be fulfilled. The determinates of the positive linkage effect are the same. We summarise the obtained results of the Rodríguez-Clare-model in Proposition 5.5:

Proposition 5.5:
The emergence of multinationals is more likely to induce positive productivity spillovers on local competitors in the consumer good industry when (i) multinationals produce more complex goods; (ii) when the communication

---

[27] It happens when, due to a higher availability of intermediates, unit costs for good *Y* relative to unit costs for good *Z* fall below the relative world market price of good *Y*.

[28] The number of varieties produced in country *N* must be higher than a threshold value for perfect specialisation of local consumer good industry in good Y (assumed to hold).

costs between the headquarters and the foreign affiliate are higher; and (iii) when the suppliers industry has at least a minimum development level.

5.3.4 Concluding remarks

Creation of vertical linkages with local firms has often been seen as one of the reasons why multinationals might benefit a host country. In this section, we presented two theoretical models of productivity spillovers from FDI where linkages to local suppliers serve as a precondition for the spread of externalities on local competitors of multinationals.

The models show that the entry of multinational firms may increase the extent of markets for intermediates and generate more specialisation among their producers. This would benefit local firms using these intermediates and enhance their productivity. However, positive impact on locally-owned industry is not for sure. Moreover, multinationals entry can even have detrimental effects on the incumbent industry in the host country. The reason is that two opposite forces are at work: a positive backwards linkage effect and a negative competition effect. The net impact on local part of the industry competing against multinationals depends on the relative strength of these two forces.

The models indicate that the relative strength of demand linkages multinationals generate with their suppliers in the host country compared to the linkages generated by local firms crowded out of the market is of key importance. Whenever the net effect is positive, the upstream industry grows and so does the productivity of local competitors.

In the Markusen/Venables model, the linkage coefficient of the firm in the downstream industry, be it a multinational or a local firm, is measured by the ratio of demand generated in the upstream industry to the additional domestic supply of the consumer good resulting from the emergence of the firm. When a multinational has a higher linkage coefficient than a local firm, the number of specialised intermediates is higher in a new equilibrium. In the Rodríguez-Clare model, the linkage coefficient of the firm in the downstream industry is measured by the ratio of employment generated in the upstream industry to the employment generated directly by the firm.

Both models reveal that the net linkage effect of multinationals is higher with higher purchases of local intermediates compared to labour employment. Whereas this is exogenous within the first model, the second one elaborates determinants of the linkage coefficient. It is higher when (i) multinationals produce more complex goods; (ii) when communication costs between the headquarters and the foreign affiliate are higher; and (iii) when the home and host country have more similar development levels. In all these cases positive productivity spillovers on local competitors are more likely, otherwise the potential for negative spillovers is higher.

Do the models give support for the technology gap and competition hypotheses? First, do higher productivity differences between multinationals and local firms enhance the scope of positive productivity spillovers? The Markusen/Venables model does not allow for derivation of a technology gap hypothesis, since technology and productivity of multinationals are not fully-specified and comparisons with the local technology are not possible. In the Rodríguez-Clare model, productivity of multinationals is always higher than their competitors because they have access to a greater set of intermediates. With the result that positive productivity spillovers are more likely and higher when the development level of the intermediate goods industry in both country is not too different, the model gives *no support* to the technology gap hypothesis. With a too big technology gap, even negative externalities on local firms are more likely.

Second, does higher competition within the domestic industry enhance the extent of positive spillovers? Within the Markusen/Venables model, the competition level can be measured by the elasticity of substitution between varieties of the consumer good, θ; higher elasticity of substitution can be interpreted as a higher competition. The model predicts that multinationals are more beneficial for the host country if they invest in sectors characterised by low degree of competition. Hence, the model *does not* provide support for the competition hypothesis. In the Rodríguez-Clare model, perfect competition among local firms is assumed so that the competition level is not a determinant of productivity spillovers.

5.4 Spillovers through workers' mobility

There is an ample evidence confirming substantial training of local personnel in multinational firms (see Section 4.1.3). It has also been reported from host countries that some proportion of production managers, engineers and skilled workers leave multinationals to join or set up local firms. This mobility of trained workers occurs although multinationals have often been found to pay higher wages than local firms for similar job positions (Aitken *et al.*, 1996).

In this section we investigate labour mobility of technical workers and managers from multinational firms to locally-owned firms as a channel of technology transfer.[29] The purpose of the analysis is to show under which conditions such spillovers may occur. As in the previous sections, we are especially interested in finding out whether a higher technology gap and more competition facilitate

[29] Spillovers due to inter-firm mobility of researchers will be discussed in Section 5.5.

positive spillovers as postulated by the technology gap and competition hypotheses.

5.4.1 Technology transfer through workers' mobility

Theoretical modelling of productivity spillovers through labour mobility is just emerging. The two existing formal approaches (Glass/Saggi, 1999; Fosfuri *et al.*, 1998) are based on identical arguments, and they supplement each other quite well when examining determinants of such a technology transfer. In this section, we outline the structure of these arguments relying chiefly on the Glass/Saggi model. In order to simplify presentation, we focus on the most basic version of the model and discuss extensions in turn.

Consider an industry in country *S* producing a homogenous consumer good. It hosts a multinational firm competing with a local firm. Firms employ only local workers and have a constant-returns-to-scale production technology. They face a perfectly elastic supply of labour (from elsewhere in the economy) at a wage equal to one (by normalisation). The main assumptions of the model are as follows:

(G.1) The multinational firm possesses a superior technology for producing output: it requires less units of labour per unit of output than the local firm does.

(G.2) All local workers hired by the multinational immediately acquire training how the superior technology works - they get *informed*. Then, if they start working with the local firm, they are more productive than *uninformed* employees, *i.e.* those who have never been trained by the multinational. However, such a technology transfer is incomplete: informed workers are not as productive with the local firm as previously with the multinational one.[30] Let the multinational need one unit of labour in order to produce one unit of output, and the local firm Θ^T units of informed labour or Θ^N units of uniformed labour for one unit of output. Technology transfer embodied in the informed workers that switched employers is reflected in lowering unit labour requirement: $\Theta^N > \Theta^T$, but since it is incomplete $\Theta^T > 1$. Θ^T measures *technological backwardness* (technology gap) of the local firm which still exists even with technology transfer. A lower Θ^T indicates a higher *absorptive capacity* of the local firm in implementing more productive technology.

(G.3) Consider a three-period Cournot competition game. In the first period, the multinational firm chooses and publicly announces the wage it will pay to

[30] Some part of managerial, organisational and production-related abilities, skills and techniques might be inappropriate for a firm which cannot rely on headquarter services from a parent company as the foreign affiliate does.

all its workers, w_m. In the second period, the local firm decides whether to offer a higher wage than w_m in order to attract informed workers and improve its own productivity. If this is the case, it faces a perfectly elastic supply of informed workers at the offered wage. In the final stage, the firms simultaneously choose the level of output in order to maximise individual profits.

We look for the sub-game perfect equilibrium of the model in pure strategies. It is straightforward to solve the model through backward induction.

Outputs and profits in equilibrium: Let x_i denote the output of firm i with i = m (for multinational) or l (for local). The total supply is given by $X = x_m + x_l$, whereas the total demand is $p = p(X)$. Assuming that the profit function π_i is strictly concave in x_i and twice differentiable, $i = m, l$, we get the usual first-order conditions (FOCs) for profit maximisation (marginal revenue equals marginal costs)

$$\frac{\partial \pi_i}{\partial x_i} = p(X) + x_i p'(X) - c_i = 0 \qquad i = m, l \tag{5.35}$$

where c_i are constant marginal costs of firm i which depend on the technology used by the firm. The second-order conditions (SOCs) are $\frac{\partial^2 \pi_i}{\partial x_i^2} = 2p'(X) + x_i p''(X) < 0$. The profit maximising outputs are conditional on the firm's own marginal costs and those of the competitor, $\pi_i(c_i, c_j)$.

Wage setting by the local firm: In order to reduce its marginal (equal to average) costs, the local firm can attract informed workers by offering them a wage higher than the multinational does.[31] Then, the local firm offers $w_l = w_m + \iota$ where ι is an arbitrary small positive amount.[32] The decision whether to hire informed or uninformed workers depends on which is the cheaper method of production.

The local firm has marginal costs equal to $\Theta^T w_l$ when it produces with informed workers (when the technology transfer take place) and Θ^N with uniformed workers (no technology transfer). Hence, the local firm wishes to attract informed workers whenever $\Theta^T w_l < \Theta^N$ or equivalently $w_l < \Gamma \equiv \Theta^N / \Theta^T$. The ratio Γ gives the potential for productivity improvement through hiring informed workers: Γ lies between 1 (fully ineffective technology transfer,

[31] When marginal costs are constant, minimising them ensures profit maximising.

[32] Since ι is arbitrary small, we omit it in all following expressions.

$\Theta^T = \Theta^N$) and Θ^N (perfect technology transfer, $\Theta^T = 1$).We obtain the following result:

If the wage offered to informed workers by the multinational firm is sufficiently low so that $w_m < \Gamma$, then the local firm finds it more profitable to produce with the superior technology and offers wage $w_l = w_m$ for informed workers in order to attract them. If $w_m \geq \Gamma$ the local firm employs uniformed workers, because the old technology causes lower marginal costs.

***Wage setting by the multinational firm*:** In principle, the multinational firm could always curtail technology transfer: since the relative productivity of uninformed to informed workers with the local firm, Γ, is public knowledge, the multinational could always keep informed workers by offering them $w_m = \Gamma$. This wage is high enough to prevent technology transfer to occur. However, paying a wage premium over a standard wage in the host country ($w_m = \Gamma > 1$) increases marginal costs and could lower profits. When does paying a wage premium raise the multinational firm's profit?

When the multinational firm tolerates technology transfer to the local firm (*T* equilibrium), it does not need to pay any wage premium to its employees. The marginal costs are equal to $c_m^T = 1$ for the multinational firm and $c_l^T = \Theta^T$ for the local firm. When the multinational prevents technology transfer (*N* equilibrium), its marginal costs are $c_m^N = w_m = \Gamma$ and the rival's costs are $c_l^N = \Theta^N$. The following table gives a quick overview over the main conditions of production by the multinational and the local firm (the first number in brackets refer to the multinational):

Type of equilibrium	Workers employed	Wages	Marginal costs
Technology transfer (T equilibrium)	(informed, informed)	$(1,1)$	$(1,\Theta^T)$
No Technology transfer (N equilibrium)	(informed, uninformed)	$(w_m,1)$	$(\Theta^N/\Theta^T,\Theta^N)$

The profit functions for both types of firms in each equilibrium are given by

$$\left(\pi_m^T, \pi_l^T\right) = \left(x_m^T(p(X)-1), x_l^T(p(X)-\Theta^T)\right) \qquad \text{with technology transfer}$$

$$\left(\pi_m^N, \pi_l^N\right) = \left(x_m^N(p(X)-\Gamma), x_l^N(p(X)-\Theta^N)\right) \qquad \text{with no technology transfer}$$

In each case, the profit of the multinational firm depends positively on Θ^T - the technological disadvantage of the local firm relative to the multinational one in case of the technology transfer. When technology transfer occurs, a higher Θ^T implies higher costs of the local firm, lower output and higher profits for the multinational. Without technology transfer, an increase in Θ^T lowers the wage premium to the informed workers and the cost buried by the multinational firm to keep them. This increases the profit.

If the local firm is able to reduce its marginal costs to the level of the multinational firm ($\Theta^T = 1$ and $\Gamma = \Theta^T$), then the profit of the multinational firm is higher when it allows informed workers to switch, *i.e.* $\pi_m^T(1,1) > \pi_m^N(\Theta^N, \Theta^N)$. This is because an uniform increase of (constant) marginal costs in a Cournot equilibrium lowers profits of both firms (see Varian, 1992, ch.16). On the contrary, if $\Theta^T = \Theta^N$, technology transfer does not change marginal costs of any firm. The profits are the same independent whether a labour movement does take place or not, $\pi_m^T(1,\Theta^T) = \pi_m^N(1,\Theta^N)$.

Taking into account the characteristics of the profit function for the multinational firm, we conclude that either the multinational firm always prefers technology transfer since $\pi_m^T(1,\Theta^T) > \pi_m^N(\Gamma,\Theta^N)$ for all Θ^T, or it allows technology transfer for small Θ^T and restricts it for high Θ^T. The second strategy is optimal if the profit functions for the multinational in *T* and *N* equilibrium intersect. Then, there exists a threshold level of Θ^T, labelled $\widetilde{\Theta}$, such that

$$\begin{aligned}
&\pi_m^T(1,\Theta^T) > \pi_m^N(\Gamma,\Theta^N) && \text{for } \Theta^T < \widetilde{\Theta} \\
&\pi_m^T(1,\Theta^T) < \pi_m^N(\Gamma,\Theta^N) && \text{for } \Theta^T > \widetilde{\Theta} \qquad (5.36)\\
&\pi_m^T(1,\widetilde{\Theta}) = \pi_m^N(\Theta^N/\widetilde{\Theta},\Theta^N) &&
\end{aligned}$$

For the existence of such a $\widetilde{\Theta}$, the profit function π_m^T has to intersect the profit function π_m^N at $\Theta^T = \Theta^N$ from above. The formal condition requires that an increase in a the local firm own cost must have a larger negative impact on its output than a decrease in its rival's costs.[33] If this is fulfilled and $\widetilde{\Theta}$ is unique, the model provides a following rule for the multinational:

Proposition 5.6:
If the local firm is able to improve its productivity sufficiently through hiring informed workers ($\Theta^T < \widetilde{\Theta}$), then the multinational should allow technology transfer and pay the wage $w_m^T = 1$. If the technology transfer is highly imperfect ($\Theta^T \geq \widetilde{\Theta}$), the multinational should curtail workers' mobility by offering a wage premium to informed workers, $w_m^T = \Gamma$.

---

[33] The existence condition for $\widetilde{\Theta}$ is $\partial x_l^T / \partial \Theta^T > \partial x_l^N / \partial \Theta^T + 1/p'$.

When technology transfer to the local firm is highly imperfect in the above sense, the wage premium which prevents technology transfer is sufficiently low, and paying it is the profit-maximising strategy for the multinational firm. Preventing technology transfer when the local firm can become highly productive, requires paying a high wage premium which lowers the profits below the level with technology transfer.

The existence of $\tilde{\Theta}$ is postulated in Figure 5.4. It is drawn for linear demand, $p(X) = A - X$ and the threshold level is $\Theta^T = 2$.[34] Technology transfer occurs only if the local firm has the ability to lower its technology gap, $\Theta^T / 1$, to less than two.

What about the profits of the local firm in each equilibrium? It can be shown that its profit is always higher when technology transfer takes place, no matter how high Θ^T is, $\pi_l^T(1,\Theta^T) > \pi_l^N(\Gamma,\Theta^N)$. Hence, the local firm always prefers technology transfer over no technology transfer.

However, this is not so for local workers. When technology transfer is optimal for the multinational firm, then neither it nor its local rival does pay any premium to the workers over the wage in the rest of the economy. In this situation, only the local firm profits from technology transfer whereas workers prefer the curtail of technology by the multinational firm. The interest of the workers are in line with those of the multinational when it prohibits technology transfer and not in line with the local firm.

Figure 5.4:
Profits of the multinational firm and technology transfer

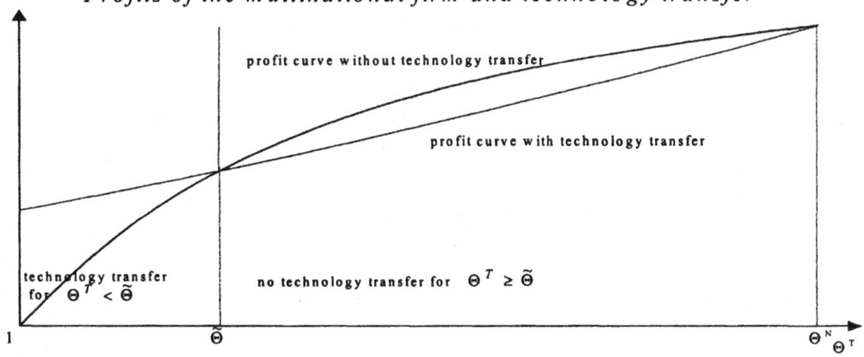

To summarise: in a quite simple theoretical framework we have obtained the result that technology transfer occurs and profits of the local firm increase, only

[34] Figure 5.4 is drawn for n=2, A=10 and $\Theta^N = 5$.

when the local firm is able to improve its productivity with the new technology to a sufficiently high extent. When the technology transfer is highly imperfect, the multinational firm is able to curtail labour mobility by offering its employees high enough wages.

5.4.2 Determinants of the technology transfer

We look now at the conditions under which technology transfer improving productivity of local firms occurs.

Technology gap: Which role does the initial technology gap between the multinational and the local firm, as measured by Θ^N, play for the decision whether to allow technology transfer or not? When Θ^N is sufficiently small such that $\Theta^N < \tilde{\Theta}$, technology transfer will take place independently how efficient it is. With $\Theta^N \geq \tilde{\Theta}$ technology transfer occurs only for industries possessing the ability to sufficiently reduce the productivity gap relative to the multinational firm (Θ^T must be lower than $\tilde{\Theta}$). For industries where it is not possible, technology transfer is curtailed and the productivity of the local firm stays constant. Hence, positive productivity spillovers through workers' mobility are more likely for industries characterised by a small initial productivity gap. This finding is also supported by Fosfuri *et al.* (1998). Hence, both models derive an 'opposite' technology gap hypothesis and give no support to the standard one.

The role of competition: Consider a domestic industry with *n-1* symmetric local firms and one multinational with a superior technology. The other assumptions of the basic model hold. Glass and Saggi show that a higher competition reflected in a higher *n* lowers the threshold level for productivity with technology transfer $\tilde{\Theta}$. For linear demand, it depends entirely on the number of firms in the market, $\tilde{\Theta} = n/(n-1)$. Hence, in industries characterised by higher competition, technology transfer independent of the absorptive capacity of the industry becomes less likely. Similarly, the range of $\Theta^T < \tilde{\Theta}$ gets smaller, and technology transfer occurs in a smaller set of industries. Hence, with a higher level of local competition, technology transfer becomes less likely. It occurs only in industries with a small initial technological gap or if the absorptive capacity of the local industries is very high.

Fosfuri *et al.* obtain the same result, although they model increased competition as a rise in elasticity of substitution between goods produced by the multinational and the local firm. Hence, both models predict that positive productivity spillovers through labour turnover are less likely when the industry is characterised by a tougher market competition. The models give support to the 'opposite' competition hypothesis.

Moreover, the model by Fosfuri *et al.* (1998) allows tracing the role of additional characteristics of the local industry. Positive spillovers are more likely to occur (i) the higher transport costs and tariffs are; and (ii) the higher the educational level of the local workforce is. The first result confirms the finding the role of communication costs as in the Rodríguez-Clare model discussed in Section 5.2. When training supplied by the multinational is a necessary condition for local workers to be employed and become *informed* about the more productive technology, a better education implies lower training costs. Then, even if the multinational firm looses its informed worker who is attracted by the local competitor, the costs of training a second one are also lower. This facilitates workers' mobility and productivity spillovers.

5.4.3 Concluding remarks

In this section we have presented a model where productivity spillovers from FDI might occur due to labour mobility. If the multinational firm has a superior technology relative to its local rival, local employees of the multinational learn these techniques and are also more productive after they are with the local firm. The local firm's productivity and profits are higher when technology transfer occurs. Hence, within the model there is no room for negative impact of the entry of the multinational firm on local firms – negative productivity spillovers cannot arise.

The multinational firm is perfectly able to prevent its loss of informed workers by offering them a high enough wage premium. A wage premium lowers profits of the multinational, but if they are still higher than those earned when the local firm gets a tougher rival due to technology transfer, the multinational firm prevents technology transfer.

Productivity spillovers are more likely when the initial productivity of the local firm relative to productivity of its rival is higher, when the domestic competition level is lower, or when the local firm has the ability to improve its relative productivity to a sufficient extent.

Concluding this section, we find that the models examining labour turnover as a channel for the spread of productivity spillovers lead to results inconsistent with the technology gap and the competition hypotheses.

5.5 Spillovers into local technology creation

This section focuses on FDI impact on own technology which helps local firms upgrade their technological level and improve productivity creation in the host country. We explore the role FDI plays in promoting R&D in form of imitation, adaptation and implementation of new products and manufacturing processes by local firms. The aim is to present the state-of-the-art of economic modelling and discuss the main determinants of positive technological spillovers being identified by this strand of literature.

In Section 5.2 we have already presented a model of economic growth in the host country due to technological spillovers from FDI. The technology used there was assumed to be a public good, accumulation of which is automatic and does not bear any costs. Similarly in models of firms' linkages in Section 5.3, local production of a wider range of intermediate goods is restricted by local demand and not by a lack of technological knowledge: technology for producing new varieties of intermediates is a public good available in the economy even when these goods are not being produced at the moment. But this idea contradicts empirical facts about technology creation and transfer as discussed in Section 3.2. Technology creation is a product of a conscious research process undertaken by specialised firms. The R&D process is costly, so establishing and protecting the rights to exploit inventions exclusively are in the interest of innovators. However, despite legal protection of innovations in form of patents, trademarks, and copyright laws, imitation of technology is widespread[35]. For less developed countries, it is a popular and sometimes even a subsidised way of local technology upgrading.

Technological *imitation* is the part of industrial research (R&D) aiming at copying of designs for products and processes invented by other firms. It comprises re-engineering and adaptation of existing successful innovations to the use of competing manufactures.

Modelling industrial R&D builds a central element of economic models of technological change developed in the 90th. In the so-called 'endogenous growth theory', innovation proceeds either by developing new producer respectively consumer goods, or by improving the quality of existing products and techniques (see Grossman/Helpman, 1991). This is a costly, intentional activity undertaken by specialised firms in the industrial R&D sector. The treatment of imitation parallels modelling of innovation.

There exists a vast theoretical literature which studies the role of imitation in transferring technology to the South. Grossman/Helpman (1991, ch. 11), Segestrom *et al.* (1990), Taylor (1993), and Barro/Sala-i-Martin (1997) are a few examples of models which underpin a positive role of imitation for growth in a non-innovating country. However, the models abstract from FDI.

Models of endogenous growth with FDI and imitation are much more seldom. Helpman (1993) provides the first dynamic general equilibrium analysis of this phenomenon, but he focuses on tightening of intellectual property rights, and, for simplicity, assumes free imitation. Lai (1998) follows Helpman's approach

[35] Mansfield *et al.* (1981) finds in a study of imitation in the drug, chemical, electronics and machinery industries that 34 out of 48 innovations have been copied despite legal protection.

in assuming zero cost of imitation, so the rate at which Northern firms transfer their production activities into the South (the rate of multinationalisation) does not impact the imitation rate.

In what follows we present the state-of-the-art of theoretical literature on FDI impact on costly R&D activities in the host economy. In Section 5.5.1 we introduce the two standard models of endogenous growth and show how product development leads to productivity growth. Section 5.5.2 studies how FDI might exercise a positive impact on the imitation rate undertaken by local firms in the host country, whereas Section 5.5.3 points out the determinants of this impact. We summarise the results in Section 5.5.4 and finally conclude.

5.5.1 Technological progress through R&D

The 'new' theory of growth proposed two models in which technological progress arises in response to profit considerations of competing manufacturers: one with expanding variety of products and one with upgrading quality of products (see Grossman/Helpman, 1991).[36] Both settings allow incorporation of FDI and modelling of its impact on technological progress in the host country. In this section, we first present basic concepts and assumptions employed to describe the production side of the economy, and then derive the links between the rate of technological progress and productivity growth.[37]

The positive impact from the emergence of multinationals worked out in Section 5.2 goes back to the fact that FDI facilitates development of local producers of intermediates, and higher availability of intermediates benefits local competitors. This is also the channel through which FDI positively affect their rivals in a dynamic context: facilitating imitation of intermediates used exclusively by multinationals enhances productivity growth in local firms. In what follows, we derive a relationship between the rate of technological growth and the rate of innovation through (i) expanding product variety, and (ii) rising product variety.

The model of expanding product variety

Consider an industry (c-industry) which produces a consumer good with a Cobb-Douglas production function using labour, L, and a composite good, I, which is assembled from a continuum of differentiated intermediates.

---

[36] Barro/Sala-i-Martin (1995) interprets the variety-of-products model as a metaphor for breakthrough innovations and the quality ladder model as for refinements of existing innovations.

[37] In a general equilibrium model, the consumption side is modelled by a representative household. It is endowed with a fixed amount of production factors and accumulates wealth in the form of shares in firms. The household maximises a Cobb-Douglas type of utility subject to an intertemporal budget constraint.

Intermediate goods are produced by the i-industry which is marked by monopolistic competition:[38]

$$X_C = AL^{\beta} X_i^{1-\beta} \qquad \text{with} \qquad X_i = \left(\int_0^n x_j^{1-\beta} dj \right)^{1/(1-\beta)} , \ 0 < \beta < 1 \tag{5.37}$$

Defining the total physical amount of intermediates employed in the c-sector, $X_I \equiv \int_0^n x_j dj$, we obtain the production function for good C:

$$X_C = An^{\beta} L^{\beta} X_I^{1-\beta} \tag{5.38}$$

Let technological progress occur through R&D that aims at developing new products. It is reflected in a permanent rise of n over time. In a standard manner, we define the growth rate of *total factor productivity (TFP growth)* as

$$TFP\ growth = \frac{\dot{X}_c}{X_c} - \left(\beta \frac{\dot{L}}{L} + (1-\beta) \frac{\dot{X}_I}{X_I} \right) \tag{5.39}$$

where dots over variables denote their derivatives with respect to time. Substituting for the growth rate of output, we immediately obtain

$$TFP\ growth = \frac{\dot{A}}{A} + \beta \frac{\dot{n}}{n} \tag{5.40}$$

The growth rate of TFP is positively related to the endogenous rate of product development. The coefficient β represents the share of labour in income.[39]

Consider labour productivity in the c-industry. Equating price to marginal productivity in the production of the final good gives the demand for the jth variety of the intermediate good, x_j, with $x_j = A^{1/\beta}(1-\beta)^{2/\beta} L$. Substituting for x_j in Eq. (5.37) and solving for growth rates, we obtain the following expression for the growth rate of labour productivity:

$$\gamma_{X_C/L} = \frac{1}{\beta} \frac{\dot{A}}{A} + \frac{\dot{n}}{n} \tag{5.41}$$

Hence, as long as there are new products which can be used as intermediates, the labour productivity of firms in the c-industry enhances. Whenever foreign direct investment has a positive impact on the rate of product development for the locally owned c-industry, foreign firms enhance productivity of locally owned firms.

[38] The formulation goes back to Barro/Sala-i-Martin (1995, Ch.6).

[39] Note that the growth rate of total factor productivity only partially reflects the growth rate of the number of varieties which drives growth in this model. The rest is embodied in the intermediates that use the new technology.

The model of rising product quality

In this type of models, competitive firms in the final good industry (c-industry)) use labour, L, and a set of intermediate goods coming from the i-industry.[40] Potentially, each type of intermediate goods can be produced in an unlimited number of vertically differentiated varieties or 'qualities'. By assumption, a higher quality of the same intermediate provides more services when it is used as an input in the production of the consumption good. The number of varieties is usually assumed to be fixed. Let the production function in the c-industry take the form

$$X_c = A\,L^{\beta} \sum_{j=1}^{J} (\widetilde{X}_j)^{1-\beta} \qquad 0<\beta<1 \tag{5.42}$$

A is the (constant) exogenous level of technology. $\widetilde{X}_j$ is the quality-adjusted amount of the jth type of the differentiated good I employed in the c-industry, $\widetilde{X}_j = \sum_{0}^{k_j} \lambda^k x_{jk}$.

By assumption, an intermediate product of a higher quality provides λ as many services as the product of the quality directly lower ($\lambda > 1$), and the measure of services in the c-industry of the currently highest quality of the jth type is λ^{k_j}. Due to the competition between producers of different qualities of the jth type of the intermediate good, only the good with the highest quality will be available for production in the c-industry.[41] x_{jk_j} denotes the quantity of the jth type of the middle good with the highest quality. Now, the production function for the good C is given by

$$X_c = A\,L^{\beta} \sum_{j=1}^{J} (\lambda^{k_j} x_{jk_j})^{1-\beta} \qquad 0<\beta<1 \tag{5.43}$$

In order to derive the demand for the jth variety of the intermediate, x_{jk_j}, firms equate their marginal products, $\partial X_c / \partial x_{jk_j} = (1-\beta) A\, L^{\beta} (\lambda^{k_j})^{1-\beta} (x_{jk_j})^{-\beta}$, to the price of the input. Assuming limit pricing, units of all varieties cost λ. Then, the demand for the jth variety is given by $x_{jk_j} = \left(\frac{1-\beta}{\lambda}\right)^{1/\beta} A^{1/\beta} L \lambda^{k_j(1-\beta)/\beta}$ in each sector.

---

[40] The following formulation of the model is due to Barro/Sala-i-Martin (1995, Ch.7). Aghion/Howitt (1992) and Grossman/Helpman (1991, Ch.4) introduced the quality ladder model into the economic literature.

[41] Grossman/Helpman (1991, Ch. 4) shows how the technological leader in the jth sector through limit pricing drives the followers from the market.

Let $X_I \equiv \sum_{j=1}^{J} x_{jk_j}$ denote the total quantity of intermediates employed in the c-industry and

$$Q \equiv \sum_{j=1}^{J} \lambda^{k_j(1-\beta)/\beta} \tag{5.44}$$

define an aggregate quality index of intermediates. The production function for the good C can then be written as $X_c = A\ L^{\beta}\ X_I^{1-\beta} Q^{\beta}$.

It implies that the total factor productivity growth is given by

$$TFP\ growth \equiv \frac{\dot{X}_c}{X_c} - \left(\beta\frac{\dot{L}}{L} + (1-\beta)\frac{\dot{X}_I}{X_I}\right) = \frac{\dot{A}}{A} + \beta\frac{\dot{Q}}{Q} \tag{5.45}$$

The total factor productivity growth is now the sum of the exogenous technological progress, $\dot{A}/A$, and the growth rate of the aggregate quality index of the middle goods employed, $\dot{Q}/Q$, weighted by the elasticity of labour β.

The labour productivity in the c-industry depends positively on the aggregate quality index of the intermediates $X_c/L = A^{1/\beta}((1-\beta)/\lambda)^{(1-\beta)/\beta} Q$. It follows that the growth rate of the labour productivity in the final good production is positively related to the rate of technological progress incorporated in the arrival of goods of higher quality

$$\gamma_{X_c/L} = \frac{1}{\beta}\frac{\dot{A}}{A} + \frac{\dot{Q}}{Q} \tag{5.46}$$

Expression (5.45) strongly resembles expression (5.41) in the model of expanding product variety. The present model states that the rate of the productivity growth in the c-industry increases when the quality of intermediates rises. Hence, the arrival of FDI has a positive impact on the productivity of local firms in the c-industry when it rises the innovation (or imitation) rate for intermediate goods.

Modelling R&D

Each firm entering the i-industry has first to develop a blueprint for its own product.[42] Blueprints are protected by patents, so a firm which developed a new brand produces it as a monopolist during its lifetime. If the patent protection is perfect, there is no duplication of research: it would be unreasonable for a firm to develop an already existing product and share the market with the previous

[42] Equivalently, there is a specialised R&D sector where firms under perfect competition develop blueprints and sell them to firms in the i-industry at prices which equal R&D marginal costs.

producer. However, imitation of existing products might be profitable if imitation costs are not prohibitively high and a successful imitator has lower production costs than the innovator.

To start up its own production, at time t_R a firm must carry the R&D costs, F_R, $R=I$ (innovation) or C (imitation, copying) covered by a loan granted by households. If imitation is a success, a firm earns positive current profits which allow it to service debt resulting from R&D expenses. However, with free entry and exit into the i-industry, the expected present value of profits at the time of innovation, t_R, is equal to R&D costs

$$F_R = \int_{t_R}^{T} E(\pi_t) D_t dt \qquad (5.47)$$

with D_t representing a discount factor at time t , and T is the time when the technology becomes obsolete. For example, if the interest rate is a constant r and the profit flows are nonstochastic, the discount factor simplifies to $e^{-r(t-t_R)}$ and the zero-profit condition to $F_R = \pi / r$.

In models with an expanding variety of products, there is a monopolistic competition in the i-industry. A firm has some monopoly power and charges profit maximising prices above marginal costs which ensure positive profits at any instant of time. Since different brands of the good I are no direct substitutes, the entry of new firms into the i-industry does not make existing products obsolete, $T = \infty$.

In models with upgrading of the quality of products, a good of superior quality is a close substitute for a good of lesser quality. Since its productivity in the c-industry is higher, the producers of good C are willing to pay a premium for quality which gives incentives for the i-industry to invest in product development. The firm which has a monopoly over the latest technology receives a flow of profits.[43] But profit flows are only temporary, since ongoing innovation makes old goods obsolete, $T < \infty$.

In the next section we show how multinationals might affect the profitability of local imitation and how this changes the rate of productivity growth in the local c-industry.

[43] The outcome of a price competition between the imitator and original innovator depends on the relation between marginal costs of both firms. If the imitator enjoys only a relative small cost advantage, it sets a "limit price" just below its competitor's costs. If the marginal costs' ratio is sufficiently low (lower than λ), the imitator can charge a monopoly price.

5.5.2 Facilitating local R&D in the presence of FDI

The list of theoretical models focusing on how FDI may affect local technology creation within the endogenous growth framework is very short. Borensztein *et al.* (1998) and Baldwin *et al.* (1999) rely on the expanding variety model, whereas Connolly (1997, 1998) and Glass/Saggi (1998, 1999) apply the rising quality (quality ladder) model. For the first two authors, imitation in the host country does not result in crowding out of the previous producer through the successful imitator: both produce a slightly different variety. The other papers concentrate on imitation leading to crowding out, *i.e.* they analyse how products imitated by local firms substitute for goods previously delivered by multinationals.

In what follows, we briefly review the models. We are interested in determinants of the scope of spillovers into R&D, especially whether the models support the contagion, the technology gap and the competition hypotheses.

In Borensztein *et al.* (1998), FDI occurs in the intermediate goods industry (marked by monopolistic competition) when Northern firms transfer productive facilities to the South and adapt Northern products to the economic environment of the South. The presence of multinationals from the more advanced North is assumed to lower the costs of imitating goods previously produced in the North. Hence, manufacturing intermediates by foreign firms is a source of cost-saving spillovers to the local R&D sector developing intermediates.

Undertaking imitation requires fixed set-up costs F_C. How does the presence of multinationals impact these costs?[44] The idea about cost-saving spillovers can be formally represented by assuming that the imitation costs are falling with the rising proportion of varieties produced by multinationals in the South, n_m / n_S. Moreover, let the imitation costs be *ceteris paribus* lower for more backward countries. Relative backwardness is measured within the model by the number of varieties of the intermediate good produced in the South, n_S, relative to the number of varieties available in the developed North, n_N.[45] This property of imitation costs holds when Northern intermediates varied in terms of how costly they were to adapt for use in the South. When the goods which are easier to

[44] The industrial structure in the South is modelled in a standard way: The final good in the c-industry is produced under competitive conditions with a Cobb-Douglas production function given by Eq. (5.37) The total number of varieties of the differentiated input available in country *S*, n_S, is produced either by local firms or by multinationals, with $n_S = n_m + n_l$. Consumers maximise standard intertemporal utility. For a comprehensive treatment of technological diffusion and growth in two-country model of this type, but without multinationals, see Barro/Sala-i-Martin (1995).

[45] South is technologically behind the North in the sense that innovation take place only in the North and at every instant of time. $n_S < n_N$

imitate would be copied first, then the imitation cost F_C at the margin would increase with the number already imitated (Barro/Sala-i-Martin, 1995). Combining both hypotheses leads to the following formulation of the imitation costs:

$$F_C = F(n_m / n_S, n_S / n_N) \tag{5.48}$$

where $\frac{\partial F_c}{\partial(n_m / n_S)} < 0$ and $\frac{\partial F_c}{\partial(n_S / n_N)} < 0$.

Borensztein *et al.* shows that on a balanced growth path the costs of imitation are constant. Hence, the presence of multinationals remains constant and the rate of imitation in the South equals the rate of product development in the North. For a given size of labour force, the growth rate of the Southern economy is determined by the growth rate of imitation in the following way:

$$\gamma_S^* = \frac{1}{\delta}\left[\frac{\beta(1-\beta)^{(2-\beta)/\beta} A^{1/\beta} L}{F_C^*} - \rho\right] \tag{5.49}$$

where $F_C^* = F_C((n_m / n_S)^*, (n_S / n_N)^*)$ and the stars denote the steady-state values. Equation (5.48) shows that a higher proportion of multinationals in the Southern i-industry increases the rate at which new intermediates are imitated and produced by domestic firms. This rate is also higher for more backward countries – with lower n_S / n_N - the South also tends to grow faster. Since TFP growth of the domestic economy and its labour productivity growth are proportional to the rate of imitation (see Eqs. (5.40-5.41)) FDI has a beneficial impact on these variables.

The above model leads to interesting results, but some important issues have to be clarified. The presence of multinationals lowers the costs of imitation of Northern goods, but the question remains: which firms imitate, multinational or local? Since the number of local firms steadily grows (in the steady-state at the same rate as the number of multinationals), local firms in the i-industry introduce imitated Northern goods. Hence, besides productivity spillovers on firms in the c-industry due to a higher rate of intermediates development with FDI, there are also positive spillovers from FDI on the local i-industry.

The authors do not really motivate their choice of the factors determining the size of spillovers into R&D. Obviously, they have accepted the contagion and the technology gap hypotheses. What can these assumptions be justified within the present model? As a possible explanation of the cost-saving impact of higher FDI on imitation within the model, one can argue that local imitators of Northern goods may avoid some part of adaptation costs when they are able to observe a higher number of multinationals which have already adopted Northern design and successfully manufacture them in the South. In addition, the turnover of researchers previously employed by multinationals and familiar with adaptation of Northern goods to local firms conducting imitation may also lower imitation costs by the latter. However, it is not obvious that the mobility of researchers is higher when the proportion of multinationals is higher. We have already analysed incentives to attract workers of multinationals in Section 5.4. Incentives to attract R&D workers have been analysed for the first time only very recently by Gersbach/Schmutzler (1999). The scope of foreign presence is not a determinant of the level of spillovers in any of these models. Hence, the contagion hypothesis underlying the present model is only weakly justified.

Within the model, the technology gap hypothesis is assumed to hold with respect to the R&D spillovers. For productivity spillovers on firms in the c-industry, Eq. (5.48) shows that the rate of productivity growth with multinationals is higher for countries with a higher labour force L. Borensztein *et al.* interpret L as a human capital stock embodied in the local labour force. But countries rich in human capital are likely to have a better developed i-industry, their technology gap tends to be smaller. This could alterate the relation between changes in technology gap and changes in productivity spillovers, but is beyond the scope of the model.

Baldwin *et al* (1999) focuses on R&D spillovers only and analyses FDI in the c-industry which is monopolistically competitive. Firms (multinational and local) require local labour and a blueprint for its own variety of a differentiated good C to start production. Blueprints are developed through costly R&D; the fixed costs are given by F_C units of labour. Whenever multinationals emerge in equilibrium, they lower the fixed set-up costs of imitation of Northern goods by local firms in the c-industry in an almost identical way as in the Borensztein model (see Eq. (5.48)): with a higher degree of multinationality, n_m / n_S, imitation costs are lower, $F_C = F(n_m / n_S)$ where $\frac{\partial F_c}{\partial (n_m / n_S)} < 0$.[46] The scope of foreign presence, n_m / n_S, is a constant parameter.

The paper shows that the growth rate at which local firms imitate and introduce new products depends positively on the degree of multinationality. Moreover, labour productivity growth in the c-industry is higher. Hence, the assumption of positive spillovers from FDI increasing productivity of labour in the R&D sector in accordance to the contagion hypothesis, results in a higher rate of productivity growth of locally owned competitors of the multinationals.

[46] The authors assume that horizontal multinationals economise on a trade off between proximity (supplying a foreign market with goods produced domestically saves transportation costs) and scale (operating one plant in the host and one in the home country causes additional costs). This motive for FDI has been intensively analysed by Horstmann-Markusen and Brainard (for a discussion, see Zukowska-Gagelmann, 1997).

In this brief review of models within the expanding variety framework, we have demonstrated that the assumption of FDI reducing costs of local imitation results in higher rates of growth of the locally-owned part of the economy and higher rates of growth of labour productivity in local firms as compared to the case without multinationals. When R&D spillovers increase with a higher degree of multinational presence, as postulated by the contagion hypothesis, the growth rates of the local economy are higher.

Within a *quality ladder framework*, Connolly (1997, 1998) deals with how FDI facilitate imitation of Northern intermediates by local firms in the i-industry, whereas Glass/Saggi (1999) are interested in imitation of consumer goods produced by multinationals in the South.[47]

Consider production of final goods in the c-industry in the South, as described in Connolly (1997). Competitive firms use local labour and a set of intermediate goods coming from the local i-industry. The structure of the i-industry is described in Section 5.4.1. Potentially, each type of intermediate goods can be produced in an unlimited number of vertically differentiated varieties or 'qualities'. By assumption, a higher quality enhances the level of services when it is used as an input in the production of the consumption good. Let the production function in the c-industry take the form given by Eq. (5.43)

$$X_c = AL^{\beta} \sum_{j=1}^{J_s} (\lambda^{k_j} x_{jk_j})^{1-\beta} \quad \text{with} \quad 0 < \beta < 1 \tag{5.50}$$

All Southern firms involved in R&D undertake imitation of Northern intermediates with a higher quality than those locally produced as long as the cost of imitation is not higher than the cost of innovation. Research is undertaken by followers, since the leading local firm which possesses the patent for the highest available variety k_j has a smaller incentive (in terms of profits) than other firms to substitute it through higher quality. The intensity of local R&D is a result of profit considerations of a potential imitator who, as described in Section 5.4.1, maximises the expected present value of profits successful imitation would yield.

Consider the *j*th sector within the i-industry in the South where the presently highest available quality is k_j. Let ι_{k_j} denote the probability per unit of time, that a quality rung k_j becomes obsolete due to a successful imitation of the rung k_j+1. Specifically, the probability ι_{k_j} follows a Poisson process described by:

$$\iota_{k_j} = F_{I,k_j} \phi_{k_j} \upsilon_{k_j} g_j h_j \tag{5.51}$$

[47] Strictly speaking, Connolly (1997) focuses on imports of Northern capital goods as a factor facilitating imitation. He derives an empirical equation which is tested in Connolly (1998) with FDI as an additional factor affecting imitation costs.

The above equation is based on the following assumptions:

(C.1) The probability of successful imitation depends positively on resources devoted to reverse engineering, F_{I,k_j};

(C.2) The past experience in imitation of Northern goods is assumed to enhance the learning potential of the Southern jth industry, ϕ_{k_j}, and to positively affect future imitation. More specifically, let $\phi_{k_j} = \phi\lambda^{k_j}$ with ϕ being a positive constant. The higher the present state of the art quality, the greater is the learning experience of Southern firms since the chain of past qualities already imitated is longer;

(C.3) Further, let the probability of imitation depend ceteris paribus negatively on the complexity of the good targeted, υ_{k_j}. Let us assume that the complexity of the quality level targeted by imitation is $\lambda^{1/\beta}$ times higher than of the quality with the presently highest rung. Then, $\upsilon_{k_j} = \upsilon\lambda^{-k_j/\beta}$ with υ a positive constant;

(C.4) With the decreasing pool of potential goods to imitate, the imitation is more difficult. Hence, the probability of imitation depends negatively on the South/North technology ratio in sector j, $GAP_j \equiv \lambda^{k_{jS}} / \lambda^{k_{jN}}$, and $g_j = g\ (GAP_j)$ with $\partial g / \partial GAP_j > 0$;

(C.5) Gathering information about Northern technology is easier when the economic interaction between the North and the South is greater. Connolly (1997) considers imports of intermediates from the North as a measure of interaction. In a subsequent work, Connolly (1998) introduces FDI as an additional factor facilitating imitation. This is given by the $h_j = h_j(FDI)$ where $\partial h_j / \partial FDI > 0$ and FDI is total inflow of foreign direct investment into the South. The author does not endogenise FDI; it is not clear in which industry multinationals emerge, neither their resource requirement nor interaction with local firms has been modelled.

The above specifications lead to the following formulation of the probability for successful imitation:

$$\iota_{k_j} = F_{I,k_j}\phi\ \upsilon\lambda^{-k_j(1-\beta)/\beta}\ g(GAP_j)h(FDI) \tag{5.52}$$

The flow of the profit earned by an imitator improving the state of the art in the jth sector from $k_j - 1$ to k_j is $\pi_{k_j} = (p_{k_j} - 1)x_{k_j}$ where p_{k_j} is the price of the just imitated variety, x_{k_j} denotes its sales and the marginal cost of its production is normalised to 1. Substituting for the price and output (see Eq. (5.43 and below) we obtain

$$\pi_{k_j} = \lambda^{(\beta-1)/\beta}\Pi_1\lambda^{k_j(1-\beta)/\beta} \qquad \text{with } \Pi_1 = \frac{\lambda-1}{\lambda}(1-\beta)^{1/\beta}A^{1/\beta}L. \tag{5.52}$$

Profit-making firms are valued at the stock market where agents equalise expected returns from buying a share of a firm to the interest rate on a riskless bond, r_S. Let the expected present value of profits for the firm which imitated the k_j rung (computed at the time of the imitation) be $E(v_{k_j})$. In a time interval dt the investor obtains dividends $\pi_{k_j}dt$. On the other hand, with probability ι_{k_j} a subsequent k_j+1 imitation would occur, in which case the k_j firm would be crowded out, and its owner would suffer a capital loss of $E(v_{k_j})$. The no-arbitrage condition reads $\pi_{k_j} - \iota_{k_j}E(v_{k_j}) = rE(v_{k_j})$ and together with Eq. (5.53) it gives the following expression for the expected present value of profits:

$$E(v_{k_j}) = \frac{\pi_{k_j}}{r+\iota_{k_j}} = \lambda^{(\beta-1)/\beta}\Pi_1\frac{\lambda^{k_j(1-\beta)/\beta}}{r+\iota_{k_j}} \tag{5.54}$$

If there is free entry of Southern firms into the imitating activity, and the imitation occurs, then expected revenue from imitation of the rung k_j equals imitation costs (Eq. (5.47))

$$F_{I,k_j-1} = \iota_{k_j-1}E(v_{k_j}) \tag{5.55}$$

The resources devoted to imitation of the rung k_j are positively related to the probability that the research will be a success, and negatively to the probability of the successful imitation of the rung k_j+1 undertaken by followers. Substituting for $E(v_{k_j})$ from Eq. (5.55) and for $F_{I,k_j-1}/\iota_{k_j-1}$ from Eq. (5.52) we obtain the following expression for the probability of successful imitation of the rung k_j:

$$\iota_{k_j} = \lambda^{(\beta-1)/\beta}\Pi_1\lambda^{k_j(1-\beta)/\beta}\frac{F_{I,k_j-1}}{\iota_{k_j-1}} - r = \Pi_2 g\,(GAP_j)h(FDI) - r \tag{5.56}$$

where $\Pi_2 \equiv \phi\upsilon\lambda^{(\beta-1)/\beta}\Pi_1$. Notice that on a balanced growth path the ratio of Southern to Northern technology level being measured by GAP_j* is constant and equal for all sectors. Since the interest rate is constant as well, the probability of imitation does not vary with k_j - it is constant across sectors and over time in a given sector.[48]

[48] This is a special case due to the chosen form of ϕ_j. For a discussion of a general case, see Barro/Sala-i-Martin (1995, ch. 7).

In the absence of exogenous technological progress, the TFP growth in the c-industry is proportional to the growth rate of the overall quality index of intermediates. The expected proportional change of the quality index Q_S (see by Eq. (5.44)) due to a single imitation is $\lambda^{(1-\beta)/\beta}-1$. Its expected change per unit of time is given by

$$E\left(\frac{\Delta Q_S}{Q_S}\right)=\iota_{k_j}\left(\lambda^{(1-\beta)/\beta}-1\right) \tag{5.57}$$

Assuming the number of sectors to be large, the growth rate of the quality index Q_S can be approximated with Eq.(5.57)[49]. We obtain

$$\frac{\dot{Q}_S}{Q_S}=\left(\lambda^{(1-\beta)/\beta}-1\right)\left(\Pi_2 g\ (GAP^*)h(FDI)-r\right) \tag{5.58}$$

Connolly shows that a balanced growth path for the South exists at which Southern output grows with the same rate as the aggregate technological level given by Eq.(5.57). Along this path, the technology gap remains constant and both economies grow at the same rate, given by the Northern rate of innovation. The steady-state technology gap, $(Q_S/Q_N)^*$, depends positively on the scope of FDI: higher FDI implies a lower cost of imitation.

5.5.3 Concluding remarks

In Section 5.5, we have reviewed theoretical models of how FDI may promote own R&D in less developed host countries. The notion is that the emergence of multinationals lowers the (expected) costs of imitation of foreign products, be it due to demonstration effects, be it due to the mobility of researchers from foreign to local firms. The few models elaborated until now adopt the contagion and the technology gap hypothesis, and examine how the steady-state growth rate in the South would be affected by higher FDI inflows. The results of these models support conclusions from Section 5.2: opening to FDI allows the host country to enhance its steady-state growth rate and to stabilise its income position. Whereas the growth rate depends on the technology creation in the North, the steady-state income ratio is positively affected by the extent of FDI. Similar results about the role of the *rate of FDI inflows* have also been obtained by Glass/Saggi (1999) without relying on any specific assumptions on the scope of cost saving FDI imposes on local imitation.

The analyses of FDI impact on local R&D point out that the host country has to invest its own resources to capture benefits from the foreign technology. Thus, if the local firms decide not to invest in technology improvement and imitation,

[49] The Law of Large Numbers implies that the aggregate quality index grows in a smooth manner despite a stochastic character of imitation in a single sector.

spillovers are absent. Hence, benefits from FDI are not automatic and not free. The same point has been raised by Parente/Prescott (1994) in their model of economic development through adoption of the foreign technology.

R&D conducted by local firms may also be essential for the quality (or age) of technology multinationals transfer to their affiliates in host countries. Empirical evidence indicates that these technologies, despite being more advanced than indigenous ones, still lag behind the technological state-of-the-art in more developed countries (see Mansfield/Romeo, 1980). Teece (1976) and Kumar (1994) demonstrated that the costs of technology transfer to foreign affiliates are substantial, but decline with the age of technology. These facts are an empirical basis for a model by Glass/Saggi (1998). They assume that if technology gap between the North and the South is higher than a threshold, the costs of technology transfer by multinationals prevent transfer of the state-of the-art technologies. Imitation by local firms, by shrinking the technology gap, permits multinationals to transfer more advanced technologies. Hence, local imitation is a necessary condition for a quicker upgrading of domestic technology and closing of the technology gap. The ability to imitate techniques and products manufactured by multinational firms can be interpreted as a sign of the 'absorptive capacity' of the South. The lack of imitation leads to a slow technology transfer and transfer of relatively 'old' technologies by FDI.

Wang/Blomström (1992) discusses another reason why local R&D is essential for a transfer of modern technologies to the Southern affiliates. Whenever local firms invest in adaptation of new technologies, the goods produced by the two types of firms become closer substitutes for each other, and local firms provide a threat of stronger competition for multinationals. Then, in order to mitigate this competition pressure, multinationals transfer technologies more rapidly and the more modern ones. In general, technology transfer via FDI is positively related to the level of host country firms' R&D investment.

5.6 Conclusions

In the present chapter, we have surveyed the theoretical literature studying FDI-related technological spillovers on the local part of the host country. We have focused our review on the new generation of models which trace spillovers emerging through three various channels: linkages with local suppliers, mobility of workers and impact on local research.

The models which analyse technological spillovers due to linkages with local suppliers do not generally support the contagion hypothesis. The overall impact of foreign firms on the local part of the industry is beneficial only when the positive backwards linkage effect overcompensates the negative competition effect. This situation is more likely when the technology gap between multinationals and local firms is not too high. It contradicts the technology gap hypothesis. In addition, the overall effect is more likely to be positive under low competition. This is at odds with the competition hypothesis.

When mobility of workers and managers is the channel for spillovers to local firms, then the discussed models support the potentially beneficial impact of FDI. However, the models lead to conclusions contradicting the technology gap and the competition hypothesis.

With FDI creating spillovers into local research, local firms may benefit in terms of their productivity growth but only as far as they conduct own R&D. This class of models assumes that the contagion and the technology gap hypothesis with regard to the imitation costs hold.

In sum, the theoretical models discussed here show that the emergence of positive spillovers is not automatic. The models stress that local characteristics of the industry, and local R&D efforts determine the ability of the host country to benefit from its opening to FDI.

The models of the impact of FDI developed so far assume the existence of an initial technological gap *vis a vis* multinationals, the lack of capability to host multinationals with state-of the-art technology and the lack of capability to conduct innovation and to be the parent country of multinationals. Indeed, these are typical features of less developed countries, including transition economies. However, the models abstract from any imperfections in the capital markets, from inefficiencies present within the existing firms, as well as from the institutional and political framework of the host country. Instead, they assume that the implementation of new technologies and the creation of new firms is limited neither by a protection of intellectual property rights, nor by political and macroeconomic uncertainty nor by financial constraints. These are crucial assumptions for the spillovers to arise within the models' framework. However, the reality in less developed countries does not fit well to the above assumptions.

Consider transition countries: from the central planning period, most of them inherited an inefficient, oversized and technologically backward state-owned manufacturing sector. The adjustment of these firms to the increased competitive pressure is considerably limited not only by various considerations of social and polit-economic nature, but also because of the lack of capital to finance investments. The lack of own financial resources, underdeveloped national capital markets and no access to external financing hinders investment not only in the incumbent firms but also the creation of small and medium size private firms. The firms' ability to finance investment in order to reap spillovers seems to be essential in practice. However, this issue has not yet been incorporated into theoretical modelling. Further research on the emergence of FDI-related spillovers should concentrate on how the development of capital markets determine the absorptive capacity of the host country.

Another extension of the present modelling could consist of the endogenisation of the type of FDI. In reality, multinationals in less developed countries not only rely on technologies behind the present technological frontier, but often restrict their engagement to outsourcing or assembling activities only. This implies that what local employees can learn about the technology is not enough to imitate and marketise them. The low proportion of local managers and researchers active for multinationals essentially limits technology transfer. It would be important to analyse simultaneously the decision of multinationals on the art of FDI they conduct and the emergence of spillovers. Rodríguez-Clare (1996) and Wang/Blomström (1992) are only first attempts in this field. Incorporation of spillovers into a Grossman/Helpman framework (1991) could be viewed as another appealing research direction.

Still another issue for modelling spillovers is a dynamic extension of the existing static theories. Indeed, most of the models discussed in this chapter exclude the process of upgrading the absorptive capacity of local firms, factor accumulation in the host country and changing profiles of FDI (e.g. in reaction to the changing local framework). A theory of economic development and the role of FDI and FDI-related spillovers in industrial upgrading as proposed by Ozawa (1992) has not been formalised so far. The possible framework for this analysis could be a product cycle model, as in Glass/Saggi (1997) or in Segerstrom *et al.* (1990).

Summing up our survey, more conceptual work is needed to explore the role of FDI in economic development process on its different stages. The increased interest in this issue, documented in a rapidly growing number of theoretical contributions in the last years, allows us to expect continuous improvement in our understanding of this issue in the near future.

Appendix 5.A:

The standard model of monopolistic competition in a differentiated goods industry

This appendix introduces a standard model of a market structure called *monopolistic competition,* which is assumed in some of the theoretical models presented in Chapter 5. Here, we describe all assumptions of the underlying model and derive equilibrium conditions in detail.

Let us assume that an industry manufacturing a final good C (c-industry for short) employs an intermediate input I produced by the i-industry. The intermediate input is horizontally differentiated, *i.e.* it comes in a continuum of varieties, which imperfectly substitute for each other in the production of the good C. Let the production function for good C take the following form:[50]

$$X_c = \left(\int_0^n x_j{}^\alpha dj \right)^{1/\alpha} \qquad 0 < \alpha < 1 \qquad \text{(A.1)}$$

where x_j denotes the quantity of the jth variety of the intermediate input employed. The set of varieties available to the producers of the good C is given by the interval $[0, n]$. We refer to n as a "number" of available varieties.

All inputs enter the production function for C symmetrically. Since the marginal productivity of intermediate input j is independent of the employed quantity of another variety k, they are neither direct substitutes nor direct complements. The elasticity of substitution between any two intermediate inputs, ε, is defined as $\varepsilon := -\dfrac{\partial \ln(x_k / x_j)}{\partial \ln(X_c^k / X_c^j)}$, where X_c^j is the partial derivative of the production function for C with respect to the jth variety. From Eq. (A.1), ε equals approximately (for large n) $1/(1-\alpha)$, and $\varepsilon > 1$. The elasticity of substitution, ε, is constant and identical for any two varieties of the differentiated input. A higher ε means that different varieties are better substitutes in the production of the final good. In other words, a high ε reflects a low degree of product differentiation in the i-industry as viewed by the producers of the final good, with ε going to infinity for perfect substitutes.

Consider how the total factor productivity in the c-industry changes with the number of available varieties. If they all bear equal prices (which turns to be true in equilibrium), producers of the final good will employ the same amount of each variety, $x_j \equiv x$, for all j. From Eq. (A.1), this implies that $X_c = n^{1/\alpha} x$.

---

[50] Monopolistic competition as a market structure for industries with differentiated products was formalised by Spence (1976) and Dixit/Stiglitz (1977) who proposed this functional form for a utility function. Ethier (1992) applied this specification to production theory.

Under the assumption that all intermediate goods are measured in a common physical unit, we may define the total quantity of the composite intermediate good as $X_I = nx$. Then, the output of the c-industry can be expressed by $X_c = n^{(1-\alpha)/\alpha} X_I$ with the total factor productivity given by $n^{(1-\alpha)/\alpha}$. It shows that spreading a given total quantity of employed inputs, X_I, over a wider range of varieties, n, increases the total factor productivity in the c-industry. This effect creates an incentive to demand and employ all available varieties of the differentiated input.

Proposition A.1:
The total factor productivity in the production of a final composite good C rises as the specialisation in the production of inputs, given by the number of available varieties, n, increases.

In what follows, we describe in turn demand and supply for intermediate goods and analyse equilibrium conditions in order to derive the number of varieties of *I* produced in equilibrium.

Demand side:

Demand for a given variety of the differentiated good comes from the producers of the final good C. Let us assume perfect competition in the c-industry.[51] Since the production function for good C is linear homogenous, the optimisation problem of a representative producer can be described as minimising expenditures per unit of the produced output:

$$\min_{\tilde{x}_j} \int_0^n p_j \tilde{x}_j dj \qquad \text{so that} \qquad X_c = \left(\int_0^n \tilde{x}_j^{\alpha} dj \right)^{1/\alpha} \geq 1 \tag{A.2}$$

where $\tilde{x}_j$ denotes a demand for a variety *j* of the differentiated input per unit of the final good C, and p_j is the price of a variety *j*. The Lagrangean is $L = \int_0^n p_j \tilde{x}_j dj + \lambda(1 - \int_0^n \tilde{x}_j^{\alpha} dj)$.[52]

The first order conditions (FOCs) for this problem is the budget constraint $\int_0^n \tilde{x}_j^{\alpha} dj = 1$ and

$$p_j = \lambda \alpha \tilde{x}_j^{\alpha - 1} \tag{A.3}$$

[51] Seethe last section for a discussion of this assumption.

[52] Note that the budget constraint in (A.2) implies $\int_0^n \tilde{x}_j^{\alpha} dj = 1$

where λ is the Lagrange multiplier associated with the problem. For interpretation, divide the jth condition by the kth one, $j,k \in [0,n]$ to get

$$\frac{p_j}{p_k} = \frac{\tilde{x}_j^{\alpha-1}}{\tilde{x}_k^{\alpha-1}} \tag{A.4}$$

The right-hand side gives the technical rate of substitution (a ratio of marginal product of variety j to marginal product of variety k while maintaining a constant level of output. On the left-hand side the price ratio gives economic rate of substitution between the two varieties holding costs constant. Both rates are equal in firm's optimum. The budget constraint states that using optimal quantities of all varieties (per unit of output) just allows to produce a unit of output.

Together, the FOCs give the following expression for the unit demand of the variety i

$$\tilde{x}_i = p_i^{-\varepsilon}\left(\int_0^n p_j^{1-\varepsilon}\,dj\right)^{\varepsilon/(1-\varepsilon)} \qquad i \in [0,n] \tag{A.5}$$

Demand for a specific variety i of the differentiated input is a negative function of its own price. It depends also on prices of all other available varieties. If they are priced equally (which turns to be true in equilibrium), the amount of each variety demanded per unit of the final good is the same: $\tilde{x} = \tilde{x}_i = n^{-1/\alpha}$.

Free entry and exit into the c-industry in reaction to instantaneous profit levels ensures that firms' profits are zero in equilibrium. Then, the exogenous price of one unit of good C, p_C, matches its minimum attainable production costs. Using equation (A.5) we obtain

$$p_C = \int_0^n \tilde{x}_j p_j\,dj = \left(\int_0^n p_j^{1-\varepsilon}\,dj\right)^{1/(1-\varepsilon)} \tag{A.6}$$

From the viewpoint of the final good producers, the right-hand side of the above equation may be seen as an aggregate price index (a shadow price) for intermediate inputs, q_i, defined over all available varieties

$$q_i := \left(\int_0^n p_j^{1-\varepsilon}\,dj\right)^{1/(1-\varepsilon)} \tag{A.7}$$

Zero profits ensure that the unit price of the final good just equals the price index of intermediate inputs employed to produce this unit, $p_C = q_i$.

The total demand for a specific variety of the intermediate input depends on the total demand for good C.[53] Let E denote the total nominal income spent on the final good C. Then, the total real demand is given by E/p_C. Using (A.6), the total demand for a single variety of the intermediate good, x_i, $i \in [0,n]$ induced by the production of good C is

$$x_i = \tilde{x}_i \frac{E}{p_C} = p_i^{-\varepsilon} \left(\int_0^n p_j^{1-\varepsilon} dj \right)^{-1} E = p_i^{-\varepsilon} p_C^{\varepsilon-1} E \qquad \text{(A.8)}$$

With zero profits in the c-industry, all income spent on good C will be spent eventually on intermediate inputs. Then, the total volume of intermediate goods purchased is equal to E/q_i and Eq. (A.8) gives

$$x_i = p_i^{-\varepsilon} q_i^{\varepsilon-1} E \qquad \text{(A.9)}$$

Equation (A.8) and (A.9) specify the demand function faced by a producer of a single variety i of the differentiated good. Note, that from Eq. (A.9), the own price elasticity $\frac{\partial x_i}{\partial p_i} \frac{p_i}{x_i}$ for each variety is equal to $-\varepsilon$.[54] The income elasticity of demand equals to unity.

Supply side

The i-industry manufactures a differentiated intermediate good (or producer services) in n varieties. We assume that each variety is produced with the same technology under increasing returns to scale. A single firm in the i-industry has to choose a variety to be produced and its price in order to maximise profits given the competition of all other firms in the industry. The firms act simultaneously and non-cooperatively. Sharing a market for a specific variety with another firm or producing two varieties lead to profits which are smaller than they would be in case of manufacturing a unique variety as a monopolist. Therefore each firm specialises in producing one specific variety and each known variety is produced only by one firm.

We focus on a representative firm producing the ith variety of the intermediate input. It sets own prices so as to maximise profits taking the variety choice and prices of other firms as given

$$\max_{x_i} \{ p_i x_i - C(w, x_i) \} \qquad \text{(A.10)}$$

[53] It is itself either a function of consumers' preferences (if C is a consumption good) or is derived from the demand of a downstream industry.

[54] This holds if the size of the set of differentiated varieties is large enough, so that isolated variation of the variety price does not change the price index.

where $C(w,x_i)$ is the cost function (the same for each variety) derived from the increasing-returns-to-scale technology, and w is the vector of input prices employed in the production of the *i*th variety. $C(w,x_i)$ is assumed to have the usual properties of a cost function (see Varian, 1992, chapter 5.4).

Profit maximising requires that marginal costs must equal marginal revenue (FOC). Facing demand given by (A.8), the *i*th firm charges price p_i so that

$$p_i\left(1-\frac{1}{\varepsilon}\right)=c(w,x_i) \tag{A.11}$$

where $c(w,x_i)$ stands for the marginal costs. Since the price elasticity of demand for the *i*th variety, ε, is higher than 1, in equilibrium each firm charges a price that exceeds marginal costs (*a mark-up pricing rule*)

$$p_i=c(w,x_i)\frac{\varepsilon}{\varepsilon-1}=\frac{c(w,x_i)}{\alpha} \tag{A.12}$$

Proposition A.2:

Firms in the i-industry charge a constant mark-up over marginal costs of production, $\frac{p_i-c(w,x_i)}{c(w,x_i)}=\frac{1}{\varepsilon-1}=\frac{1-\alpha}{\alpha}$ ***which is higher when different varieties less perfectly substitute for each other in the c-industry (*** ε ***and*** α ***are lower).***

Equilibrium conditions

Assuming free entry and exit in the i-industry in response to instantaneous profit levels, each firm profit, $\pi_i=p_ix_i-C(w_i,x_i)$, is zero in equilibrium. Using the demand function for each variety (A.8) and the profit-maximising pricing rule of a firm (A.12), the zero-profit condition defines the equilibrium number of firms in the i-industry, n, as well as the purchased quantity of each variety, x_i.

Proposition A.3:
In Nash equilibrium with equal cost functions for all firms in the i-industry, each variety of the differentiated intermediate good is priced and demanded equally.

Labour as a unique production factor in the i-industry

Let us consider now a special case of the cost function: to produce one unit of an intermediate input the firm requires a fixed input, F, of a primary resource (*labour*) and each additional unit of the intermediate good requires one additional unit of labour. Pricing according to the mark-up rule (A.12), gives a common price for each variety of the intermediate good

$$p_i = \frac{w}{\alpha} = \frac{\varepsilon - 1}{\varepsilon} w \qquad i \in [0, n] \tag{A.13}$$

where w stands now for wage. The profit-maximising price does not depend, *ceteris paribus*, on the total demand for the intermediate good.

The overall price index for the composite intermediate good is derived from (A.7)

$$q_i = n^{1/(1-\varepsilon)} \frac{w}{\alpha} \tag{A.14}$$

The shadow price of the composite input for the producers of the final good decreases when the number of available varieties, n , increases.

All varieties are demanded in the same quantity given by equation (A.9)

$$x = \frac{E/n}{w/\alpha}, \tag{A.15}$$

Higher total income spent on good C will be symmetrically distributed for the purchases of all varieties of the intermediate input (E/n). The purchased quantity of each intermediate input is then inversely related to its price and equal for each variety. It decreases with the higher available variety of the intermediate good for a given total demand for the final good C.

Until now, we have taken the number of available varieties of the differentiated intermediate good as given. Now, we are ready to derive it explicitly from the zero-profit condition for firms in the i-industry. Consider profits of a representative firm producing a single variety of the differentiated input. Under the above assumptions about the cost function, using equations (A.13) and (A.15) gives the optimum level of profit for a single firm

$$\pi_i = p_i x_i - w(F + x_i) = \frac{E}{n} - w\left(F + \frac{E/n}{w/\alpha}\right) \tag{A.16}$$

which is decreasing in the number of firms, n. Whenever incumbents reap positive profits, entry of new producers (n increases) scales the profits of the existing firms down until they are equal to zero. Similarly, when the number of firms is too high so they make losses, the exit of some producers let the profits of the remainders increase. Then, the sales revenues, $(p_i - w)x_i$, are just high enough to cover the fixed costs, wF. In Nash equilibrium, the output of each variety of the intermediate good is given by (use A.13)

$$x_i = \frac{\alpha}{1-\alpha} F = (\varepsilon - 1) F \tag{A.17}$$

In equilibrium, the total number of firms operating in the i-industry is (see A.16)

$$n = (1-\alpha)\frac{E}{wF} = \frac{1}{\varepsilon}\frac{E}{wF} \tag{A.18}$$

This completes the description of the equilibrium. In what follows, we discuss it by analysing its comparative-static properties.

Consider the role played by the elasticity of substitution between different varieties ε. Recall that high ε means a low degree of product differentiation in the i-industry. Use Eqs. (A.12), (A.17) and (A.18) to get:

Proposition A.4:
When intermediate varieties are better substitutes for each other in the production of the good C (ε is higher), the equilibrium number of them is smaller, the output sold by each firm in the i-industry increases, and the achieved mark-ups fall.

What about the size of the market for intermediate inputs? Obviously, it is measured by the income, E, spent on the final good since eventually it is all spent on the intermediates.

Proposition A.5:
The equilibrium number of firms in the i-industry increases when the size of the market for intermediate inputs rises. The price and the output of each variety of the intermediate good do not change.

Since a degree of specialisation in production of intermediate inputs, as measured by n, positively affects the total factor productivity in the production of the final good, $n^{(1-\alpha)/\alpha}$, the size of the market puts a limit on the productivity of the industry producing the final good. Expanding the market for intermediate inputs increases the total factor productivity of the industry using this inputs.

Further remarks:

- In the partial equilibrium model of monopolistic competition as presented above, wage in the economy and income spent on the final good C are exogenously given. This may be changed in a general equilibrium model, *e.g.* related to the degree of specialisation in the production of intermediates (see Rodríguez-Clare, 1996).
- So far, we have assumed perfect competition in the industry producing the final good. In doing so, we focused on a representative producer, and assumed no profits in equilibrium. But zero profits due to free-entry-and-exit assumption prevail also when the c-industry is monopolistically competitive. Imagine that each firm in the c-industry produces one variety of a differentiated final good C from available varieties of the intermediate good.

Let the production function for each variety of the final good be given by Eq. (A.1). With free entry and exit into the c-industry, profits are zero. Minimising costs by the firms in the c-industry implies derived demand of a single producer of good C for each variety i of the intermediate good which is also given by Eq. (A.9). The same analysis prevails for the market equilibrium in the i-industry. Propositions 1-4 hold.

Appendix 5.B:

Comparative statics of the Markusen/Venables model (1999) with exogenous multinationals

This appendix proves the result (5.26) in Section 5.3.2 which specifies the condition under which the entry of multinationals has a positive impact on the number of local firms. I assume that the host country was initially in a stable equilibrium E and ask how n and n_l adjust after multinational has appeared. Formally, I derive dn_l / dn_m in a simultaneous equilibrium.

The equilibrium condition for the i-industry is given by Eq. (5.25). Totally differentiating it, we derive

$$\mu_l(F_l + x_l)dn_l + \mu_m(F_m + x_m)dn_m + n_m\mu_m dx_m = -\varepsilon K_3 q_i^{-\varepsilon-1}dq_i \tag{B1}$$

where $K_3 = (1-1/\varepsilon)^{-\varepsilon} > 0$ and

$$dq_i = -\frac{\varepsilon}{(\varepsilon-1)^2}n^{\varepsilon/(1-\varepsilon)}dn<0 \quad \text{from Eqs. (5.2) and (5.6).} \tag{B2}$$

We express dx_m as a function of dn:

$$dx_m = x_m(\theta-\eta)dq_c / q_c > 0 \quad \text{from Eq. (5.11)} \tag{B3}$$

$$(\theta-\eta)\frac{\partial q_c}{q_c} = \theta\frac{\partial p_l}{p_l} > 0 \quad \text{from Eqs. (5.10) and (5.14)} \tag{B4}$$

$$dp_l = \frac{\theta}{\theta-1}\mu_l dq_i > 0 \quad \text{from Eq. (5.13)} \tag{B5}$$

Substituting dx_m into Eq. (B1) results in

$$\mu_l(F_l + x_l)dn_l + \left(\frac{\theta^2}{\theta-1}n_m\mu_m x_m\frac{\mu_l}{p_l} + K_3\varepsilon q_i^{-\varepsilon-1}\right)dq_i = -\mu_m(F_m + x_m)dn_m \tag{B6}$$

Totally differentiating the price index for the c-industry (Eq. (5.9)) gives

$$(1-\theta)q_c^{-\theta}dq_c = p_l^{1-\theta}dn_l + (1-\theta)p_l^{-\theta}dp_l + (dn_m + dn_e)p_e^{1-\theta} \tag{B7}$$

We assume that the entry of multinationals is accompanied by a fall in the number of exporters supplying the host country since some of them become multinationals and relocate their production to the host country. Let $dn_e = \max(-n_e, -\zeta dn_m)$ where ζ stands for the replacement rate of foreign imports through production by multinationals, $\zeta \geq 0$. Substituting for dq_c and dp_l from Eqs. (B3) and (B4), using Eqs. (5.19), (5.23) and the equilibrium condition for the c-industry, $x_l = 1$, we get after rearranging

$$p_l x_l dn_l + \left(\frac{\theta^2}{\theta-\eta} K_1 \frac{\mu_l}{p_l} q_c^{1-\eta} - \theta n_l \mu_l x_l\right) dq_i = -(1-\zeta) p_m x_m dn_m \tag{B8}$$

Equations (B6) and (B8) form a linear system in two variables dn_l and dq_i (or dn via Eq. (B2)) with the change in the number of multinationals being exogenously given. We solve for dn/dn_m and get

$$\frac{dn}{dn_m} = \frac{K_4}{\Delta}\left[\frac{\mu_m (F_m + x_m)}{p_m x_m (1-\zeta)} - \frac{\mu_l (F_l + x_l)}{p_l x_l}\right] \tag{B9}$$

where $K_4 = -\frac{(\varepsilon-1)^2}{\varepsilon}(1-\zeta) p_l x_l p_m x_m n^{\varepsilon/(\varepsilon-1)} < 0$ and

$$\Delta := \mu_l (F_l + x_l)\left(\frac{\theta^2}{\theta-\eta}\frac{\mu_l}{p_l} K_1 q_c^{1-\eta} - \theta n_l \mu_l x_l\right) - p_l x_l \left(\frac{\theta^2}{\theta-1} n_m \mu_m x_m \frac{\mu_l}{p_l} + K_3 \varepsilon q_i^{-\varepsilon-1}\right). \tag{B10}$$

The sign of Δ is given by the above expression, evaluated at the stable equilibrium E. The equilibrium at E is stable when at E the zero-profit curve for local firms in the c-industry meets the zero-profit curve for firms in the i-industry from below: $\left.\frac{dn_l}{dn}\right|_{\pi=0,E} > \left.\frac{dn_l}{dn}\right|_{\pi_l=0,E}$. As I showed below, in the stable equilibrium $\Delta < 0$ holds. From it, we obtain that the impact of the entry of multinationals on the number of firms in the i-industry is positive if and only if the expression in brackets is positive.

The proof that $\Delta < 0$ at the stable equilibrium E.

First, I calculate the slope of the curve $\pi_l = 0$ in equilibrium. For given n_m and n_e, differentiating the price index for the c-industry (Eq. (5.9)) leads to

$$dn_l = (1-\theta)\left[\left(\frac{q_c}{p_l}\right)^{1-\theta}\left(\frac{dq_c}{q_c} - \frac{dp_l}{p_l}\right) - (n_m + n_e)\left(\frac{p_m}{p_l}\right)^{1-\theta}\frac{dp_l}{p_l}\right] \tag{B11}$$

Substituting for $(n_m + n_e)\left(\frac{p_m}{p_l}\right)^{1-\theta}$ from Eq.(5.9) and for $\frac{dq_c}{q_c}$ in equilibrium from (B4), we obtain

$$\frac{dn_l}{dp_l} = \frac{(1-\theta)}{\theta \mu_l}\frac{\left(\frac{\theta^2}{\theta-\eta}\frac{\mu_l}{p_l} K_1 q_c^{1-\eta} - \theta n_l \mu_l x_l\right)}{p_l x_l} \tag{B12}$$

or equivalently

$$\frac{dn_l}{dn}=\frac{\varepsilon}{(\varepsilon-1)^2}n^{\varepsilon/(1-\varepsilon)}\frac{\left(\frac{\theta^2}{\theta-\eta}\frac{\mu_l}{p_l}K_1q_c^{1-\eta}-\theta n_l\mu_l x_l\right)}{p_l x_l}. \tag{B13}$$

Next, for given n_m the slope of the curve $\pi=0$ in stable equilibrium can be derived from (B1)

$$\mu_l(F_l+x_l)dn_l+n_m\mu_m dx_m=\frac{1-\theta}{\theta\mu_l}\varepsilon K_3 q_i^{-\varepsilon-1}dp_l \tag{B14}$$

Substituting for dx_m from (B3)-(B4), we obtain

$$\frac{dn_l}{dp_l}=\frac{1-\theta}{\theta\mu_l}\frac{\left(\frac{\theta^2}{\theta-1}n_m\mu_m x_m\frac{\mu_l}{p_l}+K_3\varepsilon q_i^{-\varepsilon-1}\right)}{\mu_l(F_l+x_l)} \tag{B15}$$

or equivalently

$$\frac{dn_l}{dn}=\frac{\varepsilon}{(\varepsilon-1)^2}n^{\varepsilon/(1-\varepsilon)}\frac{\left(\frac{\theta^2}{\theta-1}n_m\mu_m x_m\frac{\mu_l}{p_l}+K_3\varepsilon q_i^{-\varepsilon-1}\right)}{\mu_l(F_l+x_l)}. \tag{B16}$$

The graphical condition for point E to be a stable equilibrium reads that the slope of the $\pi=0$ curve is higher than the slope of the $\pi_l=0$ curve. This implies $\left.\frac{dn_l}{dn}\right|_{\pi=0,E}>\left.\frac{dn_l}{dn}\right|_{\pi_l=0,E}$. Using (B13) and (B16), we get as a stability condition

$$\frac{\left(\frac{\theta^2}{\theta-1}n_m\mu_m x_m\frac{\mu_l}{p_l}+K_3\varepsilon q_i^{-\varepsilon-1}\right)}{\mu_l(F_l+x_l)}>\frac{\left(\frac{\theta^2}{\theta-\eta}\frac{\mu_l}{p_l}K_1q_c^{1-\eta}-\theta n_l\mu_l x_l\right)}{p_l x_l}. \tag{B17}$$

This implies that Δ evaluated at stable equilibrium has a negative sign.

Chapter 6:

Productivity spillovers from FDI in Polish manufacturing 1993-1997

6.1 Introduction

In this chapter, we examine the impact of foreign direct enterprises operating in Poland on the performance of the domestic industry from 1993 through 1997. We focus our analysis on detecting and characterising productivity spillovers on locally-owned firms. Following the existing empirical literature, we test whether the scope of productivity spillovers is properly described by the contagion, the technology gap and the competition hypotheses.

This examination has a three-fold motivation. First, as discussed in Section 4.3, there are only few studies on the role of FDI in generating productivity spillovers in backward countries. This stands in contrast to the presently widespread beliefs in the positive impact of foreign investment on the upgrading of technology in host countries. The present work is one of the first attempts to identify spillovers in a transition country: earlier, Djankov/Hoekman (1999) found a significantly negative impact of intra-industrial foreign presence on the local firms' performance in the Czech Republic over the 1992-96 period. For China in the 1990-92 period, Kinoshita (1998) could not find any support for the hypothesis that the mere presence of foreign firms increases the productivity growth rates of local firms.

Second, this paper is unique in studying the role of the competition level - both from domestic firms and imports - and of the ownership status for the ability of local firms to reap productivity spillovers. Hence, our results contribute to the present discussion of the relative dynamism of different ownership sectors in transition countries.

Third, and contrary to the studies for the Czech Republic and China, we do not rely on a limited industrial survey but use a comprehensive data set covering about 90 per cent of all domestic firms.

The course of this chapter is as follows: Section 6.2 discusses the regulatory framework related to FDI in Poland in the 1980s and the early 1990s. Section 6.3 presents foreign and local firms in Polish manufacturing in more detail by comparing their characteristics and economic performance. Section 6.4 develops an empirical methodology for testing productivity spillovers on local firms. The main results are listed and discussed in Section 6.5. Here, we also report on the robustness of our empirical findings. Section 6.6 shortly concludes. Appendix 6.A describes in more detail the data and the variables used.

6.2 FDI-related policies

For Poland, 1992 was the first year of a rise in GDP after a few years of stagnation and a dramatic decline at the onset of transition to a market economy (see Table 6.1). Over the period 1990-91, real domestic product fell by almost 18 per cent, but between 1993 and 1997, the average annual growth rate of real GDP was 5.8 per cent - one of the highest in Europe. Due to a shift in economic policy which is now conducive to macroeconomic stability, liberalisation of trade and privatisation, foreign capital has slowly discovered business opportunities in Poland. The annual inflow of foreign direct investment (FDI), which was negligible until 1989, increased continuously from USD89 million in 1990 up to about USD7500 million in 1998.

Table 6.1:
Poland 1990-98: Main Economic Indicators

Poland	1990	1991	1992	1993	1994	1995	1996	1997	1998
GDP (per cent change)	-11.6	-7.0	2.6	3.8	5.2	7.0	6.1	6.8	4.8
Industrial production (per cent change)	-24.2	-8.0	2.8	6.4	12.1	9.7	8.3	11.5	4.8
Trade balance (per cent of GDP)	6.1	0.1	0.6	-2.7	-0.9	-1.5	-6.1	-8.3	-9.1
Inflation (per cent)	585.8	70.3	43.0	35.3	32.2	27.8	19.9	14.9	11.8
Unemployment (per cent)	6.5	12.2	14.3	16.4	16.0	14.9	13.2	10.3	10.4
FDI inflows (mn USD)	89	100	300	600	500	1100	2800	3000	7500

Source: BCE, 1999

The legal framework

The Polish economy re-opened to FDI in 1976 – first by allowing small establishments by Polish expatriates in a few sectors. Cautious step-by step liberalisation followed, but until 1989 most sectors remained blocked to foreign capital and the legislation concerning FDI was repressive for the other sectors.

The first radical reform of the law referring to firms with foreign capital was undertaken at the end of 1988. For the first time, wholly foreign-owned companies have been permitted. The number of sectors open to foreign investors increased but individual permits or feasibility studies restricted access in practice. Together with comprehensive market reforms undertaken in 1990, these measures resulted in an increase of the number of joint-ventures registered at the end of December 1990 up to 2,400 – the number was multiplied more than forty-three-fold since January 1989. A provision of extended tax holidays for all firms for 3 to 6 years seem to have played an important causal role, especially for short-term oriented projects in trade and services. Despite the policy of attracting foreign capital through generous tax incentives, the FDI inflow with 11 and 89 million USD in 1989 and 1990, respectively, was still very low.

A substantial change in legislation, providing more advantageous conditions for foreign investors, was the law on companies with foreign participation amended in the middle of 1991. The new law lifted the general requirement of administrative permit previously necessary for foreign investors, with the exception of defence, real estate dealing, operation of sea and airports, wholesale trading of imported consumer goods and provision of legal services. The law guaranteed (i) foreign investment protection against nationalisation or actions bringing effects similar to nationalisation; (ii) unlimited transfer of profits and dividends; and (iii) immediate repatriation of the invested capital.

Since 1991, Poland like other most advanced transition countries, which then signed the Europe Agreement with the European Communities and their Member States, has started to introduce the principle of 'national treatment' according to which foreign and locally-owned firms should receive equal treatment.[1] This lead to a wide reduction of tax rebates and abolishment of tax holidays. However, the law introduced incentives which were conditional on the investor's fulfilling of a number of requirements. In general, tax incentives were awarded if the investment boosted jobs or exports, or was located in regions of high structural unemployment or introduced modern technologies, or exceeded a minimum level of capital investment (2 million ECU).[2]

The investment law was further liberalised in 1993 and 1996, when Poland became a full member of the OECD. The then-existing list of sectors closed to FDI was reduced to only one, and the existing negative discrimination of foreign investors through permits was (almost) removed[3]. Only in the field of telecommunication and broadcasting, foreign participation is still limited to minority-owned joint ventures. Since 1994, legal protection of intellectual property rights is adjusted to the standards in the OECD countries.

From 1995 on, the government has actively encouraged FDI in the so-called special economic zones which are regions of high structural unemployment. Investors (not exclusively foreign) may benefit from income tax exemptions, if they fulfil employment requirements. 13 out of 17 now existing special zones was created only in 1997.

---

[1] According to OECD (1994), this is one of the basic principles on which an national FDI framework should be based on.

[2] However, granting tax exemptions is quite restricted: in a 1997 survey of 877 foreign firms, only 25 per cent of them benefited from them.

[3] The only exception is running casinos and gambling houses.

FDI and privatisation

Foreigners can invest in Poland through greenfield projects, joint ventures with a local partner or participation in the privatisation of state-owned enterprises. In practice, the first two modes, particularly greenfield investment, *i.e.* the creation of a new wholly-owned subsidiary, are the most frequently used.[4] Although there are numerous legal possibilities for foreign privatisation, over the whole period 1990-97 foreign investors have been engaged only in about 200 firms out of 4233 privatised (agricultural firms excluded) (Wlodarczyk, 1998). Only 19 per cent share of FDI over 1995-97 was related to privatisation, confirming that it has not been the most popular mode of FDI, unlike in Hungary until 1995 and throughout in the Czech Republic, Croatia and Bulgaria (UNCTAD, 1998). However, the role of foreign privatisation is much higher than can be judged by the numbers above: foreign investors mostly participated in privatisation of large state companies (130 out of 200).

Trade policy

In trade policy, radical liberalisation took place at the very beginning of transformation in 1990. This included the abolishment of the state foreign trade monopoly, the introduction of internal convertibility of the domestic currency and the phasing-out of the majority of quantitative restrictions and licensing requirements on both exports and imports.

Further major cuts in trade barriers was introduced due to commitments under the Uruguay Round (from 1995 on), Europe Agreement (from 1992 on) and the accession to the OECD (from 1996 on). The average rate of effective protection in manufacturing has fallen from 10.2 to 4.3 per cent between 1994 and 1998, but has remained at the double-digit level for the food, apparel and transport equipment industry. These are precisely the industries where the majority of foreign capital have been invested (compare to Table 2.4).[5]

This is not a spurious correlation, but a result of the FDI-related policy: Poland, against the general trend of reducing trade impediments, actively implemented

---

[4] This is the outcome of two industrial surveys among foreign investors: An OECD (1994) survey was conducted in 1992-93 with investors from Austria, France, Germany, Japan, United Kingdom and the United States. Meyer (1995) interviewed 268 firms from the United Kingdom and Germany in winter 1994/95.

[5] According to PAIZ (1999), the sectors with the highest cumulative FDI inflows were food, beverages and tobacco products manufacturing (18.5 per cent), transport equipment manufacturing (14.2 per cent) and pulp, paper and paper products manufacturing, as well as publishing and printing (6.5 per cent). The second most significant sector after manufacturing was financial intermediation; up to the end of 1997 foreign companies invested 3,130.4 million USD in this section. The lowest amount of foreign capital was attracted by primary industries like agriculture (15 million USD), and mining and quarrying (16.2 million USD).

discriminatory trade policies as FDI incentives. These were tailor-made measures aimed to attract large foreign investors by reducing their risk of competition from imports or lowering their costs in form of duty-free imports of components (UNCTAD, 1997).[6]

6.3 Local and foreign firms in Poland 1993-1997

6.3.1 The data

The empirical analysis is based on unpublished firm data compiled by the Polish Central Statistical Office (GUS) on an annual basis for 1993-97.[7] Since the release of individual firm data is prohibited by Polish law, data are aggregated up to the three-digit level of the EKD (the Polish correspondence to the International Standard Industrial Classification, ISIC).[8] We restrict ourselves to manufacturing firms and note that over one half (54 per cent) of all foreign capital invested in Poland till 1997 went into manufacturing (GUS, 1998a).

In order to simplify notation we call three-digit activities *industries* and two-digit activities *branches*. Within Polish manufacturing, there are 14 branches and 103 industries. Additionally, we adopt Neven's classification of industries according to their factor intensity (Neven, 1994). This procedure sorts out all three-digit industries into 5 *sectors* characterised by different relative intensity of human capital, physical capital and labour. Sector I consists of high tech industries intensive in human capital. Sector II is intensive in human capital but uses little physical capital. Sector III is labour intensive and needs relatively little capital. Sector IV includes industries intensive in labour and capital. The final Sector V consists of industries that are intensive in both human capital and capital (but less than Sector I). The full list of industries, branches and sectors can be found in Appendix 6.B.

Within each industry, we distinguish 2 exclusive types of domestic enterprises: *locally-owned (local) and foreign-owned (foreign, multinational)*. Firms with at least 10 per cent of shares owned by foreigners are defined as 'foreign', those without foreign capital as 'locally owned'.[9] In 1997, only for 2 per cent of all

---

[6] The spread of such practices in all transition countries has been intensively analysed in Messerlin (1994).

[7] Data prior to 1993 were collected due to another accounting method and in another sectoral breakdown. Thus, they are not comparable to latter figures.

[8] Aggregated three-digit data are not provided if they refer to less than 3 firms or if one firm contributes to more than three quarters of the value of the variable in question. For the list of industries for which data are available, see the appendix.

[9] In the existing empirical literature, some authors define foreign firms as those where at least 15 per cent (Blomström/Wolff, 1994; Sjöholm, 1997) or 20 per cent (Djankov/Hoekman, 1998) of the equity is owned by foreigners. Others are even more restrictive: one third of the equity should be owned by a single foreign entity (Aturupane *et al.*, 1997). The last definition is more in accordance with standard definitions of FDI and foreign direct enterprises as

domestic firms with foreign capital was the share of foreign ownership less than 10 per cent. Foreigners were majority owners in 73 per cent of all Polish firms with foreign capital, and the sole owners in 49 per cent of these firms (see Table 6.2). Substantial amounts of foreign capital have been invested almost entirely in majority-owned foreign firms.

Table 6.2:
Ownership Structure of Foreign Firms in Poland, 1997

Share of foreign capital in equity capital of the firm (per cent):	Share in the total number of foreign firms (per cent)	Share in the total foreign capital invested (per cent)	Average amount of capital invested per foreign firm (millions of PZL)
=100	49	61	2.19
(50-99]	24	31	2.21
(25-50]	22	8	0.62
(10-25]	3	0	0.44
(0-10]	2	0	0.10

Source: GUS, 1998a

In total, 3-digit industry data are provided for 6 non-exclusive types of enterprises: *domestic, foreign, all local, local survivors, state survivors and private survivors*. Annual data for domestic firms, *i.e.* local and foreign, describe the whole Polish industry. Local survivors are local firms which operated over the whole period 1993-1997. As compared to the set of all local firms, enterprises which exit the market within this period or those that have entered the market after 1993 have been excluded. Local survivors are subdivided into 'state survivors' and 'private survivors'. The former ones are defined as those with state ownership ranging above 50 per cent of shares over the whole period in question, and in the latter type private ownership is above 49 per cent of shares in each year.

Some descriptive statistics for different types of enterprises are provided in Table 6.A.1 in Appendix 6.A. Our sample consists of 15327 domestic firms in 1993 and 20007 domestic firms in 1997. In 1993, there are 12460 local firms in the sample (81 per cent), whereas in 1997 the share of locally-owned firms was slightly lower with 80 per cent (15921 local firms).[10] In different years, the data set covers about 90 per cent of all Polish manufacturing firms, 86 to 97 per cent of manufacturing output, and 85 per cent of total employment.[11] Approximately 10 per cent of all manufacturing workers in 1993 were employed in foreign

proposed by IMF (1993) and OECD (1992), but the ownership threshold is set even higher. Here, we apply a lower ownership threshold since in a transition country the direct investment usually gives the foreign investor a position of a strategic investor and control, independently of the scope of his engagement.

[10] The share of firms with foreign capital in the total number of locally-owned firms in Polish economy increased from 10.1 per cent in 1993 to 25 per cent in 1997 (GUS, 1998a).

[11] The information is gathered by GUS only from firms with more than 5 employees.

firms with the share increasing to 20 per cent in 1997. Foreign and local firms varied in many aspects: in 1993 foreign firms were half as big as local ones and almost six times smaller than state firms as measured by employment. Expansion of employment in foreign firms and reduction in local ones led to the convergence of firm's size: in 1997, both types of firms are similarly big (112 versus 115 employees).

There are big differences in the output structure between local and foreign firms. Foreign firms are engaged more intensively than local firms in the automotive industry (branch 34), manufacturing of tobacco products (16), manufacturing of furniture (36), pulp and paper industry (21) as well as in producing radio and television equipment (32). Their output position is under-proportional in petroleum and coal (23), manufacturing of primary metals (27) and manufacturing of transport equipment (35).

Do foreign firms contribute to sectoral restructuring of domestic production through a different activity pattern than this of the incumbent state firms? Figure 6.1 provides an indicator of the similarity between output structure in two different types of firms, *the similarity index*.[12] If the output structure is the same for two types of firms, the index takes a value of 1. The more different the output structure is the smaller the value of the index. The figure suggests that in 1993 the structure of manufacturing output of foreign firms resembles most the output structure of private firms and least the output structure of state firms. Till 1997, the values of similarity indices has got smaller, except for the index of similarity between foreign and all domestic firms. It results from an overall increase in output share of foreign firms in the domestic manufacturing from 12 to 29 per cent over the 1993-97 period. The sectoral output structure of foreign enterprises is still most similar to the one of private firms. Hence, this short analysis supports the view that foreign firms help restructure the domestic manufacturing sector.

[12] The similarity index between output structure of *i*th and *j*th firm is defined as $S_t^{i,j} = \sum_k \min(s_{k,t}^i, s_{k,t}^j)$, where $s_{k,t}^i$ is the share of industry *k* in the overall output of the *i*th type of firms in the year *t*.

Figure 6.1:
Similarity index of output structure between foreign firms and various types of local firms, 1993 and 1997

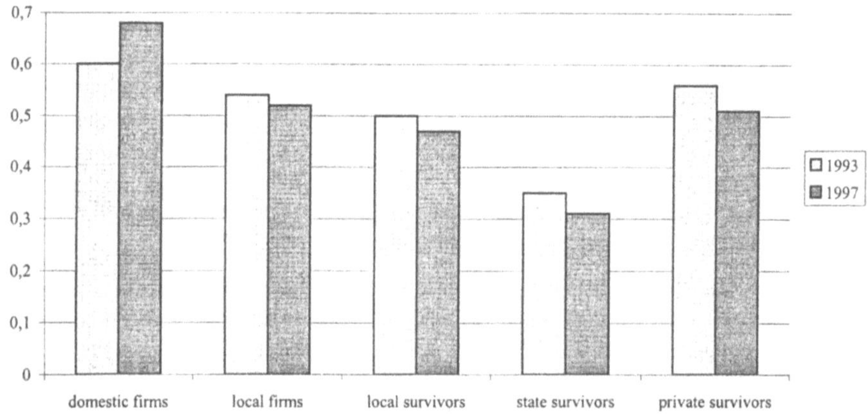

Note: The similarity index has been calculated using data for 3-digit industries.

6.3.2 Relative performance of foreign firms

As Table 6.3 makes clear, the presence of foreign firms increased significantly in all but one branch of industries over the investigated period.[13] For the total Polish industry, all indicators of the foreign presence more than doubled between 1993 and 1997 and range now between 20 per cent and 30 per cent depending on the measure applied. However, the distribution of foreign firms is highly uneven.

In 1993, the highest share of foreign firms in domestic industry output for a single three-digit industry was about 60 per cent, and it jumped to 95 per cent in 1997. In 1993, manufacturing of motor vehicles (341), manufacturing of other transport equipment (355) and manufacturing of pulp, paper and paperboard (211) were the industries with the highest foreign presence (59 per cent, 54 per cent and 48 per cent of gross output, respectively).[14] In 1997, the most foreign-dominated industry was tobacco manufacturing (160) with 95 per cent followed by manufacturing of motor vehicles (341) and manufacturing of radio and

[13] The only exception is branch 23 (petroleum refineries and manufacture of coke) which was administratively closed to the penetration of foreign firms.

[14] The numbers in brackets identify a three-digit industry according to EKD, see Appendix 6.A.

television equipment (323) with 94 per cent and 91 per cent, respectively. Moreover, between 1993 and 1997 the number of industries with foreign share in output lower than 5 per cent has sunk from 26 to 15 (out of 100 industries for which data are available), and the median share has increased from 10 per cent to 21 per cent.

Table 6.3:
Sectoral Distribution of Foreign Firms in Poland 1993-1997

	Share of gross output in foreign firms in domestic industry gross output		Share of employment in foreign firms in domestic industry employment		Share of capital stock in foreign firms in industry capital stock	
Industry [a]	**1993**	**1997**	**1993**	**1997**	**1993**	**1997**
15 - Food	0.12	0.29	0.10	0.20	0.13	0.39
16 - Tobacco	0.04	0.95	0.03	0.84	0.02	0.90
17 - Textiles	0.07	0.10	0.04	0.07	0.06	0.13
18 - Apparel	0.27	0.31	0.20	0.23	0.22	0.27
19 - Leather and footwear	0.09	0.09	0.06	0.09	0.03	0.09
20 - Wood	0.14	0.32	0.11	0.18	0.12	0.42
21 - Paper	0.37	0.67	0.26	0.38	0.42	0.76
22 - Printing and publishing	0.27	0.39	0.15	0.27	0.16	0.31
23 - Petroleum and coke	0.00	0.00	0.00	0.01	0.00	0.01
24 - Chemicals	0.09	0.26	0.06	0.15	0.05	0.17
25 - Rubber and plastics	0.17	0.45	0.10	0.34	0.10	0.48
26 - Non-metallic mineral products	0.15	0.36	0.09	0.26	0.14	0.46
27 - Primary metals	0.06	0.10	0.05	0.06	0.03	0.06
28 - Fabricated metal products	0.12	0.24	0.07	0.11	0.07	0.24
29 - Machinery	0.09	0.16	0.04	0.08	0.02	0.12
30 - Office and computing machinery	0.34	0.19	0.17	0.27	0.06	0.26
31 - Electrical machinery	0.16	0.37	0.13	0.27	0.13	0.42
32 - Radio and television equipment	0.35	0.73	0.26	0.40	0.28	0.56
33 - Instruments	0.11	0.37	0.06	0.13	0.06	0.15
34 - Vehicles	0.53	0.85	0.22	0.56	0.40	0.76
35 - Other transport equipment	0.03	0.19	0.02	0.13	0.02	0.15
36 - Miscel. manufacturing	0.29	0.44	0.21	0.35	0.16	0.42
37 - Recycling	0.21	0.16	0.14	0.17	0.10	0.15
Sector I	0.12	0.34	0.10	0.19	0.08	0.21
Sector II	0.10	0.38	0.07	0.17	0.06	0.29
Sector III	0.14	0.27	0.12	0.19	0.08	0.24
Sector IV	0.14	0.30	0.09	0.20	0.11	0.29
Sector V	0.16	0.37	0.16	0.31	0.20	0.50
Total manufacturing	0.14	0.33	0.10	0.20	0.10	0.31

Note: [a]- a two-digit activity according to EKD; sectors according to Neven (1994)

The role of foreign firms as measured by their share in domestic industry output is higher than measured by their contribution to domestic industry employment.

This implies that labour productivity in foreign firms is on average higher than the productivity of the total domestic industry. Similarly, the fact that the share of foreign firms in domestic capital stock is higher than their share in employment means that (both on average and in the majority of investigated branches) they use more capital intensive technologies than domestic industry as a whole.

These observations allow the conclusion that labour productivity and relative capital intensity of foreign firms is, on average, higher than that of local firms. This is confirmed further by Table 6.4, which shows the firms' labour productivity and capital-labour ratio in relation to the overall capital-labour ratio of the industry at the beginning of the investigated period.

In 1993, productivity of foreign firms was, on average, 1.4 times higher than that of locally owned firms and exceeded the latter in all but one branch (petroleum and coal). The difference was highest in manufacturing of motor vehicles, machinery, office and computing machines, where foreign firms were more than twice as productive as their locally owned counterparts. Among Polish firms, labour productivity in 13 out of 22 industries is higher in state firms as compared to private firms.

One explanation for this result is the higher capital-labour ratio of the state firms in these industries. Only in food, tobacco and primary metals industries are state firms more productive than foreign rivals. To a large extent, this is related to their higher capital intensity. The higher capital-labour ratio of state-owned in comparison to foreign firms also holds for total manufacturing. This might result from old, ineffective capital stock which is still booked in state firms.

Did the locally owned firms catch up in terms of productivity with foreign firms operating in Poland over the investigated period? The data in Table 6.5 indicate that it is definitely not the case for manufacturing as a whole. In 1997, foreign firms in Poland were twice as productive as locally owned ones. However, for a number of branches, the lead of foreign firms decreased, and local firms have now even a productivity lead in manufacturing of office and computing machinery.

The capital intensity of production in locally-owned part of Polish manufacturing has fallen relatively to capital intensity of foreign firms over the period investigated, but for state firms in some branches it is still higher than that of foreign ones. This, in connection with low relative productivity, is consistent with the presence of high sunk capital costs in state firms, resulting from capital immobility between industries. Hit by a loss of demand during transition, these firms tried to survive predominantly by shedding labour – this improved their labour productivity figures and increased their capital intensity.[15]

[15] Unfortunately, data on capital utilisation are not available.

Table 6.4:
Comparison of Labour Productivity and Capital-Intensity Levels Between Foreign and Local Firms in Poland, 1993

	Gross Output per Employee by Segment as a Fraction of the Overall Gross Output per Employee of the Domestic Industry				**Capital-Labour Ratio by Segment as a Fraction of the Overall Capital-Labour Ratio of the Domestic Industry**			
	Foreign	Locally Owned			Foreign	Locally Owned		
Industry [a]		All	State [b]	Private [c]		All	State [b]	Private [c]
15 - Food	1.2	1.0	2.0	0.8	1.3	1.0	1.1	0.8
16 - Tobacco	1.2	1.0	2.3		0.8	1.0	0.9	
17 - Textiles	1.9	1.0	0.8	1.1	1.5	1.0	0.9	0.7
18 - Apparel	1.3	0.9	0.6	0.9	1.1	1.0	0.8	0.9
19 - Leather and footwear	1.5	1.0	1.0	1.0	0.5	1.0	1.1	0.6
20 - Wood	1.2	1.0	0.9	0.9	1.1	1.0	1.0	0.5
21 - Paper	1.5	0.8	1.2	0.6	1.6	0.8	1.5	0.3
22 - Printing and publishing	1.8	0.9	0.8	0.9	1.1	1.0	1.1	0.7
23 - Petroleum and coke	0.3	1.0	1.1	0.1	0.7	1.0	1.0	0.0
24 - Chemicals	1.6	1.0	1.1	0.8	0.8	1.0	1.2	0.3
25 - Rubber and plastics	1.6	0.9	1.2	0.7	1.0	1.0	1.4	0.4
26 - Non-metallic mineral products	1.8	0.9	0.8	0.9	1.6	0.9	0.9	0.4
27 - Primary metals	1.2	1.0	1.4	0.7	0.5	1.0	1.6	0.2
28 - Fabricated metal products	1.6	1.0	1.3	0.9	1.0	1.0	1.6	0.5
29 - Machinery	2.0	1.0	0.9	1.0	0.6	1.0	1.2	0.3
30 - Office and computing machinery	2.0	0.8	0.6	0.6	0.3	1.1	1.7	0.7
31 - Electrical machinery	1.3	1.0	0.8	0.7	1.1	1.0	0.7	0.9
32 - Radio and television equipment	1.4	0.9	0.4	1.3	1.1	1.0	1.4	0.4
33 - Instruments	1.9	0.9	0.9	1.1	1.1	1.0	3.0	0.6
34 - Vehicles	2.4	0.6	0.5	0.4	1.8	0.8	1.9	0.3
35 - Other transport equipment	1.6	1.0	1.2	1.0	1.0	1.0	0.4	0.3
36 - Miscel. manufacturing	1.4	0.9	0.8	0.9	0.8	1.1	0.3	0.9
37 - Recycling	1.5	0.9	0.8	1.0	0.7	1.0	1.4	0.4
Sector I	1.2	1.0	1.2	0.9	0.8	1.0	1.3	0.3
Sector II	1.5	1.0	0.9	0.8	0.8	1.0	1.1	0.5
Sector III	1.2	1.0	1.1	0.8	0.6	1.0	1.2	0.5
Sector IV	1.6	0.9	1.5	0.7	1.2	1.0	1.6	0.4
Sector V	1.0	1.0	2.0	0.8	1.3	0.9	1.1	0.7
Total manufacturing	1.4	1.0	1.3	0.8	1.1	1.0	1.3	0.5

Note: [a]- 2-digit activity according to EKD respectively sectors according to Neven (1994), [b]- state survivors, [c]- private survivors

The observed reduction of productivity gaps between foreign and local firms in some branches is, to a large extent, due to the rise of relative productivity of private firms. They perform even better than foreign firms in office and computing machinery, recycling and leather and footwear industry, though they produce less capital intensively.

Table 6.5:
Technological Convergence Between Foreign and Local Firms in Poland, 1993-97

	Ratio of Gross Output per Employee Between Local and Foreign Firms						**Ratio of Capital-Labour Ratio Between Local and Foreign Firms**					
	All		**State** [b]		**Private** [c]		**All**		**State** [b]		**Private** [c]	
Industry [a]	**1993**	**1997**	**1993**	**1997**	**1993**	**1997**	**1993**	**1997**	**1993**	**1997**	**1993**	**1997**
15 - Food	0.8	0.6	1.7	1.2	0.7	0.5	0.7	0.4	0.9	0.5	0.6	0.4
16 - Tobacco	0.8	0.3	1.9				1.3	0.6	1.2			
17 - Textiles	0.5	0.7	0.4	0.6	0.6	0.8	0.7	0.6	0.6	0.5	0.5	0.5
18 - Apparel	0.7	0.6	0.4	0.5	0.7	0.6	0.9	0.8	0.8	0.9	0.8	0.8
19 - Leather and footwear	0.6	1.0	0.6	0.8	0.7	1.0	2.1	1.0	2.1	1.2	1.2	0.8
20 - Wood	0.8	0.5	0.8	0.4	0.8	0.5	0.9	0.3	0.9	0.4	0.4	0.2
21 - Paper	0.6	0.3	0.9	0.2	0.4	0.3	0.5	0.2	0.9	0.3	0.2	0.1
22 - Printing and publishing	0.5	0.6	0.4	0.4	0.5	0.5	0.9	0.8	1.0	0.8	0.6	0.6
23 - Petroleum and coke	3.4	3.0	3.7	3.6	0.3		1.5	0.8	1.5	1.0	0.0	
24 - Chemicals	0.6	0.5	0.7	0.6	0.5	0.4	1.2	0.8	1.4	1.1	0.3	0.3
25 - Rubber and plastics	0.6	0.6	0.7	0.5	0.4	0.5	1.0	0.6	1.5	0.6	0.5	0.4
26 - Non-metallic mineral products	0.5	0.6	0.5	0.4	0.5	0.7	0.6	0.4	0.6	0.4	0.3	0.3
27 - Primary metals	0.8	0.6	1.1	0.7	0.6	0.6	1.9	1.0	3.0	1.4	0.4	0.4
28 - Fabricated Metal products	0.6	0.4	0.8	0.4	0.5	0.4	1.0	0.4	1.7	0.6	0.5	0.3
29 - Machinery	0.5	0.5	0.4	0.4	0.5	0.5	1.8	0.7	2.2	0.9	0.5	0.3
30 - Office and computing machinery	0.4	1.6	0.3	0.5	0.3	2.7	3.4	1.0	5.1	0.9	2.1	0.8
31 - Electrical machinery	0.7	0.6	0.6	0.5	0.5	0.5	0.9	0.5	0.6	0.4	0.8	0.3
32 - Radio and television equipment	0.6	0.2	0.3	0.1	1.0	0.3	0.9	0.5	1.3	0.7	0.3	0.3
33 - Instruments	0.5	0.3	0.5	0.2	0.6	0.3	0.9	0.8	2.7	1.4	0.5	0.8
34 - Vehicles	0.2	0.2	0.2	0.2	0.2	0.2	0.4	0.4	1.0	1.4	0.2	0.2
35 - Other transport equipment	0.6	0.7	0.8	0.5	0.6	0.9	1.0	0.9	0.4	0.5	0.3	0.3
36 - Miscel. manufacturing	0.6	0.7	0.6	0.6	0.7	0.7	1.4	0.8	0.4	0.3	1.1	0.7
37 - Recycling	0.6	1.0	0.5	1.0	0.7	1.2	1.4	1.1	1.9	1.8	0.5	1.0
Sector I	0.8	0.5	1.1	0.5	0.7	0.4	1.3	0.8	1.6	1.1	0.4	0.3
Sector II	0.7	0.3	0.6	0.2	0.5	0.3	1.3	0.5	1.4	0.6	0.6	0.3
Sector III	0.8	0.6	0.9	0.5	0.6	0.6	1.6	0.7	1.8	1.0	0.7	0.5
Sector IV	0.6	0.6	1.0	1.0	0.4	0.4	0.8	0.6	1.3	1.3	0.4	0.3
Sector V	1.0	0.7	2.0	1.3	0.8	0.6	0.7	0.4	0.9	0.5	0.5	0.4
Total manufacturing	0.7	0.5	1.0	0.7	0.6	0.4	0.9	0.6	1.2	0.9	0.5	0.3

Note: [a]- 2-digit activity according to EKD respectively sectors according to Neven (1994), [b]- state survivors, [c]- private survivors

The above analysis has shown that, for total manufacturing and almost all industries, foreign owned firms in Poland have a labour productivity lead against local firms. Between 1993 and 1997, this difference increased for all types of locally owned firms at the aggregate level. For some industries, productivity convergence could be detected, but twice as often for private than for state firms.

6.4 Empirical specifications

The previous section demonstrated that there are substantial technological differences between foreign and locally-owned firms in Polish manufacturing and that the relative productivity of local firms follows an industry-specific time path. Does a higher presence of foreign firms help local firms to raise their productivity? In other words, are intra-industrial productivity spillovers at work?

Our general approach to investigate this question is to regress productivity growth across three-digit industries in different types of local firms on measures of foreign presence within the domestic industry. We say that *positive (intra-industrial) productivity spillovers* on local firms have been detected if the coefficient for the foreign-presence-variable is positive and significant. We interpret negative coefficients associated with this variable as the existence of *negative productivity spillovers*.

6.4.1 Econometric framework

Our econometric model is quite analogous to the one used in previous empirical studies of productivity spillovers, which were discussed in Section 4.2.[16] Consider the Cobb-Douglas production function for output in the industry i in the period t, Y_{it},

$$Y_{it} = A_{it} L_{it}^{\alpha} K_{it}^{1-\alpha} \qquad i = 1,...,n \qquad t = 1,...,T \qquad 1 > \alpha > 0 \tag{6.1}$$

where L_{it} is total labour input and K_{it} is total capital input of the industry. A_{it} gives the industry-specific technological level at time t. It stands for all factors affecting output other than tangibles: in the first place, technological change and organisational capital like management practices and labour organisation.

Define labour productivity as a ratio of total output to labour input, $LP_{it} \equiv Y_{it} / L_{it}$, and labour productivity growth, ΔLP_{it}, as $\Delta LP_{it} = \Delta y_{it} - \Delta l_{it}$ where lowercase letters denote log differences of the corresponding uppercase symbols. After taking first differences of the log version of equation (6.1) we obtain

$$\Delta LP_{it} = \Delta a_{it} + (1-\alpha)\Delta(K/L)_{it} \tag{6.2}$$

where $\Delta(K/L)_{it} \equiv \Delta k_{it} - \Delta l_{it}$ gives the change in the capital-labour ratio of the industry.

[16] For a discussion of some shortcomings of the present econometric approach, see Section 4.2.3.

The first term on the right side of Eq. (6.2), $\Delta a_{it} \equiv \ln(A_{it} / A_{it-1})$, gives the change of technological level of the industry i within the period t. We assume that it results from the interaction of different factors operating at different levels of aggregation: (i) common for the whole economy, (ii) common for sector j to which industry i belongs to, and (iii) specific to the industry i. Let the way how these factors contribute to productivity growth be given by the following model

$$\Delta LP_{it} = c_{jt} + \Delta y_{it} + \Delta a_{it}^{i} + (1-\alpha)\Delta(K/L)_{it} \tag{6.3}$$

For a transition economy, the interpretation of the proposed model is as follows. The term c_{jt} captures aggregate forces specific to the sector j within the period t. Some of these factors can be classified as real, aggregate demand shocks, which affect all industries at a given time: fiscal and monetary policies, dis-hoarding of inventories and imports in the presence of moderate and falling inflation and real appreciation of the national currency (see Table 6.1). However, most of these factors affect the various sectors in a highly differentiated way. For example, consider changes in the price of capital, labour, intermediates and imported inputs. It seems reasonable to assume that the impact of these changes depends on the relative factor intensities of the industries. Hence, we specify the term c_{jt} as a sectoral dummy variable – identical for all three-digit industries with similar relative intensity of factors used which belong to the same sector of the Neven classification (Neven, 1994). Further sector-specific shocks may be found on the supply side (institutional changes, trade liberalisation and access to imported technologies, better management practices), as well as on the demand side (the new structure of relative prices, availability and development of new goods and services).

Even in the absence of restructuring and efficiency gains, the factors mentioned above have a strong impact on measured productivity. For example, positive demand shocks usually result in a higher measured productivity only because of a higher factor utilisation which cannot be easily observed.[17] This problem may be serious in a transition country because of a widespread existence of considerable amounts of idle resources within firms inherited from the period under planned economy. In order to capture the impact of industry-specific demand shocks on the productivity change, Eq. (6.3) includes an additional variable, $\Delta y_{it} \equiv \ln(Y_{it} / Y_{it-1})$, which measures the growth rate of output of the industry.

---

[17] Within the production function framework given by Eq. (6.1), we may assume that the factor input is given by its physical stock (number of employees and value of capital stock, respectively) multiplied by its utilisation level which is the same for both production factors. Then, the term c_{jt} captures explicitly the change of the overall level of capacity utilisation within the period t. This representation is widely accepted in the business cycle literature (see Bernanke/Parkinson, 1991).

In order to test the existence of productivity spillovers, we assume that technological externalities associated with the intra-industrial presence of foreign firms are reflected in the term Δa_{it}^{l} in Eq. (6.3). More specifically, we test whether productivity change of local firms is a function of a foreign presence-variable (*FDI*) and some other characteristics of the industry

$$\Delta a_{it}^{l} = f\,(FDI_i,\ ownership,\ GAP_i,\ competition_i) + \varepsilon_{it} \qquad (6.4)$$

where ε_{it} is an idiosyncratic disturbance to productivity in industry *i* at period *t;* ε_{it} is $NID(0,\delta^2)$. In Eq. (6.4), *ownership* specifies which type of the firms (domestic, local, foreign, local survivors, state survivors or private survivors) the data refer to; *GAP* is a measure of the technological backwardness of the local firms relative to foreign firms in the same industry; *competition* measures the combined effect of external and internal competition within the industry. More details about how these variables have been constructed are given in Appendix 6.A.

The main problem when using our data set for calculating productivity arises from the lack of information on the use of intermediates for the whole period. For this reason, we cannot compute value added as our measure of output and use total factor productivity as our measure of the technological level. However, in our investigation of 2-digit industries based on data published in GUS (1998b), we detect correlation coefficients between the growth rates of gross value added and of gross output for the 1993-97 period of around 0.8.[18] Therefore, the choice of gross output may be a good approximation.

In the following section, we present and discuss hypotheses about the impact of foreign presence and the other industry-specific characteristics on the productivity growth of local firms.

6.4.2 Hypotheses on productivity spillovers from FDI

The present paper tests 3 main hypotheses on productivity spillovers associated with the intra-industrial foreign investment:

(1) The contagion hypothesis
Productivity spillovers from the activity of foreign firms on local part of an industry are increasing with higher foreign presence within the domestic industry.

(2) The technology gap hypothesis
Productivity spillovers from the activity of foreign firms on local part of an industry increase with the technological gap between local and foreign firms.

[18] In Section 6.5.4, we bring another argument in favour of the robustness of our results with respect to the chosen output measure.

(3) The competition hypothesis
Productivity spillovers from the activity of foreign firms on local part of an industry are higher in more competitive markets.

The arguments for and against these hypotheses has been given in previous chapters of this work. We have concluded there that empirical findings summarised in Chapter 4 and theoretical models analysed in Chapter 5 give different suggestions about the expected impact of the key determinants of the scope of productivity spillovers: foreign presence, relative backwardness of local firms and competition level. Generally, theoretical models do not exclude the possibility of negative spillovers due to a detrimental competition effect on local firms. They also contradict the technology gap and the competition hypotheses (Table 6.6).

Table 6.6:
Expected impact of various determinants of productivity spillovers

	Empirical hypotheses	Theoretical models of Chapter 5
Foreign presence	Positive *(Contagion hypothesis)*	Positive or negative (M/V) Positive or negative (R-C) Positive (G/S)
Relative technological backwardness of local firms	Positive *(Technology gap hypothesis)*	Negative (R-C) Negative (G/S)
Competition level within the industry	Positive *(Competition hypothesis)*	Negative (M/V) Negative (G/S) Positive (W/B)

Note: M/V – Markusen/Venables (1999); R-C – Rodríguez-Clare (1996); G/S – Glass/Saggi (1999); W/B – Wang/Blomström (1992)

Studying productivity spillovers in a transition country requires a few additional considerations. Firms can undertake a variety of measures to improve productivity in organisational, financial or technological fields. They may try to reduce costs and increase productivity through scaling down enterprise activities. Indeed, most transition countries have seen state enterprises cutting obsolete production lines, shedding labour, selling non-productive assets, reducing waste and improving management (World Bank, 1997). This is the so-called 'defensive restructuring'. Its objective is the firm's survival over a crisis period. In contrast, strategic restructuring is not only survival-oriented, but it involves innovative business strategies and the introduction of new product lines and processes.[19] It requires new investments, and it requires financing sources.

In the case of Poland, as well as most other transition countries with underdeveloped financial markets, low profitability of firms reduces not only the possibility of self-financing of investment projects, but also the very chance for strategic restructuring. As a consequence, competitive pressure from direct

[19] For the distinction of strategic and defensive restructuring, see Grosfeld/Roland (1995).

investment (and from opening to imports) on state firms and the new emerging private sector may crowd out locally owned enterprises. If this is the case, both a higher foreign presence and a severe competition are detrimental to productivity growth of local firms – contrary to the contagion and the technology gap hypotheses.

The measured labour productivity change gives the net contribution of many different factors (change in utilisation ratio, quality of inputs, deepening of capital-labour ratio, reduction of X-inefficiency) and not only technological progress. Since aggregated rather than firm-level data are available for our econometric analysis, this paper is unable to test the relative importance of different channels through which foreign firms affect the performance of local firms. Furthermore, data do not reveal the precise way how the firms react – by downsizing or by investing in products, processes or people, by exporting to less competitive foreign markets or by specialising in low-tech products for the domestic market.

Consequently, we define our primary objective as testing for the existence of productivity spillovers from FDI in accordance with the three hypotheses formulated above. At the same time, we test indirectly whether the positive effects of the foreign presence stressed by the literature on technology diffusion could materialise in Poland, and whether they dominate the negative effects attributable to the increased competition.

6.4.3 Estimation procedure

Combing Eqs. (6.3) and (6.4), we specify our first statistical model to be estimated in the following way:

$$\Delta LP_i = \beta_{0j} + \beta_1 FDI_i + \beta_2 (GAP_i * FDI_i) + \beta_3 \Delta y_i + \beta_4 \Delta (K/L)_i + \varepsilon_i \tag{6.5}$$

The model is estimated for different subsets of local firms with data aggregated over firms within a three-digit industry. The dependent variable is the log difference of labour productivity in 1997 and 1993. In accordance with the analysis of aggregate shocks in Section 1, we include sector-specific constants β_{0j}, where $j=1:5$ denotes sector the ith industry belongs to in the Neven classification. *FDI* stands for the average share of foreign firms' output in domestic output over the 1993-1996 period, *GAP* is constructed as the ratio of labour productivity of foreign firms to the labour productivity of local firms within the same 3-digit industry minus one.[20]

First, we test the contagion hypothesis alone and set $\beta_2 = 0$. Significant and positive value of estimates for β_1 support the contagion hypothesis. Significant

[20] Appendix 6.A describes the chosen variables. See also Section 4.3.1.

and negative estimates of β_1 reject the contagion hypothesis, since they mean that a higher intra-industrial foreign presence is associated with a lower productivity growth in local firms.

Second, we test simultaneously the contagion and the technology gap hypothesis by estimating Eq. (6.5) without any parameter restrictions. The marginal effect of a higher foreign presence on productivity growth is given by $\beta_1 + \beta_2 GAP_i$, *i.e.* it increases (decreases) with the initial technology gap whenever the estimated β_2 is positive (negative). A positive β_2 supports the technology gap hypothesis. Positive values of the whole term for all levels of initial technology gap give unlimited support to the contagion hypothesis. Opposite signs of the estimates for β_1 and β_2 indicate the existence of thresholds effects: the impact of a higher foreign presence may be diametrically different for low as compared to high technology gap industries. The threshold value is given by $GAP_i = -\beta_1 / \beta_2$.

The technology gap hypothesis is also confirmed if we find that spillovers coefficients are lower for low-gap industries than for high-gap industries. To check this empirically, we divide all industries into two groups, using the median value of the *GAP*-variable as a selection criterion for each type of local firms. Industries are characterised by a low technological gap when the industry-specific *GAP* is lower than median, and a high technological gap in the opposite case. Checking the technology gap hypothesis consists of estimating the following model:

$$\Delta LP_i = \gamma_{0j} + \gamma_1 FDI_i + \gamma_2((GAP\_L)_i * FDI_i) + \gamma_3 \Delta y_i + \gamma_4 \Delta(K/L)_i + \varepsilon_i \quad (6.6)$$

The variable $(GAP\_L)_i$ is a dummy variable which is 1 if in 1993 the local firms in the *i*th industry have a technology gap that is smaller than the median value for all domestic industries, and it is 0 for all other industries. The slope of the regression line is γ_1 for industries with a high technology gap and $\gamma_1 + \gamma_2$ for the others. There is no statistical reason to reject the contagion hypothesis if both terms are significant and positive. If $\gamma_1 > \gamma_1 + \gamma_2$, the technology gap hypothesis cannot be rejected.

Third, we test the competition hypothesis by estimating equations (6.5) and (6.6) separately for industries characterised by low and high competition, where the median value of the competition index for all industries in 1993 serves as the separation criterion. Significantly different coefficients for these two subsets of industries are interpreted as support for the hypothesis that competition matters a lot for the scope of spillovers. A higher positive value of the spillovers coefficient for industries subject to more severe competition supports the competition hypothesis.

With one observation for each industry, we have a cross-section data set and apply the OLS estimation procedure. However, there is heteroscedasticity in our data as the test of White (1980) shows for almost all estimated models. In this case, OLS estimators are still unbiased and consistent, but they are inefficient. Efficient estimation with GLS requires precise knowledge of the nature of heteroscedasticity. Estimation with improperly weighted least square estimator gives inefficient results, and in small or moderate-sized samples it remains uncertain whether GLS estimators are more efficient than OLS ones (Greene, 1993, ch.14). Since the endogenous variable in our model are growth rates, we are unsure about the nature of heteroscedasticity. We solve this problem in a standard way by correcting the estimation of the covariance matrix according to the White (1980) procedure and calculating heteroscedasticity corrected standard errors and t-values.

6.5 Results

6.5.1 FDI and local productivity growth

Descriptive statistics of the samples are given in Table 6.A.2, some correlation coefficients in Table 6.A.3. On average, Polish manufacturing improved its performance over the period 1993-97 – labour productivity increased over 60 per cent.[21] Productivity growth was higher for private firms than for state ones. Exit and entry of local firms resulted in a higher productivity change for the local part of the industry than it was the case for local survivors. For each type of local firms and the domestic industry as a whole, the productivity change was higher in industries characterised by relatively high competition. Interestingly, in highly competitive industries, the technology gap to foreign firms was significantly higher for all types of local firms. This is consistent with the empirical observation by Mansfield/Romeo (1980) and the model by Wang/Blomström (1992) presented in Section 5 which indicate that multinationals transfer more modern techniques to their foreign affiliates in industries under higher competitive pressure.

First, we examine the impact of FDI on productivity growth in the Polish industry as a whole (local and foreign firms together), estimating Eq.(6.5) with data for all domestic firms. The results are presented in Table 6.7. Since the *FDI* coefficients are highly significant and positive, industries with a higher foreign presence experienced a higher productivity growth (col. 1). The scope of the FDI impact on growth depends only weakly significant on the initial technology gap: it is higher for more backward industries (col. 2-3). The determinants of productivity growth depend on the competition level within the industry. Whereas FDI does not affect productivity growth in highly competitive industries, a higher foreign presence is associated with a higher productivity growth under low competition. For both groups of industries, the larger scope of

[21] This is equal to $e^{\Delta LP}$-1 with ΔLP taken from Table 6.A.2.

the initial technology gap seems to enhance the positive impact of a higher foreign presence.

Table 6.7:
Foreign Firms and the Performance of the Domestic Industry, 1993-1997

	All industries			High Competition			Low Competition		
Variables	(1)	(2)	(3)	(4)	(5)	(6)	(7)	(8)	(9)
FDI	0.66	0.46	0.82	0.35	0.08	0.59	0.93	0.83	0.98
	(4.27)**	(2.29)**	(3.98)**	(1.22)	(0.26)	(1.45)	(5.98)**	(3.13)**	(6.14)**
FDI*GAP		0.37			0.82			0.13	
		(1.56)			(1.82)*			(0.51)	
GAP_L*FDI			-0.28			-0.36			-0.13
			(-1.23)			(-1.08)			(-0.55)
Δ K/L	0.08	0.11	0.10	0.01	0.03	0.04	0.17	0.18	0.18
	(1.28)	(1.80)*	(1.67)*	(0.06)	(0.24)	(0.28)	(2.77)**	(2.78)**	(2.79)**
R^2	0.80	0.81	0.81	0.84	0.86	0.85	0.88	0.88	0.87
Sample size	96	96	96	48	48	48	48	48	48

Note: The endogenous variable is $\ln(LP_{1997}/LP_{1993})$. The estimates are computed with OLS and include five sector-specific constants. t-statistics (absolute values adjusted for heteroscedasticity according to White's (1980) procedure) are shown in parentheses. ** - significant at the 5 per cent level. * -significant at the 10 per cent level.

One explanation for the positive impact detected here is a higher relative productivity of foreign firms and their higher rates of productivity growth. This fact is supported by the data in Tables 6.3-6.4. The whole domestic industry benefits from a higher presence of foreign firms in terms of productivity change. Positive productivity spillovers on local firms could also contribute to this result, but within the present framework it is not possible to detect them. Since high and low competitive industries do not differ substantially as far as the average share of FDI is concerned (see Table 6.A.2) and the correlation coefficient between *FDI* and *COMP* is still negative but low (see Table 6.A.3), the differing results with respect to the FDI impact cannot be explained by a higher presence of (more productive) foreign firms in low competitive industries. Instead, we conjecture that the indirect effect of foreign firms on local firms may depend on the competitive level of the industry.

Imagine that local firms in industries characterised by high competition are too weak to reap benefits from the higher presence of foreign firms – restructuring, technology adoption and capital investment requires financial means which might be scarce for firms facing tight competition from other domestic firms and imports. For these firms, the access to soft bank credits and subsidies is usually less easy than for (state) firms in highly concentrated industries. Hence, local firms in highly competitive industries are likely to be crowded out of the market when the competition pressure of foreign firms is high. If, on the other hand, firms facing low competition (state oligopolists protected from imports) have an easier access to financial resources (own or state) which are needed for restructuring, they may be able to benefit from a higher intra-industrial foreign presence by eliminating X-inefficiencies and investing in new technologies. This would explain that the positive *FDI*-coefficient is higher for the low competition industries than the one for the sample of all industries. We will check these hypotheses below when testing for productivity spillovers on local firms in low and high competition industries.

Productivity Spillovers

We test the existence and scope of *productivity spillovers* on local firms by estimating equations (6.5) and (6.6). The results are presented in Tables 6.8 and 6.9. The fit of the regressions is satisfactory, especially for the group of high competitive industries with R^2 around 0.8. The variable Δy which stays for industry-specific demand shocks is highly significant in most specifications. Its contribution to the overall fit of regression as measured by R^2 is very high. The main findings can be summarised as follows:

- A higher foreign presence within an industry is associated with a lower productivity growth of its locally-owned part (all local firms). If the foreign share of domestic output is one percentage point higher, the productivity growth factor for local firms is 0.68 percent lower (Tab.6.8, col. 1). Hence, we cannot find support for the existence of positive productivity spillovers on local firms in accordance with the contagion hypothesis.
- The negative impact on all local firms is even higher (the *FDI*-coefficient equals –0.90) for high competitive industries, for low competitive industries, the absolute value is smaller (-0.32) but statistically insignificant (see Tab. 6.9, col. 1 and 4). Hence, we cannot find support for the existence of positive productivity spillovers on local firms in accordance with the contagion and the competition hypotheses.
- As postulated by the technology gap hypothesis, a higher initial technology gap is beneficial for the scope of productivity spillovers (Tab. 6.8, col. 2). However, since the impact of a higher foreign presence is negative (-0.98), it only means that it is less detrimental for industries with more backward local firms.[22] The technology gap hypothesis is also supported by the estimates in the column (3). Whereas no spillovers have been detected for the group of high-gap industries, the FDI impact on low-gap industries is significantly negative.

[22] With the estimated coefficients on FDI and FDI*GAP, the threshold value for local technology gap 0.33. All industries with a technology gap higher than 0.33 will benefit from a higher foreign presence. However, only one industry in the sample of all local firms satisfies this threshold.

Table 6.8:
Productivity Spillovers and Technological Gap

	(1)	(2)	(3)
	All industries		
	All local firms		
FDI	-0.68 (-2.71)**	-0.98 (-3.32)**	-0.27 (-1.02)
FDI*GAP		0.30 (2.30)**	
GAP_L*FDI			-0.66 (-2.99)**
Δ y	0.50 (2.92)**	0.49 (2.99)**	0.46 (2.89)**
Δ K/L	-0.07 (-0.63)	-0.04 (-0.42)	-0.03 (-0.29)
R^2	0.74	0.76	0.77
Sample size	96	96	96
	All survivors		
FDI	-0.41 (-1.15)	-0.95 (-2.45)**	-0.07 (-0.21)
FDI*GAP		0.42 (3.36)**	
GAP_L*FDI			-0.88 (-3.45)**
Δ y	0.42 (2.22)**	0.43 (2.42)**	0.42 (2.32)**
Δ K/L	0.12 (1.31)	0.14 (1.54)	0.14 (1.60)
R^2	0.60	0.65	0.65
Sample size	94	94	94
	State survivors		
FDI	-0.05 (-0.06)	-1.37 (-2.81)**	0.92 (1.46)
FDI*GAP		0.89 (4.57)**	
GAP_L*FDI			-1.75 (-3.83)**
Δ y	0.58 (2.67)**	0.54 (3.08)**	0.57 (3.39)**
Δ K/L	0.15 (1.53)	0.21 (3.11)**	0.19 (2.72)**
R^2	0.39	0.61	0.57
Sample size	75	75	75
	Private survivors		
FDI	-0.56 (-1.55)	-1.12 (-1.91)*	-0.39 (-1.39)
FDI*GAP		0.46 (1.68)	
GAP_L*FDI			-0.48 (-0.91)
Δ y	0.28 (0.83)	0.31 (0.87)	0.29 (0.83)
Δ K/L	0.16 (1.46)	0.14 (1.38)	0.15 (1.41)
R^2	0.41	0.44	0.42
Sample size	88	88	88

Note: The endogenous variable is $\ln(LP_{1997}/ LP_{1993})$. The estimates are computed with OLS and include sector-specific constants. t-statistics (absolute values adjusted for heteroscedasticity according to White's (1980) procedure) are shown in parentheses. ** - significant at the 5 per cent level. * -significant at the 10 per cent level.

It could be interpreted that a higher foreign presence is harmful to local firms. However, this interpretation might be negatively biased due to adverse selection: Local firms which were sold to foreign investors drop out of the sample of local firms. Since foreign privatisation took place mainly in less competitive industries and only the best performing local firms could be sold, this might explain the deterring impact of FDI on the performance of the rest of the industry. In order to control for the impact of foreign privatisation, we conduct our analyses for the group of local survivors, *i.e.* firms which operated over the whole investigated period. In addition, it allows to exclude the effect of exit and entry on the aggregate performance of the local part of the industry. We obtain the following econometric results:

- The FDI impact on the productivity of local firms which operated over the entire period considerably depends on the competitive status of the industry. The simple contagion hypothesis cannot be statistically supported for all industries – a higher foreign presence seems to be detrimental to productivity growth of local survivors, but the effect is statistically insignificant (Tab. 6.8, col. 1). We detect a strongly negative impact of a higher foreign presence in the group of highly competitive industries (Tab. 6.9, col. 1). There is no evidence for productivity spillovers under low competition.
- The size of the technology gap matters for the scope of spillovers: it reduces the negative impact of a higher intra-industrial foreign share, as formulated in the technology gap hypothesis (Tab. 6.8, col. 2). However, only for 4 out of 94 industries is the size of the technology gap so big that the existence of positive spillovers cannot be rejected. Whereas in less backward industries, the FDI impact on productivity growth is negligible, it is highly detrimental on the performance of industries with a relatively high technology gap (Tab. 6.8, col. 3).
- In the highly competitive industries, the impact of foreign firms is extremely detrimental (Tab. 6.9, col. 3). Higher initial backwardness helps neutralise this negative effect, but the spillovers are positive only in the computer industry (300), manufacturing of controlling equipment (333), primary metal industry (274, 275) and manufacturing of grain mill products (156). On the other hand, in the industries characterised by low competition and relatively high technological gaps, we detect positive productivity spillovers which are proportional to the scope of the intra-industrial activity of foreign firms. This supports the contagion, technology gap and the competition hypothesis.

The results for local firms as compared to those for local survivors indicate that for low competitive industries the problem of adverse selection may exist and contribute to the evidence of negative spillovers. Under high competition, the detrimental impact on local survivors is even higher than on all local firms. It means that exit and entry into the local industry, intensified by higher competition, has enhanced industrial productivity growth and neutralised the negative impact of competition from FDI on local survivors. With our data set, it is not possible to check whether FDI has played a role of a catalyst for this process of creative destruction.

Table 6.9:
Productivity Spillovers and Competition

	High Competition			Low Competition		
Variables	(1)	(2)	(3)	(4)	(5)	(6)
			All local firms			
FDI	-0.90 (-2.89)**	-1.18 (-3.51)**	-0.41 (-1.52)	-0.32 (-1.50)	-0.68 (-2.99)**	-0.01 (-0.02)
FDI*GAP		0.59 (2.13)**			0.26 (2.62)**	
GAP_L*FDI			-0.61 (-2.38)**			-0.63 (-2.55)**
Δ K/L	-0.06 (-0.52)	-0.02 (-0.15)	-0.02 (-0.17)	0.12 (2.52)**	0.13 (2.75)**	0.13 (2.61)**
Δ y	0.84 (3.98)**	0.76 (4.21)**	0.78 (4.00)**	0.22 (2.40)**	0.23 (2.80)**	0.21 (2.51)**
R^2	0.89	0.90	0.90	0.72	0.73	0.75
Sample size	48	48	48	48	48	48
			All local survivors			
FDI	-1.23 (-2.90)**	-1.43 (-3.69)**	-0.85 (-2.55)**	0.39 (0.88)	-0.28 (-0.49)	0.58 (1.48)
FDI*GAP		0.79 (2.32)**			0.30 (2.66)**	
GAP_L*FDI			-0.56 (-1.49)			-1.29 (-3.67)**
Δ K/L	0.00 (0.00)	0.01 (0.10)	0.02 (0.16)	0.26 (2.99)**	0.25 (2.71)**	0.25 (3.03)**
Δ y	0.83 (2.88)**	0.70 (3.51)**	0.80 (3.06)**	0.13 (1.28)	0.16 (1.80)*	0.14 (1.77)*
R^2	0.80	0.83	0.81	0.58	0.62	0.67
Sample size	48	48	48	46	46	46
			State survivors			
FDI	-1.01 (-2.03)**	-1.48 (-3.78)**	0.15 (0.33)	1.22 (1.21)	-0.64 (-0.66)	1.73 (2.21)**
FDI*GAP		1.06 (4.00)**			0.78 (2.66)**	
GAP_L*FDI			-1.27 (-3.63)**			-1.89 (-2.35)**
Δ K/L	0.16 (1.04)	0.10 (0.86)	0.14 (1.14)	0.22 (2.05)**	0.26 (2.30)**	0.26 (2.49)**
Δ y	0.46 (2.21)**	0.26 (1.92)*	0.40 (2.76)**	0.33 (1.16)	0.43 (1.73)*	0.40 (1.66)
R^2	0.69	0.82	0.79	0.41	0.60	0.58
Sample size	42	42	42	33	33	33
			Private survivors			
FDI	-0.94 (-2.04)**	-1.45 (-3.17)**	-0.54 (-1.55)	-0.29 (-0.71)	-0.75 (-0.96)	-0.22 (-0.59)
FDI*GAP		0.83 (2.76)**			0.27 (0.89)	
GAP_L*FDI			-0.91 (-1.85)*			-0.28 (-0.47)
Δ K/L	0.21 (1.86)*	0.15 (1.83)*	0.17 (1.75)*	0.13 (0.93)	0.11 (0.84)	0.12 (0.86)
Δ y	0.98 (2.67)**	0.94 (3.45)**	1.02 (3.04)**	-0.02 (-0.08)	0.00 (0.00)	-0.02 (-0.07)
R^2	0.80	0.85	0.82	0.26	0.28	0.27
Sample size	48	48	48	40	40	40

Note: The endogenous variable is $\ln(LP_{1997}/ LP_{1993})$. The estimates are computed with OLS and include sector-specific constants. t-statistics (absolute values adjusted for heteroscedasticity according to White's (1980) procedure) are shown in parentheses. ** - significant at the 5 per cent level. * -significant at the 10 per cent level.

In order to investigate how the ownership status of the firm affects the existence of spillovers, we analyse them separately for state and private firms. The findings can be summarised as follows:

- The FDI impact on productivity growth of state firms is negative but insignificant when analysed for all industries together. However, it results from the overlapping of highly significant, opposite in sign results for different groups of industries. In highly competitive industries, a higher activity of foreign firms has a negative impact on state firms (Tab. 6.9, col. 2 and 3). Consistent with the technology gap hypothesis, a higher technology gap helps reap positive spillovers; in 18 out of 42 high competitive industries, FDI affects productivity growth of state firms positively. In lowly competitive industries, we detect positive spillovers from FDI (Tab. 6.9, col. 4-6): they are high in scope (1.73) for industries with relatively high technology gap and zero for low-gap industries. The technology gap hypothesis is also supported by results of the regression (5): the scope of positive productivity spillovers increase with the technology gap.

- The FDI impact on the performance of private survivors is negative but insignificant (all industries, lowly competitive industries) or significantly negative (highly competitive industries). The FDI impact is more harmful in industries which were initially relatively more productive (Tab. 6.9, col. 2,3).

Based on our results for state and private survivors, it appears that these two types of local firms in highly competitive industries were similarly affected by the presence of foreign firms: higher intra-industrial FDI led to negative productivity spillovers. Under low competition, the effect of FDI varies diametrically: whereas positive spillovers have been detected for state firms in accordance with the technology gap hypothesis, higher FDI seems to have no impact on the productivity growth of private firms.

To summarise: we do not find statistical evidence that foreign direct investment does contribute to productivity growth of locally-owned firms within the same industry. On the contrary, we detect a detrimental impact of higher foreign presence on local productivity growth, especially for relatively less backward firms in highly competitive industries. Under low competition, the impact of FDI is less detrimental, and it seems to be positive for state survivors. Hence, our results do not support the standard hypotheses on the existence and scope of productivity spillovers.

Before we check the robustness of these results concerning the role of FDI for restructuring of local firms and comment on them, we proceed now by investigating the question whether FDI helped locally-owned part of the Polish manufacturing to catch-up in productivity levels with the multinationals.

6.5.2 FDI and local productivity convergence

In Section 6.3.2, we detected that the process of catching up in productivity between foreign and local firms is highly uneven: in a number of industries, relative productivity of local firms improved over the period 1993-97, but it was not a general trend. We found out that the private firms could reduce their technology gap more often and to a greater extent. In this section, we examine the impact of FDI on the speed of the catching-up process. Our econometric model has the following form:

$$\Delta RLP_i = \chi_{0j} + \chi_1 FDI_i + \chi_2 RLP_i FDI_i + \chi_3 RLP_i + \varepsilon_i \qquad (6.7)$$

with RLP_i is the ratio of labour productivity of local firms to labour productivity of foreign firms within the same 3-digit industry *i*. Relative labour productivity is computed for all type of local firms in 1993 and 1997, so that $\Delta RLP_i = (LP_{i97} / LP_{i93})^{local} / (LP_{i97} / LP_{i93})^{foreign}$.[23] We estimate Eq. (6.7) for different types of local firms stepwise: By setting $\chi_1 = \chi_2 = 0$, we test whether the speed of catching up is negatively related to the initial relative productivity, as it is typically the case for a convergence process. In case of industries with diverging relative productivity, we do not formulate any expectations about the sign of the *RLP* coefficient. Next, we test how a higher intra-industrial foreign presence affects the speed of catch-up. We allow FDI to influence this rate directly and through its interaction with the *RLP* variable. A positive value of the *FDI* coefficients would suggest that FDI has helped local firms close the technology gap more rapidly, negative coefficients indicate that a higher foreign presence has hindered improving local relative productivity.

We compute separate estimations for industries which reduced their technology gap to foreign firms (productivity convergence) and for industries where the technology gap increased (productivity divergence). Since only industries with initial relative local productivity lower than 1 have been examined, the number of observations is now smaller than for examining productivity spillovers. The results are given in Table 6.10. The fit of the regression is quite high, especially for industries with productivity divergence.

- As expected for the whole domestic manufacturing, which widened its relative technology gap over the period in question (see Table 6.6), the extent of the catch up (ΔRLP) is negatively related to the initial relative productivity of local firms: more backward industries (*RLP* lower) could change their relative productivity more (Tab. 6.10, col.1). This is consistent with the technology gap hypothesis for convergence. The catch-up coefficient is higher for all local firms than for local survivors. For a given size of technology gap, the rate of catch-up is higher for private firms than for the state ones.
- In industries with productivity convergence, its scope for the whole industry was not significantly affected by the initial technology gap. In industries with productivity divergence, the change of the relative productivity is negatively affected by higher initial technological backwardness.

[23] Relative labour productivity, *RLP*, and technology gap, *GAP*, are related through *GAP=1/RLP-1*.

Table 6.10:
FDI and Productivity Convergence, 1993-1997

	All industries			Industries with productivity divergence		Industries with productivity convergence	
All domestic firms							
RLP	-2.23 (-2.56)**	-2.21 (-2.43)**	-2.16 (-2.20)**	-0.21(-8.00)**	-0.21(-7.63)**	-0.18(-0.82)	-0.21(-0.90)
FDI		-0.11 (0.26)			0.04(0.19)		-0.58(-0.74)
FDI*RLP			-0.20 (0.34)				
R^2	0.72	0.72	0.72	0.95	0.95	0.74	0.74
Sample size	78	78	78	47	47	49	49
All local firms							
RLP	-2.35 (-2.67)**	-2.31 (-2,66)**	-1.92 (-2.09)**	-0.15(-4.43)**	-0.19(-6.11)**	-0.17(-0.85)	-0.21(-0.94)
FDI		-1.07 (-2,38)**			-0.67(-3.86)**		-0.72(-0.74)
FDI*RLP			-1.83 (-2.69)**				
R^2	0.64	0.65	0.65	0.91	0.93	0.70	0.70
Sample size	78	78	78	47	47	49	49
All local survivors							
RLP	-2.19 (-2.58)**	-2.33 (-2.74)**	-1.83 (-2.23)**	-0.08(-4.05)**	-0.11(-5.34)**	-0.12(-0.55)	-0.16(-0.69)
FDI		-1.55 (-2.77)**			-0.51(-2.40)**		-0.86(-0.90)
FDI*RLP			-2.65 (-2.76)**				
R^2	0.61	0.63	0.62	0.91	0.92	0.68	0.68
Sample size	80	80	80	51	51	43	43
State survivors							
RLP	-1.59 (-2.37)**	-1.61 (-2.44)**	-1.34 (-1.93)**	-0.07(-3.35)**	-0.10(-5.24)**	0.01(0.10)	-0.07(-0.40)
FDI		-0.88 (-2.15)**			-0.69(-2.63)**		-1.98(-1.50)
FDI*RLP			-1.03 (-1.34)				
R^2	0.52	0.52	0.52	0.88	0.90	0.58	0.60
Sample size	67	67	67	45	45	30	30
Private survivors							
RLP	-2.14 (-2.73)**	-2.25 (-2.81)**	-1.80 (-2.47)**	-0.15(-2.64)**	-0.16(-2.84)**	-1.69(-1.53)	-2.05(-1.78)*
FDI		-1.62 (-1.95)*			-0.46(-2.42)**		-2.40(-1.82)*
FDI*RLP			-2.17 (-1.82)*				
R^2	0.57	0.59	0.58	0.91	0.92	0.70	0.71
Sample size	77	77	77	46	46	42	42

Note: The endogenous variable is $\Delta RLP=RLP_{1997}/ RLP_{1993}$. The estimates are computed with OLS and include sector-specific constants. t-statistics (absolute values adjusted for heteroscedasticity according to White's (1980) procedure) are shown in parentheses. ** - significant at the 5 per cent level. * -significant at the 10 per cent level.

- For total domestic manufacturing, the rate of industrial catch-up is not significantly affected by the scope of the foreign presence, independent of whether the convergence took place or not.
- Higher FDI exercised a negative impact on the rate of relative productivity change in the local part of the industry. In industries with productivity divergence, the adverse impact of FDI was higher for the state than for the private firms. In industries with productivity convergence, the impact of FDI was negative, but significantly negative only for private survivors.

Since the labour productivity growth in foreign firms is only weakly positively correlated with the scope of foreign presence (0.18), the negative impact of higher FDI on the scope of convergence cannot be explained simply by a higher extent of foreign productivity improvement in industries with much FDI. It means that the local productivity growth is not only negatively affected by a higher competition through FDI, but also that the scope of falling behind multinationals is higher in industries with a higher foreign presence. The negative affect of FDI on the productivity convergence is even more alarming than its detrimental impact on labour productivity growth. It suggests that on average locally-owned firms loose comparative advantages relative to foreign firms. They are pushed into slowly growing markets, and the building of a two tier economy is under way. Further research on this important issue based on detailed manufacturing data is needed.

6.5.3 FDI and local investment in technology

As the benefits of a higher presence of multinationals could not be found in the present performance of the local firms, we investigate whether FDI positively affects modernisation efforts of local firms. This can be done by relating local firms' investment ratio in intangible assets, such as licenses, patents, designs and trademarks, to the presence of foreign firms in various industries. Annual investment in intangibles possessed by local firms is proxied by the change in their value due to purchases and own R&D activities. For each industry and type of local firms, we calculate the investment ratio over the period 1993-97 which gives the average annual share of investment in intangibles in firms' output. We regress this measure on the *FDI*- variable, controlling for the competition level of the industry and the initial technology gap. Results are presented in Table 6.11.

The investment ratio in intangible assets is higher in industries with a greater foreign presence. This positive impact is statistically significant with regards to the whole domestic industry, but insignificant for the locally-owned firms. This is consistent with the previous results suggesting that multinationals' positive impact on the performance of Polish manufacturing has mostly a direct nature and is not a source of positive spillovers. The negative *FDI* coefficients for state firms confirm the view that productivity spillovers detected in previous regressions result from defensive restructuring in state firms, and are not a sign of investment in upgrading of their technology. Indeed, state firms invest significantly less in technology than private ones, independent from the competitive status of the industry.

The competition level is important for the behaviour of local private firms. In highly competitive industries, private survivors and *de novo* private firms invest in technologies significantly more when intra-industrial foreign presence is high.

A higher initial technology gap of the industry stimulates investment in *de novo* firms, and seems to dampen it for private survivors. This seems reasonable when taking into account that start-up investment expenditures in technology are higher than subsequent expenditures. In industries facing low competition, investment in technology of local firms is mostly unrelated to the presence of foreign firms and the productivity gap of their local rivals.

Table 6.11:
FDI and local investment in technology, 1993-97

	All industries		High competition		Low Competition	
			All domestic firms			
FDI	0.93 (2.32)**	0.86 (1.81)*	1.29 (2.42)**	1.37 (2.40)**	0.71 (1.31)	0.36 (0.55)
FDI*GAP		0.14 (0.29)		-0.26 (-0.41)		0.51 (0.82)
R^2	0.47	0.47	0.47	0.47	0.50	0.51
Sample size	96	96	48	48	48	48
			All local firms			
FDI	1.07 (1.57)	1.18 (1.14)	1.65 (1.99)**	-0.89 (-1.34)	0.65 (0.76)	0.19 (0.00)
FDI*GAP		-0.10 (-0.20)		2.18 (2.03)**		0.36 (0.63)
R^2	0.32	0.32	0.50	0.52	0.25	0.28
Sample size	96	96	96	48	48	48
			All local survivors			
FDI	0.05 (0.31)	0.16 (0.58)	0.29 (0.98)	0.40 (1.15)	-0.13 (-1.68)*	-0.17 (-1.27)
FDI*GAP		-0.08 (-0.81)		-0.25 (-0.94)		0.02 (0.55)
R^2	0.22	0.23	0.34	0.36	0.31	0.31
Sample size	94	94	48	48	46	46
			State survivors			
FDI	-0.59 (-1.65)	-0.20 (-0.75)	-0.69 (-1.43)	-0.37 (-0.90)	-0.51 (-1.03)	0.13 (0.41)
FDI*GAP		-0.24 (-0.75)		-0.47 (-1.08)		-0.28 (-1.37)
R^2	0.11	0.14	0.10	0.12	0.25	0.34
Sample size	75	75	42	42	33	33
			Private survivors			
FDI	0.93 (1.13)	1.69 (1.10)	2.16 (1.44)	3.23 (1.72)*	0.07 (0.39)	-0.23 (-0.67)
FDI*GAP		-0.68 (-0.94)		-1.62 (-1.57)		0.20 (1.19)
R^2	0.27	0.31	0.44	0.53	0.44	0.46
Sample size	88	88	48	48	40	40

Note: The endogenous variable is the average ratio of change in firm's intangible assets to output over the period 1993-97. The estimates are computed with OLS and include sector-specific constants. t-statistics (absolute values adjusted for heteroscedasticity according to White's (1980) procedure) are shown in parentheses. ** - significant at the 5 per cent level. * -significant at the 10 per cent level.

6.5.4 Sensitivity analyses

In this section, we check the robustness of the obtained results regarding the existence and scope of productivity spillovers. We investigate three issues: (i) the sensitivity of our findings to the definition of output; (ii) the sensitivity to the applied measure of productivity; and (iii) the sensitivity to the definition of foreign presence.

(i) Sensitivity with regard to the definition of output

Our basic measure of output does not contain sales in firms' own shops, since it is not possible to correct them for the revenues from the resale of purchased goods. Consequently, we underestimate gross output and labour productivity of local firms. If the importance of sales in own shops for different types of domestic firms change over the period in question, the measured labour productivity growth is affected by it. Unfortunately, we are not able to isolate this effect. However, we can check whether our results are robust with regard to the choice of output measure.

With the alternative definition of gross output, sales in firm's own shops are included. On average of all industries, gross output and labour productivity for local firms are now about 20 per cent higher, and for a number of industries up to 50 per cent higher. The two measures of output are most different for foreign firms - their ratio equals 1.4 in 1993 and 1.3 in 1997 – and for local private survivors – 1.2 in 1993 and 1.3 in 1997. This must be interpreted as a piece of evidence for the fact that foreign as well as private local firms engage not only in productive activities but also in trade with goods – imported or produced by other domestic firms. It is also an argument for our basic measure of output, which is more related to production and its efficiency than the alternative one. However, the computed measures of productivity change are highly correlated. We re-estimate econometric Eq. (6.5) with the new measures of labour productivity growth, $\Delta LP'$, and with $\Delta y'$, *FDI'* and *GAP'* which are now based on the alternative definition of gross output. The original and the new results are compared in Table 6.12.

The positive impact of a higher foreign presence on productivity growth of the domestic industry is statistically robust, hence independent of the definition of output. Moreover, all results concerning productivity spillovers have been confirmed: significantly negative spillovers for the whole group of locally-owned firms, and a negative but insignificant impact on the productivity growth of various sub-types of local firms. When testing the technology gap hypothesis, we obtain statistically identical coefficients for all domestic firms, all local firms, all local survivors and private survivors. In case of the first two types of local firms, both regressions detect a negative impact of higher *FDI* on local productivity growth, which is smaller for more backward industries. The results for state survivors differ slightly: with our basic measure of output, we find positive spillovers for 10 out of 75 most backward industries and negative spillovers for the rest; with the alternative measure of output, we find positive spillovers in accordance with the technology gap hypothesis. We explain this by pointing out that technology gaps between state and foreign firms are higher and more differentiated with the second measure of output, whereas the other variables do not very significantly.

In sum, our findings about the nature of productivity spillovers are robust with regards to a definition of output which underlies the calculations.

Table 6.12:
Productivity Spillovers: sales vs. gross output, 1993-97

Endogenous Variable:	ΔLP	ΔLP′	ΔLP	ΔLP′
		All domestic firms		
FDI	0.66 (4.27)**	0.53 (2.91)**	0.46 (2.29)**	0.35 (1.76)*
FDI*GAP			0.37 (1.56)	0.22 (1.18)
Δ K/L	0.08 (1.28)	0.11 (1.69)*	0.11 (1.80)*	0.14 (2.18)**
R^2	0.80	0.82	0.81	0.82
Sample size	96	96	96	96
		All local firms		
FDI	-0.68 (-2.71)**	-0.49 (-2.70)**	-0.98 (-3.32)**	-1.00 (-3.56)**
FDI*GAP			0.30 (2.30)**	0.33 (2.17)**
Δ K/L	0.50 (2.92)**	-0.05 (-0.53)	0.49 (2.99)**	-0.02 (-0.22)
Δ y	-0.07 (-0.63)	0.44 (3.00)**	-0.04 (-0.42)	0.41 (4.05)**
R^2	0.74	0.75	0.76	0.81
Sample size	96	96	96	96
		All survivors		
FDI	-0.41 (-1.15)	-0.18 (-0.62)	-0.95 (-2.45)**	-1.04 (-2.96)**
FDI*GAP			0.42 (3.36)**	0.41 (3.51)**
Δ K/L	0.42 (2.22)**	0.19 (1.99)**	0.43 (2.42)**	0.19 (2.89)**
Δ y	0.12 (1.31)	0.34 (2.12)**	0.14 (1.54)	0.32 (3.78)**
R^2	0.60	0.60	0.65	0.75
DW	2.09	2.18	2.17	2.18
Sample size	94	94	94	94
		State survivors		
FDI	-0.05 (-0.06)	-0.08 (-0.11)	-1.37 (-2.81)**	-0.50 (-0.86)
FDI*GAP			0.89 (4.57)**	0.30 (3.66)**
Δ K/L	0.58 (2.67)**	0.13 (1.34)	0.54 (3.08)**	0.24 (2.94)**
Δ y	0.15 (1.53)	0.54 (2.60)**	0.21 (3.11)**	0.32 (2.07)
R^2	0.39	0.39	0.61	0.55
Sample size	75	75	75	75
		Private survivors		
FDI	-0.56 (-1.55)	-0.29 (-0.88)	-1.12 (-1.91)*	-0.85 (-1.64)
FDI*GAP			0.46 (1.68)	0.44 (1.62)
Δ K/L	0.28 (0.83)	0.23 (2.95)**	0.31 (0.87)	0.20 (2.76)**
Δ y	0.16 (1.46)	0.07 (0.23)	0.14 (1.38)	0.07 (0.24)
R^2	0.41	0.48	0.44	0.55
Sample size	88	88	88	88

Note: The endogenous variables is $\ln(LP_{1997}/\ LP_{1993})$ and $\ln(LP'_{1997}/\ LP'_{1993})$. The estimates are computed with OLS and include sector-specific constants. t-statistics (absolute values adjusted for heteroscedasticity according to White's (1980) procedure) are shown in parentheses. ** - significant at the 5 per cent level. * -significant at the 10 per cent level.

(ii) Sensitivity with regard to the measure of productivity growth

Our empirical analysis could not be based on total factor productivity growth as a measure of change in the performance of local firms since data on the use of intermediates are not available over the whole period 1993-97. Instead, we have examined labour productivity growth. However, it is an open question whether both measures lead to qualitatively consistent results. We can shed some light on this issue comparing results obtained with these two measures for the period 1993-94 for which relevant data on intermediates are at hand. They allow calculating value added, *VA*, for each industry and every type of firm in 1993 and 1994. We use the change in value added per capita, $\Delta VAPC_{i94} \equiv \ln(VAPC_{i94} / VAPC_{i93}) = \Delta va_{i94} - \Delta l_{i94}$, apart from ΔLP_{i94}, as another endogenous variable when estimating Equation (6.5). More specifically, we obtain the following empirical model:

$$\Delta VAPC_i = \beta_{0j} + \beta_1 FDI'_i + \beta_2 (GAP'_i * FDI'_i) + \beta_3 \Delta y_i + \beta_4 \Delta (K/L)_i + \varepsilon_i \qquad (6.5a)$$

where FDI' stands for the share of foreign firms' value added in domestic value added in 1993 and GAP' is the 1993 ratio of the value-added-per capita for foreign firms to the value-added-per-capita for local firms within the same 3-digit industry minus one. With the model (6.5) and (6.5a), we test for the existence of productivity spillovers in accordance to the contagion and technology gap hypotheses.

The econometric results are given in Table 6.13. The impact of a higher foreign intra-industrial presence on productivity growth between 1993 and 1994 for the whole domestic industry as well as for different types of local firms is generally positive but insignificant. The analysis of value-added-per capita growth widely confirms the results obtained with labour productivity growth. Only for the group of private survivors, both measures lead to slightly different conclusions: with labour productivity growth, we believe to find statistical support for positive productivity spillovers increasing with a technology gap of local firms, whereas with growth of value-added-per capita the relevant coefficients are positive but insignificant.

In sum, labour productivity change seems a good proxy for the growth of value-added-per-capita, at least as judged on the basis of the period 1993-1994.

With the above findings, there is not a strong evidence that FDI affected the performance of locally-owned firms during the early stage of industrial recovery in Poland. Moreover, we find only a weak statistical support for the thesis that a higher foreign presence significantly enhances productivity growth of the whole domestic industry. These results differ from our findings for the longer period 1993-97. Apparently, local firms, especially private survivors and *de novo* enterprises, could adjust to higher competition in the short run and reap positive productivity spillovers whose scope was positively related to the initial technology gap. On the contrary, state firms were negatively affected by FDI. In the long-run, the results are just opposite. We can explain this pattern by different types of adjustment on the part of different firms. This will be done in Section 6.6.

Table 6.13:
Productivity Spillovers: labour productivity vs. value-added-per-capita, 1993-94

Endogenous Variable:	Δ LP	Δ VAPC	Δ LP	Δ VAPC
		All domestic firms		
FDI	0.10 (0.97)	0.15 (1.02)	0.11 (0.87)	0.06 (0.41)
FDI*GAP			-0.01 (-0.08)	0.14 (1.09)
Δ K/L	0.23 (3.54)**	0.22 (2.49)**	0.23 (3.45)**	0.22 (2.51)**
R^2	0.41	0.31	0.41	0.32
DW	2.10	1.69	2.10	1.67
Sample size	96	96	96	96
		All local firms		
FDI	0.06 (0.58)	0.13 (0.91)	-0.09 (-0.59)	-0.05 (-0.31)
FDI*GAP			0.12 (1.66)	0.16 (1.94)*
Δ K/L	0.00 (-0.06)	0.02 (0.27)	0.00 (0.10)	0.03 (0.38)
Δ y	0.71 (12.25)**	0.62 (5.60)**	0.72 (12.96)**	0.61 (5.80)**
R^2	0.87	0.84	0.87	0.84
DW	2.12	2.18	2.12	2.09
Sample size	96	96	96	96
		All survivors		
FDI	0.11 (0.73)	0.11 (0.44)	0.06 (0.36)	-0.09 (-0.41)
FDI*GAP			0.03 (0.28)	0.16 (1.67)*
Δ K/L	0.20 (2.84)**	0.12 (0.95)	0.20 (2.73)**	0.12 (0.98)
Δ y	0.47 (3.63)**	0.60 (2.68)**	0.47 (3.58)**	0.61 (2.69)**
R^2	0.49	0.33	0.49	0.35
DW	2.08	2.02	2.11	2.07
Sample size	96	96	96	96
		State survivors		
FDI	0.17 (0.63)	-0.40 (-0.49)	-0.09 (-0.34)	-0.53 (-0.66)
FDI*GAP			0.15 (0.66)	0.11 (0.83)
Δ K/L	0.42 (2.54)**	0.36 (1.88)*	0.42 (2.59)**	0.37 (1.94)*
Δ y	0.49 (1.81)*	0.78 (1.62)	0.51 (1.88)*	0.72 (1.49)
R^2	0.39	0.25	0.40	0.25
DW	2.00	1.60	2.06	1.66
Sample size	78	78	78	78
		Private survivors		
FDI	0.17 (0.88)	0.40 (1.68)*	-0.21 (-0.80)	-0.39 (-1.02)
FDI*GAP			0.28 (2.77)**	0.56 (1.59)
Δ K/L	0.02 (0.17)	-0.10 (-0.44)	0.01 (0.06)	-0.10 (-0.52)
Δ y	0.19 (1.43)	0.35 (1.13)	0.24 (1.60)	0.42 (1.43)
R^2	0.33	0.35	0.37	0.45
DW	1.94	2.14	2.00	2.08
Sample size	89	89	89	89

Note: The endogenous variables are $\Delta LP = \ln(LP_{1994}/ LP_{1993})$ and $\Delta VAPC = \ln(VAPC_{1994}/ VAPC_{1993})$. The estimates are computed with OLS and include sector-specific constants. t-statistics (absolute values adjusted for heteroscedasticity according to White's (1980) procedure) are shown in parentheses. ** - significant at the 5 per cent level. * -significant at the 10 per cent level.

(iii) Sensitivity with regard to the definition of foreign presence

To check whether our findings are sensitive with respect to the definition of the foreign presence variable, we alternatively compute *FDI* as the share of employment in foreign firms to the total domestic employment in each 3-digit industry. This second measure generally indicates a lower intra-industrial foreign presence than the first one because of a higher relative productivity of foreign firms.

Table 6.14:
Productivity Spillovers: Foreign share in domestic output vs. employment, 1993-97

Definition of FDI	Foreign share in domestic output	Foreign share in domestic employment	Foreign share in domestic output	Foreign share in domestic employment
		All domestic firms		
FDI	0.66 (4.27)**	0.71 (2.66)**	0.46 (2.29)**	0.39 (1.79)*
FDI*GAP			0.37 (1.56)	1.05 (2.87)**
Δ K/L	0.08 (1.28)	0.08 (1.13)	0.11 (1.80)*	0.13 (2.16)**
R^2	0.80	0.79	0.81	0.81
Sample size	96	96	96	96
		All local firms		
FDI	-0.68 (-2.71)**	-0.90 (-3.03)**	-0.98 (-3.32)**	-1.13 (-3.31)**
FDI*GAP			0.30 (2.30)**	0.45 (1.94)*
Δ K/L	0.50 (2.92)**	-0.04 (-0.42)	0.49 (2.99)**	0.00 (0.01)
Δ y	-0.07 (-0.63)	0.49 (3.13)**	-0.04 (-0.42)	0.45 (3.12)**
R^2	0.74	0.74	0.76	0.75
Sample size	96	96	96	96
		All survivors		
FDI	-0.41 (-1.15)	-0.52 (-1.30)	-0.95 (-2.45)**	-1.07 (-2.62)**
FDI*GAP			0.42 (3.36)**	0.67 (2.79)**
Δ K/L	0.42 (2.22)**	0.13 (1.58)	0.43 (2.42)**	0.16 (2.22)**
Δ y	0.12 (1.31)	0.42 (2.38)**	0.14 (1.54)	0.39 (2.52)**
R^2	0.60	0.60	0.65	0.66
Sample size	94	94	94	94
		State survivors		
FDI	-0.05 (-0.06)	0.09 (0.11)	-1.37 (-2.81)**	-1.24 (-2.35)**
FDI*GAP			0.89 (4.57)**	1.19 (4.19)**
Δ K/L	0.58 (2.67)**	0.15 (1.50)	0.54 (3.08)**	0.23 (3.15)**
Δ y	0.15 (1.53)	0.56 (2.87)**	0.21 (3.11)**	0.43 (2.47)**
R^2	0.39	0.38	0.61	0.59
Sample size	75	75	75	75
		Private survivors		
FDI	-0.56 (-1.55)	-0.95 (-2.19)**	-1.12 (-1.91)*	-1.53 (-2.63)**
FDI*GAP			0.46 (1.68)	0.80 (1.85)*
Δ K/L	0.28 (0.83)	0.16 (1.47)	0.31 (0.87)	0.15 (1.44)
Δ y	0.16 (1.46)	0.30 (0.91)	0.14 (1.38)	0.30 (0.90)
R^2	0.41	0.41	0.44	0.46
Sample size	88	88	88	88

Note: The endogenous variables is $\ln(LP_{1997}/ LP_{1993})$. The estimates are computed with OLS and include sector-specific constants. t-statistics (absolute values adjusted for heteroscedasticity according to White's (1980) procedure) are shown in parentheses. ** - significant at the 5 per cent level. * -significant at the 10 per cent level.

Estimation results with the basic and the alternative measure of foreign presence are summarised in Table 6.14. A higher foreign presence has a positive impact on productivity growth of the domestic industry, but its impact on local firms is generally either insignificant or negative. With both *FDI* measures, technology gap matters a lot for the scope and sign of spillovers, but using the foreign share in employment the threshold values for positive spillovers are lower, so that positive spillovers can be detected for a higher number of industries. For example, positive spillovers for state survivors are now present in 32 (instead of 18) out of 75 industries, positive spillovers for private survivors in 11 (instead of 6) out of 88 industries. Hence, we find our basic results robust with regard to the measure of foreign presence employed in the analysis of spillovers.

6.6 Conclusions

Our results do not support the standard hypotheses on the existence and scope of positive productivity spillovers form FDI on local firms. Rather, they suggest that in Poland from 1993 through 1997 foreign firms did not exercise a positive impact on the restructuring of locally owned firms. On the contrary, the evidence for negative spillovers, especially in less concentrated and protected industries, have been detected. Hence, our results are consistent with the two other existing studies of productivity spillovers in transition countries (Djankov/Hoekman, 1998; Kinoshita, 1999): in transition countries, opening to FDI has a detrimental impact on productivity growth of local firms. This shows the weakness of indigenous firms in Poland. They could not sufficiently adjust to the competitive pressure of foreign firms operating domestically and abroad.

We find support for the hypothesis that a higher initial backwardness benefits local firms, but only in the sense that it reduces the scope of the generally detrimental impact of FDI. The only group of local firms for which we detect positive productivity spillovers from FDI are state firms, especially those which were initially most backward and those in low competitive industries.

We explain it by the fact that the channels through which foreign firms affect their local rival are different in the Polish industry than those depicted by the literature which mostly refers to market economies. Apparently, negative competition effects dominate, whereas technology transfer through linkages to local firms, labour turnover and facilitating imitation are either absent or too weak to overcompensate them on average of all firms. The main reaction to a higher foreign competition seems to be downsizing and reduction of X-efficiency, rather than investing in upgrading technology.

In the case of private firms and those local enterprises which faced tight competition from local rivals and imports, the potential scope of productivity improvement through measures of defensive restructuring was smaller and quickly used. These measures contributed to positive spillovers from FDI detected for the period 1993-94, but they were not sufficient in a longer run – hence the evidence for negative spillovers over the years 1993-97.

The potential for defensive restructuring was the highest in the most technologically backwards firms, predominantly state firms traditionally facing low competition. Negative spillovers till 1994 are consistent with the empirical observation that state firms on average do not seem to adjust to the higher foreign competition and productivity losses in the short run as quickly as private one. In the longer run, thanks to their outstanding importance for regional employment, for loan performance of banks and the state budget, state firms were further financed by the government. The links to the budget were partly direct (restructuring programmes and funds), partly indirect (outstanding payments to the social security funds). This helped improve productivity through the financing of labour shedding, capital investment and marketing measures. However, since the state firms facing low competition improved their productivity and invested on average less than other types of firms, the positive spillovers of FDI for the period 1993-97 seem to result from short term measures only and not from investing in technology. This is confirmed by our analysis in Section 6.5.3: private firms and not the state ones reacted with higher modernisation investment on enhanced competition. This gives private firms better chances than state firms to compete successfully against foreign rivals in the future.

Our results are consistent with econometric findings by Bedi/Cieslik (1998). The authors have shown that Polish workers in industries with a higher foreign presence of fully-owned foreign firms do not enjoy higher wages and higher wage growth. Hence, foreign firms do not affect positively productivity and productivity growth in local firms, as would be the case under positive productivity spillovers. Our analysis gives a different picture of the role of foreign firms in Poland than limited case-studies by Bak/Kulawczuk (1996). These authors have given several examples for how foreign firms have contributed to improved marketing skills of local firms, and have facilitated their access to foreign technology. In addition, the study has also shown that, in the perception of domestic consumers, local firms upgraded their products and services in reaction to the competition from multinationals. The discrepancy between case-study analyses and econometric testing does not imply inconsistency: it shows the FDI impact on local firms from two different perspectives. Positive effects are present, but not widespread. Further research is needed to detect other determinants of positive spillovers.

Appendix 6.A

The empirical analyses were conduced for three-digit industries taking two effects into consideration. On the one hand, a more detailed breakdown would be a better guarantee that different firms within one industry really produce the same goods. On the other hand, in a more detailed breakdown it is more likely that the sales of different goods produced by one firm are classified together with the main output good even if they constitute different 4-digit activities.[24] In addition, the number of industries for which data are released shrinks the more detailed the level of aggregation since it becomes more likely that statistical secrecy regulations comes in work.

The figures cover the entire balance sheet and profit and loss statement including output, assets, employment, export shares and costs. Because of missing data (for the entire period or some years), some industries had to be discarded from the samples. The number of the remaining industries ranges between 96 (in the samples of domestic, foreign and local firms) to 75 (in the sample of private survivors). The list of excluded industries is given in Tab. 6.A.4.

Additional statistical sources are statistical yearbooks published by GUS. Data on price deflators for output of 2-digit industries (branches) are taken from the 'Statistical Yearbook of the Industry 1998' and applied to all 3-digit industries within a branch. For different types of investment goods, economy-wide price deflators are obtained either from the 'Statistical Yearbook 1998' (for investment in buildings) or from the 'Statistical Yearbook of the Industry 1998' (for machines and transport equipment).

Gross output is measured by the sum of total sales (domestic and exports), the change in inventories and the value of self-constructed assets, all expressed in the local currency (PLZ).

Labour input is measured by the average of the number of employees at the beginning and the end of each year. No adjustment for the average number of hours worked is possible. There is no information about the composition of the labour force according to its education status. There is also no data on the total wage bill of the firm which, in connection with minimum wage, could provide an alternative measure of labour input.

We measure capital input by the average of the net value of the capital stock at the beginning and the end of the year. For our purposes, the capital stock includes machinery, tools and transport equipment. We exclude buildings since their book value is hardly correlated with their productive services. According to

[24] The principle behind classification of firms is the main type of their activity. In 1996, over 85 per cent of all domestic firms indicated one exclusive type of activity at the 3-digit level, but only 42 per cent at the 4-digit level.

a present statistical regulation, the value of different components of the firms' capital stock in the balance sheet has been re-valued each year over the period. It is now expressed partly in replacement prices of a previous year (old capital goods) and partly in actual purchase prices (new capital goods bought less than 2 years before). Alternative measures of capital services proposed in the literature like energy use (see Burnside *et al.,* 1995) are available only for 1993 and could not be used in a dynamic analysis.

As our measure of foreign presence for each 3-digit industry, we adopt the share of sales of foreign firms in total domestic sales of this industry *i* (*FDI*). The results are robust with respect to the choice of alternative indicators of the foreign presence like foreign share in domestic employment and domestic capital stock. It is not possible to differentiate between FDI coming from various home countries, although it might be the case that multinationals from technology leaders create higher spillovers. The FDI-variable is lagged by one year (i.e. we take the average share of foreign firms in domestic output over the 1993-1996 period) in order to allow for adjustment lags on the side of local firms and to reduce endogeneity (higher productivity growth of local firms attracts foreign firms looking for local suppliers).

For testing the technology gap hypothesis, the variable *GAP* is constructed as the ratio of labour productivity of foreign firms to the labour productivity of local firms within the same 3-digit industry minus one. It is computed for each sub-sample of local firms (all local, all survivors, state survivors, private survivors) for each year of the 1993-97 period. Obviously, observed differences in labour productivity may result from different sources which are not necessary connected to technology. For example, foreign and local firms may work with different capital/labour ratios (quite likely since local and foreign firms face different relative factor prices) or produce on a different scale (important if returns to scale are not constant). Unfortunately, we cannot correct for it. Alternative proposals of measures for relative technology which could be found in the literature like patent fees or investment ratios (for the discussion, see Kokko, 1994) seem less appropriate since they give differences in technology only under additional restrictive assumptions.

For each type of local firms, we divide all industries into two groups, using the median value of the *GAP*-variable as a selection criterion. Industries are characterised by a low technological gap when industry-specific *GAP* is lower than the median, and high technological gap in the opposite case.

Our measure of competition level as viewed by domestic firms incorporates competition from their domestic rivals and competition from abroad. The domestic competition index for each industry (labelled *CONC* for 'concentration') is constructed for each year as the sum of squared shares of gross output for the 4 largest firms in domestic industry total output. Following

Sjöholm (1997), we define a concise index of competition (*COMP*) by multiplying the concentration index by the rate of effective protection.[25] Data on effective protection for 2-digit industries for the period 1994-1997 are taken from (Marczewski, 1998). We take effective protection for 1994 when calculating the value of the competition index for 1993. High values of *COMP* indicate a low competition level within the industry. The median value of the variable *COMP* is applied as a threshold to sort out industries with a low level of competition in 1993 from industries with a high one.

[25] If the effective rate of protection is negative, we divide it through the CONC-index. Data on imports might be viewed as a better measure of competition from abroad, but they do not allow to distinguish between imports of intermediates and technology embodied in machinery from imports of substitutes for domestic goods.

Table 6.A.1:
Main characteristics of various types of firms in Polish manufacturing, 1993-1997

	Domestic firms		Local firms		Foreign firms		Local survivors		State survivors		Private survivors	
	1993	1997	1993	1997	1993	1997	1993	1997	1993	1997	1993	1997
No of firms	15327	20007	12460	15921	2867	4081	6676	6725	1064	1058	5284	5380
No of employees (thousands)	2260	2284	2034	1825	225	459	1233	1033	489	380	477	461
Share in total domestic employment	1.00	1.00	0.90	0.80	0.10	0.20	0.55	0.45	0.22	0.17	0.21	0.20
Average firm's size (employees)	147	114	163	115	79	112	185	154	460	360	90	86
Industry[a]:	Output structure											
15	26	24	27	25	23	21	27	24	21	17	46	41
16	3	3	3	0	1	8	3	0	5	0	0	0
17	3	3	4	3	2	1	4	3	2	2	3	3
18	2	2	1	2	3	2	2	2	0	1	4	4
19	1	1	1	1	1	0	1	1	1	1	2	2
20	2	3	2	3	2	2	2	2	1	1	2	3
21	2	2	1	1	6	5	2	1	2	1	1	1
22	2	2	2	2	5	3	2	2	1	1	4	3
23	7	7	8	10	0	0	10	15	20	31	0	0
24	9	8	9	9	5	6	9	9	8	10	6	5
25	3	4	3	3	3	5	3	2	1	1	4	4
26	5	5	5	4	5	5	5	5	3	3	6	6
27	9	7	9	10	4	2	8	10	13	17	1	2
28	3	4	3	4	2	3	3	4	2	1	6	6
29	7	7	7	9	4	3	8	9	8	8	4	6
30	0	0	0	0	0	0	0	0	0	0	0	1
31	3	3	3	3	3	4	2	3	1	1	2	3
32	1	2	1	1	3	4	1	1	0	0	2	1
33	1	1	1	1	1	1	1	1	1	1	1	1
34	5	7	3	2	19	18	2	2	2	1	1	1
35	4	3	5	3	1	2	5	4	6	3	1	1
36	2	3	2	3	5	4	2	2	1	1	4	5
37	0	0	0	0	1	0	0	0	0	0	1	1
Sector I	10	10	11	10	9	11	10	11	9	11	8	7
Sector II	17	16	16	14	11	19	15	13	14	9	11	13
Sector III	13	12	13	13	13	10	13	13	11	8	13	15
Sector IV	41	43	41	44	43	40	39	43	45	56	34	34
Sector V	20	18	20	17	23	20	24	19	21	16	34	30

Note: [a]- 2-digit activity according to EKD respectively sectors according to Neven (1994)

Table 6.A.2:
Descriptive Characteristics: Means and Standard Deviations (in brackets)

	All industries	High Gap	Low Gap	High competition	Low competition
Domestic					
Δ LP	0.49 (0.29)	0.54 (0.31)	0.50 (0.29)	0.54 (0.31)	0.44 (0.25)
ΔK/L	0.51 (0.41)	0.45 (0.35)	0.50 (0.40)	0.47 (0.34)	0.56 (0.48)
FDI	0.21 (0.15)			0.22 (0.14)	0.20 (0.16)
GAP	0.62 (0.83)			0.83 (0.86)	0.40 (0.76)
Sample size	96	48	33	48	48
Local					
Δ LP	0.40 (0.33)	0.49 (0.36)	0.32 (0.28)	0.48 (0.35)	0.32 (0.27)
ΔK/L	0.38 (0.43)	0.30 (0.36)	0.36 (0.40)	0.32 (0.31)	0.43 (0.53)
GAP	0.76 (0.94)			1.00 (0.90)	0.52 (0.91)
Sample size	96	48	33	48	48
Local survivors					
Δ LP	0.34 (0.39)	0.45 (0.40)	0.29 (0.29)	0.41 (0.38)	0.27 (0.40)
ΔK/L	0.18 (0.57)	0.11 (0.35)	0,21 (0.62)	0.13 (0.32)	0.23 (0.75)
GAP	0.79 (0.99)			0.96 (0.93)	0.60 (1.03)
Sample size	94	48	31	48	46
State survivors					
Δ LP	0.25 (0.47)	0.42 (0.42)	0.12 (0.47)	0.32 (0.36)	0.16 (0.58)
ΔK/L	0.16 (0.62)	0.07 (0.52)	0.19 (0.52)	0.19 (0.52)	0.11 (0.74)
GAP	1.01 (1.08)			1.21 (1.00)	0.77 (1.14)
Sample size	75	37	30	42	33
Private survivors					
Δ LP	0.36 (0.52)	0.42 (0.63)	0.37 (0.28)	0.47 (0.45)	0.22 (0.57)
ΔK/L	0.62 (0.70)	0.73 (0.73)	0.50 (0.65)	0.53 (0.40)	0.73 (0.94)
GAP	0.90 (1.10)			0.97 (1.15)	0.82 (1.05)
Sample size	88	44	34	48	40

Table 6.A.3: Correlation between FDI and selected variables

	All industries	High competition	Low Competition
		Domestic	
Δ LP	0.35	0.15	0.58
ΔK/L	0.10	0.32	-0.02
GAP	-0.06	-0.27	0.10
COMP	-0.11		
Sample size	96	48	48
		Local	
Δ LP	-0.03	-0.02	-0.08
ΔK/L	-0.13	0.15	-0.27
GAP	0.08	-0.17	0.28
Δ y	0.37	0.41	0.35
Sample size	96	48	48
		Local survivors	
Δ LP	0.03	-0.13	0.14
ΔK/L	-0.11	0.15	-0.21
GAP	0.13	-0.20	0.39
Δ y	0.37	0.41	0.35
Sample size	94	48	46
		State Survivors	
Δ LP	0.12	-0.21	0.33
ΔK/L	-0.09	0.21	-0.31
GAP	0.15	-0.23	0.48
Δ y	0.47	0.39	0.56
Sample size	75	42	33
		Private survivors	
Δ LP	-0.08	0.04	-0.17
ΔK/L	-0.19	0.02	-0.30
GAP	0.04	-0.06	0.16
Δ y	0.37	0.47	0.36
Sample size	88	48	40

Table 6.A.4:
Classification Of All Economic Activities, 3-digit industries

D	**MANUFACTURING**
15	**MANUFACTURE OF FOOD PRODUCTS AND BEVERAGES**
151	Slaughtering, preparing and preserving meat
152	Canning, preserving and processing of fishery products
153	Processing of fruits and vegetables
154	Manufacture of vegetable and animal oil and fats[4, 5]
155	Manufacture of dairy products[4]
156	Manufacture of starches, starch products and grain mill products
157	Manufacture of prepared animal feeds
158	Manufacture of food products, not elsewhere classified (n.e.c)
159	Beverages
16	**MANUFACTURE OF TOBACCO PRODUCTS**
160	Manufacture of tobacco products [3,4,5]
17	**MANUFACTURE OF TEXTILES**
171	Preparing and spinning of yarn
172	Weaving of textiles
173	Finishing of textiles[4]
174	Manufacture of made-up textile goods except wearing apparel
175	Manufacture of textile goods, n.e.c
176	Manufacture of knitting textiles[4]
177	Manufacture of knitting textile products
18	**MANUFACTURE OF WEARING APPAREL**
181	Manufacture of wearing apparel of leather[4]
182	Manufacture of ready-made clothing and accessories
183	Dressing and dyeing of fur; manufacture of products of fur[4]
19	**MANUFACTURE OF LEATHER AND PRODUCTS OF LEATHER**
191	Tanning and dressing of leather
192	Manufacture of luggage, handbags, saddlery and harness[4]
193	Manufacture of footwear
20	**MANUFACTURE OF WOOD AND OF PRODUCTS OF WOOD AND CORK, EXCEPT FURNITURE; MANUFACTURE OF ARTICLES OF STRAW AND PLAITING MATERIALS**
201	Sawmills, planing and other wood mills
202	Manufacture of veneer and plywood sheets, wood panels
203	Manufacture of wood for constructing
204	Manufacture of packings and pallets of wood[4]
205	Manufacture of other products of wood; manufacture of articles of cork, straw and plaiting materials[4]
21	**MANUFACTURE OF PULP, PAPER AND PAPER PRODUCTS**
211	Manufacture of pulp, paper and paperboard
212	Manufacture of articles of paper and paperboard
22	**PUBLISHING, PRINTING AND REPRODUCTION OF RECORDED MEDIA**
221	Publishing
222	Printing and service activities related to printing
223	Reproduction of recorded media[4]
23	**MANUFACTURE OF COKE, REFINED PETROLEUM PRODUCTS AND NUCLEAR FUEL**
231	Manufacture of coke [1,2,3,4,5]
232	Manufacture of refined petroleum products[5]
233	Manufacture of nuclear fuel
24	**MANUFACTURE OF CHEMICALS AND CHEMICAL PRODUCTS**
241	Manufacture of basic chemicals
242	Manufacture of fertilisers and pesticides [1,2,3,4,5]
243	Manufacture of paints, varnishes and lacquers
244	Manufacture of drugs and medicines
245	Manufacture of soap and cleaning preparations, perfumes, cosmetics and other toilet preparations
246	Manufacture of chemical products, n.e.c
247	Manufacture of synthetic fibres[4, 5]
25	**MANUFACTURE OF RUBBER AND PLASTICS PRODUCTS**
251	Manufacture of rubber products
252	Manufacture of plastics products, n.e.c
26	**MANUFACTURE OF OTHER NON-METALLIC MINERAL PRODUCTS**
261	Manufacture of glass and glass products
262	Manufacture of non-structural ceramic products
263	Manufacture of ceramic plates[4]
264	Manufacture of structural clay products
265	Manufacture of cement, lime and plaster
266	Manufacture of products of cement, lime and plaster
267	Manufacture of building stones[4]

268	Manufacture of non-metallic mineral products
27	**MANUFACTURE OF BASIC METALS**
271	Manufacture of iron and steel[5]
272	Manufacture of tubes[3, 4, 5]
273	Drawing, cold rolling and folding of steel
274	Non-ferrous metal basic industries
275	Founding of metals
28	**MANUFACTURE OF FABRICATED METAL PRODUCTS, EXCEPT MACHINERY AND EQUIPMENT**
281	Manufacture of structural metal products
282	Manufacture of metal tanks and containers, manufacture of radiators and central heating bodies
283	Manufacture of steam generators
284	Forging, clossed-died forging, pressing and stamping of metals
285	Treatment and coating of metals; general mechanical engineering on a fee or contract basis[4]
286	Manufacture of cutlery, hand tools and general hardware
287	Manufacture of other fabricated metal products n.e.c
29	**MANUFACTURE OF MACHINERY AND EQUIPMENT N.E.C.**
291	Manufacture of pumps, compressors, taps and valves
292	Manufacture of other general purpose machinery
293	Manufacture of agricultural and forestry machinery
294	Manufacture of machine-tools
295	Manufacture of other special purpose machinery
296	Manufacture of weapons and ammunition[1,2,3,4,5]
297	Manufacture of domestic appliances n.e.c.
30	**MANUFACTURE OF OFFICE, ACCOUNTING AND COMPUTING MACHINERY**
300	Manufacture of office, accounting and computing machinery
31	**MANUFACTURE OF ELECTRICAL MACHINERY AND APPARATUS N.E.C.**
311	Manufacture of electrical motors, generators and electrical rotary converters
312	Manufacture of switch-boards for electrical energy
313	Manufacture of isolated wires[4]
314	Manufacture of accumulators, batteries and cells
315	Manufacture of electrical lamps and lighting
316	Manufacture of other electrical equipment n.e.c.
32	**MANUFACTURE OF RADIO, TELEVISION AND COMMUNICATION EQUIPMENT AND APPARATUS**
321	Manufacture of diodes, transistors and other electronic components.
322	Manufacture of radio, television and communication equipment and apparatus
323	Manufacture of radio and television receivers and related equipment
33	**MANUFACTURE OF MEDICAL, PRECISION AND OPTICAL INSTRUMENTS, WATCHES AND CLOCKS**
331	Manufacture of medical and instruments and equipment
332	Manufacture of professional and scientific, and measuring and controlling equipment, n.e.c
333	Manufacture of controlling equipment for industrial processes
334	Manufacture of photographic and optical goods[4]
335	Manufacture of watches and clocks[1,2,3,4,5]
34	**MANUFACTURE OF MOTOR VEHICLES, TRAILERS AND SEMI-TRAILERS**
341	Manufacture of motor vehicles
342	Manufacture of car bodies; manufacture of trailers and semi-trailers
343	Manufacture of parts and accessories for motor vehicles
35	**MANUFACTURE OF OTHER TRANSPORT EQUIPMENT**
351	Building and repairing of ships
352	Manufacture of locomotives, trams and rail transport equipment
353	Manufacture of aeroplanes[5]
354	Manufactures of motorcycles and bicycles
355	Manufacture of transport equipment, n.e.c[4]
36	**MANUFACTURE OF FURNITURE; MANUFACTURING, N.E.C.**
361	Manufacture of furniture
362	Manufacture of jewellery and related articles[4]
363	Manufacture of musical instruments
364	Manufacture of sporting and athletic goods[5]
365	Manufacture of toys[4]
366	Other manufacturing, n.e.c.
37	**RECYCLING[1,2,3,4,5]**
371	Recycling of metal products
372	Recycling of no-metal products

Source: GUS (1994); Note: The industries excluded from the analysis of: [1]-domestic firms, [2]- local firms, [3]- local survivors, [4]- state firms, [5]- private firms

Table 6.A.5:
Classification of Industries according to their Factor Intensity

Sector I	Sector II	Sector III	Sector IV	Sector V
	Less Intensive in Physical Capital		Intensive in Physical Capital	
High Tech	Human capital intensive	Labour intensive	Labour intensive	Human capital intensive
241	152	171	151	153
242	154	177	158	155
243	160	181	172	156
244	266	182	173	157
245	267	183	174	159
246	268	192	175	211
247	291	193	176	212
300	292	262	191	221
321	294	272	201	222
322	295	275	202	223
323	297	281	203	265
353	311	282	204	362
	312	293	205	
	313	335	231	
	314	342	232	
	315	351	251	
	316	352	252	
	331	361	261	
	332	363	263	
	333		264	
	334		271	
	355		273	
			274	
			283	
			284	
			285	
			286	
			287	
			341	
			343	
			354	
			364	
			365	
			366	

Note: based on Neven (1994).

Chapter 7:
Conclusions

7.1 Introduction

In this thesis, we have investigated the role of FDI for diffusion and assimilation of technologies and ideas across borders. The potential of FDI in spreading knowledge and consequently encouraging growth finds support in the now-emerging theoretical literature on spillovers and in numerous case studies. Given the relative technological backwardness of the domestic industry in the transition countries and the fact that most FDI originates from industrial countries, it was expected that foreign direct investment will alter the production possibilities of the host country by bringing new technologies and ideas as well as additional capital. In addition, the transition countries expected that the positive impact of FDI will be not only confined to the foreign affiliates, but will spill over to local firms. The spillovers should facilitate industrial restructuring and translate themselves into a higher productivity growth.

This study provides evidence that, in Poland over the period 1993-97, such expectations were not fully realised. We, indeed, found that foreign firms positively contribute to technological progress of the domestic industry as a whole. However, the magnitude of the productivity growth of the local firms is not positively related to a higher domestic activity of the foreign-owned firms. Moreover, we have detected some evidence for negative productivity spillovers, especially on private firms in highly competitive industries.

The plan of this chapter is as follows: in Section 7.2, we give our assessment of the empirical findings obtained in Chapter 6. Section 7.3 derives conclusions from our study with regard to economic and social policies supporting industrial restructuring during transition.

7.2 Assessment of the empirical findings

Our empirical investigation has shed more light on the process of the industrial restructuring in Poland in the presence of FDI. We organise our conclusions around the following issues: (i) FDI impact on industrial restructuring; (ii) the role of productivity spillovers from FDI; (iii) the revealed competitiveness of the Polish industry, (iv) the danger of over-reliance on foreign capital in the transition process.

7.2.1 FDI and the pattern of industrial restructuring in Poland

Our analysis confirms the results of the previous studies showing that the 1990 reforms initiated a significant process of structural change at the firm level (see Berg, 1994; EBRD, 1995). The intensity of this process differs considerably among various industrial and ownership sectors. Labour market analyses show that there was a sharp increase in gross job destruction and in reallocation rates in the state sector at the start of the transition (Konings *et al.*, 1996). In turn, it was the private sector which accounted for a disproportionately large fraction of all jobs created afterwards. Zukowski (1998) suggests that efficiency gains turned out to be a main driving force of the boost in output during the industrial recovery from 1992 on. The pattern of the productivity response of state enterprises has been statistically different from that of private firms: the private sector has largely outperformed the public one in terms of both productivity and sales growth. However, there exists considerable firm heterogeneity within each of these ownership sectors, reflected in simultaneous creation and destruction of jobs in both the state and private part of the Polish manufacturing.

In the light of our analysis, the expectation that foreign-owned private firms will play an important role in the process of recovery, modernisation and growth seems to be fulfilled. We could statistically confirm previous anecdotal evidence (see Bak/Kulawczuk, 1996) suggesting that domestic industries with a higher foreign presence have experienced higher productivity growth, higher investment rates in new technologies and physical capital. This is good news, confirming experience of some emerging markets, the EU periphery (Ireland, Spain, Portugal) and some other transition countries (see UNCTAD, 1997). Indeed, liberalising FDI inflows is an effective policy able to accelerate growth even in a relatively short run. In this sense, the engagement of foreign investors in Poland should be judged as a success story.

However, the positive impact of FDI on industrial restructuring in Poland comes alone from the direct positive effect of a higher presence of foreign firms, i.e. newly established foreign firms and domestic firms with foreign capital perform better than those in local hands. Over the investigated period, we find no evidence that the improved performance of local firms is due to the positive externalities from FDI. On the contrary, the higher presence of foreign firms generally led to an under-average performance of the locally-owned sector of the industry. Nevertheless, relatively stronger productivity growth among foreign firms was significant enough in aggregate to generate strong performance for industries with a higher foreign presence, offsetting weaker performance by the locally-owned firms which constitute the bulk of domestic firms. Hence the expectation of local firms overcoming their efficiency deficits due to the blessing of spillovers proved somehow naive and unrealistic.

The missing evidence of productivity spillovers allows the conclusion that liberalising FDI in Poland was not a beneficial strategy for the entire set of domestic firms. Obviously, FDI inflows could not help reach both targets: to help restructure firms privatised with the foreign investors' participation and to facilitate technological upgrading of their locally-owned competitors. In this light, opening to FDI is not a miraculous panacea for a painless modernisation and growth for all market incumbents. It is rather a process of 'creative destruction' in the Schumpeterian sense, with most winners having access to modern technology and capital and most losers among initially inefficient firms unable to improve their performance.

7.2.2 The role of spillovers for restructuring

Our empirical findings support the fears of those who claimed that the indigenous sector in Poland is too weak to reap technological spillovers from FDI. The absence of positive spillovers suggests that (i) the channels deemed in the literature to serve technology diffusion – first of all, vertical linkages to local firms and the mobility of workers, managers and researchers - have not been widely open in the period under investigation; and/or (ii) local firms could not afford financing of the necessary investment in restructuring measures.

Indeed, there is some case-study evidence from Hungary, Poland and the Czech Republic confirming little vertical linkages of foreign affiliates in these countries (Hunya, 1997, 2000). Multinationals justify it by the present poor quality standards of local suppliers. Instead of local sourcing, most foreign firms rely on imports of investment goods, inputs and technology within their international network, which is mirrored in relatively high trade deficits of the leading transition countries. In some cases, traditional foreign suppliers have followed a multinational and set up own affiliates in the host location. If the manufactured output is then exported and all profits repatriated, FDI creates a sort of a foreign enclave in the local economy. In this situation, the possibility of positive externalities is reduced to a minimum.

The labour turnover from multinational to indigenous firms could not have served as a wide channel of knowledge diffusion, since such mobility is presently unattractive for employees in foreign firms. It is not only because foreign affiliates pay considerably higher wages. In addition, they typically offer a non-taxable social package including professional training, health insurance, employers' contributions to a private pension system, free leisure time and sport activities and so on. As long as local private firms cannot follow this standard, the chances to attract well-qualified employees are slim.[26]

The second important reason for the lack of positive spillovers can be found in the limited access of indigenous firms to capital. It is well known that although efficiency can be also improved through downsizing and marketing measures,

[26] However, the new evidence from countries with a longer record of foreign participation, for example China, indicate that the policy of multinationals to reserve top positions in their affiliates for managers coming from the host country, may be a decisive factor for some top local professionals to leave.

growth in productivity will require investment in fixed capital and infrastructure, product and process innovations after static efficiency gains are exhausted. The fact that industrial employment ceased to decline and investment in fixed assets has increased significantly since 1994 may suggest that the possibilities of a productivity increase through simple rationalisation of employment have significantly diminished.

Third, restructuring in industrial enterprises is generally hindered by the slow pace of restructuring and development of the financial sector. The access to credit as a condition for successful industrial restructuring is important since most Polish firms and industries operate under hard budget constraints from the early phase in the transition process. There is some preliminary statistical evidence (Weller, 1999) supporting a positive connection between access to credit and investment.

The insufficient development of the domestic financial sector affects local firms much more negatively than the foreign ones. The latter have access to financial resources from abroad and receive credits under the risk conditions of well-established foreign enterprises. Local firms, in contrast, must rely on local capital markets, which is very tight due to insufficient domestic savings, restrictive monetary policy and the crowding-out from public debt policy. In addition, a market for venture capital to finance the development of private firms is practically absent.

Under these circumstances, the lack of positive spillovers during the early phase of FDI liberalisation and building of a market economy does not come as a surprise. It should rather be stressed that we find empirical evidence of a positive role of foreign firms on the technological investment in pure locally-owned firms, especially in private ones. With this process continuing and leading to the improved positioning of the local firms in the medium run, we should be able to find empirical support for the positive role of FDI on restructuring over a longer period of investigation than the presently taken 5 years. We recommend a further search for productivity spillovers, preferably with firm-level data, to be done as transformation proceeds.

7.2.3 Polarisation tendencies within the Polish industry

The expansion of the foreign-owned sector in Poland is accompanied by a decrease in the absolute size and the relative importance of the locally-owned firms. Between 1993 and 1997, local firms reduced their employment level by 200,000. Some industries are almost entirely in foreign hands. A wide-scale reallocation of labour from shrinking firms and sectors to growing ones proceeds, e.g. the state-owned sector has lost over a 100,000 employees. Anyhow, the evidence given in this paper in Chapter 5 shows that the Polish economy is not dominated by foreign firms. Rather, certain industries are increasingly targeted by foreign firms, due to their participation in privatisation process and greenfield investment. These industries' performance is superior to those dominated by local firms, which is a plus for the Polish industry as a whole.

An uneven performance throughout industrial firms has resulted in a dual economy in which a leading segment starts restructuring and catching up the efficiency standards typical of a comparable market economy while a declining segment lags behind in restructuring and efficiency improvements. It is typically foreign affiliates and domestic firms privatised to foreign investors which dominate the first group, whereas local firms, especially the state ones, belong in majority to the second category. In the short run, the process under way unavoidably leads to the creation of a two-tier economy: a relatively modern foreign-dominated sector and a low-tech local sector. The polarisation of the domestic economy in the presence of FDI is a process which has also been observed in other host countries, as different as Mexico, Ireland and Malaysia. The findings of Glatz/Moser (1989) point to an increasing technological gap for Austrian-owned companies vis-à-vis foreign subsidiaries since the 1960s. The same phenomenon occurs in Eastern Germany, where foreign affiliates have a higher productivity and productivity growth, higher R&D intensity and capital investment than local firms (Gerling/Schmidt, 1997).

Although we find evidence that the FDI-led upgrading of the domestic industry benefits the host country as a whole, it might have some unpleasant social and political consequences. Since growth is concentrated in foreign-dominated enclaves, usually around big industrial cities, the detrimental competition effect on relatively less efficient local firms leads to open unemployment in other regions. This has become the most important challenges for the economic and social policies in the near future.

7.2.4 Competitiveness of the Polish industry

The absence of positive productivity spillovers among local firms should be viewed as a sign of a poor competitiveness of the locally-owned Polish manufacturing. Not only are they less efficient than the firms from industrialised countries, but they are also not capable to adjust rapidly to the increased pressure through restructuring and modernisation. Given the competition test provided by the presence of foreign firms, the threat of detrimental effects of EU competition in the post-accession period is quite likely. Viewed from this perspective, the present engagement of foreign firms represents an asset for the Polish economy. First, more FDI makes a bigger part of the domestic industry competitive at the international level. Second, some successful engagement of foreign firms into the domestic economy might demonstrate to firms from the EU that co-operation, supplier contracts and participation in locally-owned firms is possible and a valuable strategy. This could change their entry strategy to the Polish market: instead of looking for market shares through exports and crowding out of local firms, integration of the local incumbents into international networks could become dominant. This would give local firms much better chances to survive the competition struggle.

7.3 Economic policy recommendations

Our analysis strongly supports the direct positive effect of the FDI on the modernisation of the Polish manufacturing. The absence of the expected indirect impact on the locally-owned firms has much to do with the economic and political environment in the early transition phase. The inherited widespread inefficiencies and an underdevelopment of market structures and institutions has definitely limited the absorptive capacity of the Polish economy and Polish enterprises. In our view, there is a room for various economic policies to support this absorptive capacity of the locally-owned firms. These policies should aim at: (i) strengthening the linkages of foreign firms with the local economy; and (ii) strengthening the adjustment capacity of local firms. While the scope of this thesis forces us to stay general, we want to touch a few important points. Some lessons drawn here follow straight from the Polish experience, whereas the others are derived from international experience and from economic plausibility.[27] We distinguish two types of such measures. First, as discussed in Chapter 2.5, the quality of the domestic political and economic environment are decisive for the magnitude of FDI inflows, their art, strategy and linkages with the local economy. Second, some FDI-related measures may additionally be used to enhance the spread of externalities from FDI.

(i) strengthening the linkages

It seems that until recently, domestic FDI-related policies neglected linkages while concentrating on incentives for attracting new investors. This holds not only for Poland but also for other leading transition countries. In order to use the restructuring and modernising potential of FDI most efficiently, governments of countries relatively successful in attracting foreign companies should now focus on measures to encourage them to make further investments in the country involving cooperation with local companies.

The absence of well-developed economic linkages between foreign and local firms has been identified as the main obstacle for the emergence of positive spillovers and for the crowding-out of local firms in the Polish case. Locally-

[27] UNCTAD (1995) distinguishes three main categories of investment-promotion activities: (i) improving a country's image as a favourable investment location; (ii) attracting investment directly; (iii) providing services to investors.

owned firms were harmed by the activity of foreign affiliates because they largely treated them as rivals instead of trying to cooperate. But they were at a competitive disadvantage, given their inherited burdens.

What can be done to enhance the attractiveness of local firms as partners for foreign affiliates? Hereby, one should take into account that FDI normally leads to the incorporation of foreign affiliates into the international network of parent companies. In general, it results in the establishment of intra-firm trade links with the parent company and other foreign affiliates world-wide. On the other hand, the ability of local firms to supply to foreign affiliates is initially low because of the poor quality and sophistication of the inputs produced and transportation bottlenecks.

Host governments can mainly contribute to the creation of linkages when they concentrate on a provision of a healthy macroeconomic framework and a stable political and legal environment. It reduces uncertainty and benefits long-term investment and business relationships, including those between firms with foreign capital and their prospective local suppliers. Low-value added FDI, with low potential for positive externalities is dominant when the planning horizon of foreign investors is shortened because of arbitrary distortions, wide-spread corruption and red-tape. Further, there is a widespread consensus that a simplification of government regulations and a stable fiscal regime create lower compliance costs for MNCs and reduce bad practices, thus benefiting the whole economy. A weak intellectual property rights regime and relatively low domestic demand discourage FDI inflows in manufacturing and technology-intensive sectors.[28] Investors with high R&D and advertising intensity are then more willing to engage in distribution or open a representative office than to undertake local production. This all reduces the probability and the extent of linkages.

The host country policy can also improve the quality of the local framework by undertaking activities in the following fields:

- provision of local public infrastructure to attract FDI and improve the creation of local firms in the geographic neighbourhood of the foreign location;
- strengthening of the local financial sector through: consolidation, a prudent supervision over the developing stock markets and banks, a solid fiscal policy.
- taking actions to improve the country's image among foreign investors; stressing advantages of a long-term involvement as opposed to quick windfall profits;

[28] Smarzynska (1999) finds that firms with low R&D outlays relative to sales are more likely to invest in transition countries.

- support for the organisation of information bourses, fairs and exchange fora for firms in different regions;
- consequently follow the EU-accession policy; based on the experience of Portugal and Spain, a general upswing in FDI can be expected when the transition countries become members. The reason would be a fall in the perceived investment risk, the enlargement of the market that could be freely reached and the level of internal liberalisation.

We believe that some tailor-made FDI-related measures, provisions (e.g. local content clauses) can be used for 'fine-tuning' of the sectoral and regional engagement of the foreign firms and their behaviour in the local economy, but the main burden of increasing the long-term commitment and creation of linkages should be carried by the general macroeconomic policy.

One of the most emotionally discussed FDI-related issues in the host countries is the threat for the domestic economy from over-reliance on foreign firms. A number of circumstances in which FDI inflows can have adverse welfare or employment consequences have been identified in the literature (see Gács *et al.*, 1999). The international trade literature suggests that national welfare can be reduced by FDI inflows if MNCs capture market shares from indigenous firms and reduce the latter's supernormal profits. In previously planned economies, however, the relevance of these arguments is very limited: the potential profits in domestic sectors that were insulated from foreign competition were frequently absent because of X-inefficiencies.

Although in the age of globalisation and EU-accession, cross-border mergers and cross-firm ownership, the 'nationality' of firms is loosing its importance, some FDI antagonists (or simply nationalists) draw a catastrophic scenario under which foreign firms might all of the sudden withdraw their capital, e.g. when cheaper locations would be found, and leave the previous host country without a functioning industrial base. Although nothing exactly comparable to the 'catastrophe' scenario related to FDI has occurred in the past, the risk of firms' closure may be minimised if strong linkages with the indigenous economy have been developed and if agglomeration economies are truly important. In this way, absolute advantage which were economised by FDI in the early phase of engagement may over time transform into comparative advantage. Since the danger of relocation is greatest with cost-sensitive low value-added FDI, governments should increase the commitment of foreign investors by including them in the policy-formulation process.[29] If the foreign sector, through the provision of opportunities for learning-by-doing and through generated tax revenues, has helped the economy to 'climb the ladder of comparative

[29] Furthermore, the evidence to date suggests that foreign firms have been less likely to decline, and to close down, during periods of economic difficulty than it is the case with indigenous firms (Barry/Bradley, 1997).

advantage' by developing its physical and human capital infrastructure, then its very presence will have reduced the adjustment costs. The economy would remain a relatively attractive base for whatever forms of FDI available, and indigenous industry would be stronger than it would otherwise have been.

One of the lessons from the Irish and Spanish experience with FDI is that, over time, production of foreign affiliates may shift towards greater complexity (new products, emerging technologies) creating a more symbiotic relationship with the rapidly modernising indigenous sector. Indeed, Vernon's product cycle model fits the stylised Irish facts rather well: early FDI in simple standardised products ('screw-driver' operations), recent shifts to maturing products (e.g. the Intel pentium chips) and a potential for attracting more R&D activity in the area of new products.

(ii) strengthening of the adjustment capacity of local firms

The transition countries badly need to develop an infrastructure to increase the potential of local firms to absorb MNCs' externalities. We think that the following measures may contribute to the achievement of this target:

- a consequent enforcement of the hard budget constraint for all types of firms, independent from their ownership;
- targeted support to modernisation and investment in technological upgrading in the incumbent local firms; governmental guaranties for such credits should be considered;
- support for financial and government institutions providing venture capital and the creation of private firms as suppliers to foreign affiliates;
- public investment in upgrading of the level of national education; incentives for a long-life learning of the labour force;
- support for R&D institutions; emphasising successful cooperation between universities and the business community;
- a balanced approach between foreign and locally-owned firms: support for joint-ventures;
- support for the institutions building consensus and partnership between local employees and foreign employers;

In the early transition phase, it was and still is a major polit-economical problem to find enough acceptation for the fact that the process of upgrading, modernisation and growth is inseparably connected to the fall of some uncompetitive firms. In order to support FDI-led modernisation, the governments should address the necessary adjustment costs resulted. Although traditional, passive labour market policies must be supported, the focus should be on:

- providing the possibilities of further learning and qualification for unemployed persons; financial support and low-interest rates credits for a life-long education;
- facilitating regional mobility of workers through privatisation of land and real estate, legal support for the development of real estate markets;
- development of an efficient transportation infrastructure in agglomerations and between regions; privatisation of the telecommunication systems; removal of some bureaucratic and legal impediments against foreign participation in this process.

Generally, the role of the host country should be to develop mechanisms to smooth the adjustment when it is necessary rather than to postpone it or to offer protection against the adjustment pressure. Under the competitive pressure from high-quality imports and FDI, such adjustment is unavoidable on a part of local firms. It would be the most detrimental strategy for the country's long-term prospects if the government would base its FDI-policy on narrow nationalistic views or partial interests of the industrial lobby.

7.4 Outlook

FDI is deemed as one of the main factors underlying the strong growth rates experienced by the Spanish and Irish economy for the last 15 years. In fact, the rising inflows of foreign capital made possible by the liberalising measures introduced allowed the deep transformation of an economy until then characterised by its relative backwardness and an almost total lack of openness, being one of the most important channels leading to the integration of the economy in world markets. In addition, the accession to the EC has involved a boost in FDI, that would reflect the favourable prospects for the country's economic future faced with the challenges of the Single European Market.

On the whole, CEECs will increasingly rely on FDI. Capital imports are not an alternative, since FDI does not consist primarily of capital flows, but rather of the flow of managerial, technological and organisational know-how. Relying on technology imports embodied in finished goods or via licensing is not a viable strategy, as it applies only to mature technologies. Those technologies relevant for growth are principally developed by MNCs and can only be gained through the participation in MNCs networks. As future members of the European Union, transition countries have a good opportunity to participate in these gains.

References:

Aghion, P. and P. Howitt (1992): A Model of Growth through Creative Destruction, *Econometrica 60*, 2, 323-351.

Aitken, B. and A. Harrison (1993): Does proximity to foreign firms induce technology transfer? Policy Research Working Paper, The World Bank.

Aitken, B. and A. Harrison (1994): Do domestic firms benefit from foreign direct investment? Evidence from panel data, Policy Research Working Paper No. 1248, The World Bank.

Aitken, B., Harrison, A. and R.E. Lipsey (1991): *Are there spillovers from Foreign Direct Investment? Evidence from Panel Data for Venezuela*, The World Bank.

Aitken, B., Harrison, A. and R.E. Lipsey (1996): Wages and foreign ownership. A comparative study of Mexico, Venezuela, and the United States, *Journal of International Economics 40*, 345-371.

Altomonte, C. (1997): FDI flows to CEECs – legal system issues, LICOS-KUL, mimeo.

Altomonte, C. (1998): FDI in the CEECs and the theory of real options: an empirical assessment, LICOS-KUL, mimeo.

Aturupane, C., S. Djankov and B. Hoekman (1997): Determinants of Intra-Industry Trade between East and West Europe, CEPR Discussion Paper No. 1721.

Audretsch, D.B. (1994): Small Firms and R&D Spillovers: Evidence from Italy, CEPR Discussion Paper No. 927.

Audretsch, D.B. (1995): The Innovation, Unemployment and Competitiveness Challenge in Germany, CEPR Discussion Paper No. 1152.

Bak, M. and P. Kulawczuk (1998): Wplyw inwestycji zagranicznych na gospodarke Polski (FDI impact on Poland's economy), Warszawa: PAIZ.

Baldwin, R., H. Braconnier and R. Forslid (1999): Multinationals, Endogenous Growth and Technological Spillovers: Theory and Evidence, CEPR Discussion Paper No. 2155.

Barro, R.J. (1998): Notes on Growth Accounting, NBER Working Paper No. 6654.

Barro, R.J. and X. Sala-i-Martin (1995): *Economic Growth,* McGraw-Hill Inc.

Barro, R.J. and X. Sala-i-Martin (1997): Technological Diffusion, Convergence, and Growth, *Journal of Economic Growth 2*, 1-26.

Barry, F. and J. Bradley (1997): FDI and Trade: The Irish host-country experience, in: The Economic Journal, 107, p. 1798-1811.

Basu, S. and Fernald, J.G. (1995): Aggregate Productivity and The Productivity of Aggregates, NBER Working Paper 5382.

BCE (1999): *Statistical Database*, http://www.bcemag.com/.

Bedi, A.S. and A. Cieslik (1998): Foreign Direct Investment, Wages and Wage Growth: The Case of Poland, Warsaw University, mimeo.

Behrman, J. and H. Wallender (1976): *Transfer of Manufacturing Technology within Multinational Enterprises*, Ballinger (Cambridge, Mass).

Benacek, W., D. Shemetilo and A. Petrov (1998): Restructuring and Measurment of Efficiency in Firms in Transition, CERGE-EI Working Paper No. 127.

Berg, A. (1994): Does Economic Reform Cause Structural Adjustment? Lessons from Poland, *Journal of Comparative Economics*, 18, 376-409.

Bernanke, B.S. and M. L. Parkinson (1991): Procyclical Labour Productivity and Competing Theories of the Business Cycle: Some Evidence from Interwar US Manufacturing Industries, *Journal of Political Economy 99*, 439-59.

Bertschek, I. (1995): Product and Process Innovation as a Response to Increasing Imports and Foreign Direct Investment, *Journal of Industrial Economics* XLII, 341-57

Blomström, M. and A. Kokko (1997): How Foreign Investment Affects Host Countries, Policy Research Working Paper No. 1745, The World Bank.

Blomström, M. and E.N. Wolff (1994): Multinational Corporations and Productivity Convergence in Mexico, in: Baumol and Nelson and Wollf (eds): *Convergence of Productivity: Cross-National Studies and Historical Evidence*, Oxford University Press, 263-284.

Blomström, M. and F. Sjöholm (1998): Technology Transfer and Spillovers: Does Local Participation with Multinationals Matter?, CEPR Discussion Paper No. 2048.

Blomström, M. and H. Persson (1983): Foreign Investment and Spillover Efficiency in an Underdeveloped Economy: Evidence from the Mexican Manufacturing Industry, *World Development*, *Vol. 11*, 493-501.

Borensztein, E., J. De Gregorio and J-W. Lee (1998): How does foreign direct investment affect economic growth?, *Journal of International Economics* 45, 115-135.

Braga, H. and L. Willmore (1991): Technological Imports and Technological Effort: An Analysis of Their Determinants in Brasilian Firms, *Journal of Industrial Economics* XXXIX, 421-32.

Brecher, R.A. and C.F. Diaz Alejandro (1977): Tariffs, foreign capital and immiserising growth, *Journal of International Economics 7*, 317-322.Brenton, P., F. Di Mauro and M. Luecke (1998): Economic Integration and FDI: An empirical Analysis of Foreign Investment in the EU and in Central and Eastern Europe, Kiel Working Paper 890.

Brunetti, A., G. Kisunko and B. Weder (1997): Institutions in Transition. Reliability of Rules and Economic Performance in Former Socialist

Countries, Universität des Saarlandes, Europa-Institut Forschungsbericht 9708.
Buckley, P.J. and M. Casson (1976): *The Future of the Multinational Enterprise*, New York: Holmes and Meiers.
Burnside, C., M. Eichenbaum and S. Rebelo (1995): Capital Utilization and Returns to Scale, *NBER Macroeconomics Annual 1995* (MIT Press), 67-124.
Cameron, G. (1996): Innovation and economic growth, London School of Economics and Political Science, Centre for Economic Performance, Discussion Paper No. 277.
Cantwell, J. (1991): A survey of theories of international production, in: C.R. Pitelis and R. Sugden, (eds.): *The nature of the Transnational Firm*, London: Routledge.
Caves, R.E. (1974): Multinational Firms, Competition, and Productivity in Host-Country Markets, *Economica*, vol.41, 176-193.
Caves, R.E. (1996): *Multinational Enterprise and Economic Analysis*, Cambridge: Cambridge University Press.
Clerides S.K., S. Lach and J.R. Tybout (1998): Is learning by Exporting important? Micro-dynamic evidence from Colombia, Mexico and Morocco, *The Quarterly Journal of Economics*, 903-947
Coe, D.T. and E. Helpman (1995): International R&D Spillovers, *European Economic Review*, Vol.39, 859-887.
Coe, D.T., E. Helpman and A.W. Hoffmaister (1997): North-South R&D Spillovers, *Economic Journal*, *Vol.107*, 134-149.
Connolly, M.P. (1997): Learning to Learn: The Role of Imitation and Trade in Technological Diffusion, Duke University, Economics Department, Working Paper No. 97-25.
Connolly, M.P. (1998): The Dual Nature of Trade: Measuring Its Impact on Imitation and Growth, Federal Reserve Bank of New York, Working Paper 44.
Corsepius, U. and R. Schweickert (1991): Entwicklungsfinanzierung durch Direktinvestitio-nen statt Auslandsverschuldung; in: J. Siebke (ed.) *Monetäre Konfliktfelder der Weltwirtschaft*, 195-207.
Das, S. (1987): Externalities, and Technology Transfer through Multinational Corporations. A Theoretical Analysis, *Journal of International Economics 22*, 171-182.
De Mello, L.-R. (Jr) (1999): Foreign direct investment-led Growth: evidence from time series and panel data, *Oxford Economic Papers 51*, 133-151.
De Mello, Luiz R, Jr. (1997): Foreign Direct Investment in Developing Countries and Growth: A Selective Survey, *The Journal of Development Studies*, Vol.34, No.1, 1-34.

Denison, E.F. (1967): *Why Growth Rates Differ*, Washington D.C.: The Brookings Institution.

Dixit, A.K. and J. Stiglitz (1977): Monopolistic Competition and Maximum Product Diversity, *American Economic Review 67*, 3, 297-308.

Djankov, S. and B. Hoekman (1999): Foreign Investment and Productivity Growth in Czech Enterprises, Working Paper No. 2115; The World Bank.

Drábek, Z. and A. Smith (1995): Trade Performance and Trade Policy in Central and Eastern Europe, CEPR Discussion Paper No. 1182, London.

Dunning, J.H. (1973): The Determinants of International Production, *Oxford Economic Papers 25*, 289-336.

Dunning, J.H. (1992): *Multinational enterprises and the global economy*, Wokingham: Addison-Wesley Publishing Company.

Dunning, J.H. (1997): *Alliance Capitalism and Global Business*, Routledge (London).

Dunning, J.H. and M. Rojec (1993): Foreign privatization in Central and Eastern Europe, CEEPN Technical Paper Series No.2, Lubljana.

EBRD (European Bank for Reconstruction and Development) (1995): *Transition report 1995. Investment and Enterprise Development*, London.

EBRD (European Bank for Reconstruction and Development) (1999): *Transition report 1999. Ten years of transition*, London.

EC (European Commission) (1997): *For a stronger and wider Union. Agenda 2000*, Vol.1, Part Two, DOC 97/6, Strasbourg.

Engelbrecht, H-J. (1997): International R&D spillovers, human capital and productivity in OECD economies: An empirical investigation, *European Economic Review*, 41, 1479-1488.

Ethier, W.J (1982): National and International Returns to Scale in the Modern Theory of International Trade, *American Economic Review 72*, 3, 389-405.

Findlay, R. (1978): Relative backwardness, Direct Foreign Investment, and the Transfer of Technology: A simple dynamic model, *The Quarterly Journal of Economics*, 1-16.

Fingleton, J., E. Fox, D. Neven and P. Seabright (1997): *Competition Policy and the Transformation of Central Europe*, CEPR (London).

Fosfuri, A., M. Motta and T. Ronde (1998): Foreign Direct Investment and Spillovers through Workers' Mobility, Universitat Pompeu Fabra, Working Paper No. 258.

Fry, M.J. (1994): Foreign Direct Investment, Financing and Growth, in: Fischer, B. (ed.) *Investment and Financing in Developing Countries*, Nomos, 181-214.

Fry, M.J., S. Claessens, P. Burridge and M-C. Blanchet (1995): Foreign Direct Investment, Other Capital Flows, and Current Account Deficits. What Causes What?, The World Bank Policy Research Working Paper 1527.

Gács, J., R. Holzmann and M.L. Wyzan (eds) (1999): *The Mixed Blessing of Financial Inflows. Transition Countries in Comparative Perspective*, Edward Elgar.

Genco, P., S. Taurelli and C. Viezzoli (1993): Private investment in Central and Eastern Europe: survey results, EBRD Working Paper No. 7.

Gerling, K. and K-D. Schmidt (1997): Restructuring and Competitiveness in the Transition Process: Evidence from an Eastern German Firm Panel, Kiel Working Paper No.791.

Geroski, P. A. (1999): Models of Technology Diffusion, CEPR Discussion Paper No. 2146.

Gersbach, H. and A. Schmutzler (1999): Endogenous Spillovers and Incentives to Innovate, University of Heidelberg Working Paper.

Gerschenberg, I. (1987): The training and spread of managerial know-how: a comparative analysis of multinational and other firms in Kenya, *World Development*; 15, 931-939.

Gerschenkron, A. (1962): *Economic Backwardness in Historical Perspective*, Cambridge (Harvard University Press).

Glass, A.J. and K. Saggi (1997): Intellectual Property Rights, Foreign Direct Investment and Innovation, Ohio State University Working Paper 95-06.

Glass, A.J. and K. Saggi (1998): International Technology Transfer and the technology gap, *Journal of Development Economics*, 55, 369-398.

Glass, A.J. and K. Saggi (1999): Multinational Firms and Technology Transfer, World Bank Working Papers – International economics, No. 2067.

Glatz, H. and H. Moser (1989): Ausländische Direktinvestitionen und Industriepolitik, *Wirtschaft und Gesellschaft*, Vienna, 33-61.

Globerman, S. (1979): Foreign Direct Investment and 'Spillover' Efficiency Benefits in Canadian Manufacturing Industries, *Canadian Journal of Economics*, Vol. 12, 42-56.

Graham, E.M. (1992): Foreign Direct Investment, *The New Palgrave Dictionary of Money and Finance 2*, 147-149.

Graham, E.M (1996): The (Not Wholly Satisfactory) State of the Theory of Foreign Direct Investment and the Multinational Enterprise, *Economic Systems 20*, 183-206.

Greene, W.H. (1993): *Econometric Analysis,* 2nd edition, New York: Macmillan Publishing Company.

Griliches, Z (1979): Issues in assessing the contribution of research and development to productivity growth, *The Bell Journal of Economics*, 10, No 1, 92-116.

Grinols, E.L. (1991): Unemployment and foreign capital: The relative Opportunity Costs of Domestic Labour and Welfare, *Economica 58*, 107-121.

Grosfeld, I. and G. Roland (1995): Defensive and Strategic Restructuring in Central European Enterprises, CEPR Discussion Paper No. 1135.

Grossman, G.M. and E. Helpman (1991): *Innovation and Growth in the Global Economy,* Cambridge, Mass.: The MIT Press.

Gupta, M. R. (1998): Foreign Capital and Technology Transfer in a Dynamic Model, *Journal of Economics*, Vol. 67, No. 1, 75-92.

GUS (1994): Europejska Klasyfikacja Dzialalnosci (European Classification of Economic Activities), 2nd edition.

GUS (1998a): Dzialalnosc gospodarcza spolek z udzialem kapitalu zagranicznego w 1997 roku (Economic activity of foreign firms in 1997), Warszawa.

GUS (1998b): Rocznik statystyczny 1998 (Statistical Yearbook 1998), Warszawa.

Haddad, M. and A. Harrison (1993): Are there Positive Spillovers from Direct Foreign Investment? Evidence from Panel Data for Morocco, *Journal of Development Economics*, Vol. 42, 51-74.

Halbach, A.J. (1988): Multinational Enterprises and Subcontracting in the Third World: A Study of Inter-Industrial Linkages, ILO Working Paper No. 58.

Harris J.R. and M. Todaro (1970): Migration, unemployment and development: A two-sector analysis, *American Economic Review 60*, 126-142.

Harrison, A. E. (1994): Productivity, imperfect competition and trade reform. Theory and evidence, *Journal of International Economics* 36, 53-73.

HCSO (Hungarian Central Statistical Office) (1997*): Foreign Direct Investment in Hungary 1995-1996*, Budapest.

Helpman, E. (1993): Innovation, imitation, and intellectual property rights, *Econometrica 61*, 1247-80.

Hennart, J-F. (1991): The Transaction Cost Theory of the Multinational Enterprise, in Pitelis, C. and R. Sudgen (eds), *The nature of the transnational firm*, London: Routledge.

Hervé, Y. and R. Holzmann (1998): Fiscal Transfers and Economic Convergence in the EU: An Analysis of Absorption Problems and an Evaluation of the Literature, Nomos: Baden-Baden

Hirschman, A.O. (1958) The strategy of economic development, New Haven, Yale University Press.

Hunya, G. (1996): Foreign Direct Investment and Modernization in CEECs, Vienna: WIIW.

Hunya, G. (1997): Large privatisation, restructuring and foreign direct investment, in: Zecchini, S. (ed.): Lessons from the Economic Transition.

Central and Eastern Europe in the 1990s, OECD, Kluwer Academic Publishers.
Hunya, G. (1998): Integration of CEEC manufacturing into European corporate structures by direct investments, Vienna: WIIW.
Hunya, G. (2000): The role of foreign direct investment in economic recovery and transformation, *WIIW Monthly Report 1/2000*, 9-12.
Hunya, G. and J. Stankovsky (1997): *WIIW-WIFO Database, Foreign Direct Investment in Central and East European Countries and the Former Soviet Union*, Vienna: WIIW, WIFO.
Hymer, S.H. (1976): *The International Operations of National Firms: A Study of Foreign Direct Investment,* Cambridge: MIT Press.
IMF (1991): *Determinants and systemic Consequences of International Capital Flows*, IMF Occasional Paper 77.
IMF (1993): *Balance of Payments Manual,* 5th edition, 86-96.
Jenkins, R. (1990): Comparing Foreign Subsidiaries and Local Firms in LDCs: Theoretical Issues and Empirical Evidence, *The Journal of Development Studies*, Vol 26, 205-228.
Kaldor, N. (1975): What is wrong with economic theory, *Quarterly Journal of Economics 89*, 3, 347-57.
Katrak, H. (1989): Imported Technologies and R&D in Newly Industrialising Countries, *Journal of Development Economies* 42, 75-88.
Katz, J.M. (1987): *Technology Creation in Latin American Manufacturing Industries*, St. Martin's Press (New York).
Keller, W. (1996): Absorptive capacity: Understanding the creation and acquisition of technology in development, *Journal of Development Economics 49*, 199-227.
Khan, M.A. (1982): Tariffs, foreign capital and immiserising growth with urban unemployment and specific factors of production, *Journal of Development Economics* 10, 245-56.
Khawar, M. (1997): The impact of multinational corporations on a developing country: a trade off in the long run?, *The Journal of International Trade and Economic Development 6:1*, 101-112.
Kholdy, S. (1995): Causality between foreign investment and spillover efficiency, *Applied Economics*, Vol.27, p. 745-749.
Kindleberger, C.P. (1969): *American Business Abroad*, Yale University Press (New Haven and London).
Kinoshita, Y. (1998): Technology Spillovers through Foreign Direct Investment, CERGE-EI Working Paper No.39.
Koizumi, T. and Kopecky, K.J. (1977): Economic Growth, Capital Movements and the International Transfer of Technical Knowledge, *Journal of International Economics* 7, 45-65.

Kokko, A. (1994): Technology, market characteristics, and spillovers, *Journal of Development Economies 43*, 279-293.

Kokko, A., R. Tansini and M.C. Zejan (1996): Local Technological Capability and Productivity Spillovers from FDI in the Uruguayan Manufacturing Sector, *The Journal of Development Studies*, Vol.32, No. 4, 602-611.

Konings, J., H. Lehmann and M.E. Schaffer (1996): Job Creation and job destruction in a transition economy: Ownership, firm size, and gross job flows in Polish manufacturing 1988-91, *Labour Economics 3*, 299-317.

Kuczynski, M. (1992): Foreign Investment, in: *The New Palgrave Dictionary of Money and Finance 2*,166-171.

Kumar, N. (1994): *Multinational enterprises and industrial organisation: The case of India*, New Delhi: Sage Publications.

Lai, E.L.-C. (1998): International intellectual property rights protection and the rate of product innovation, *Journal of Development Economies 55*, 133-153.

Lal, A. K. (1995): Increasing returns, urban unemployment, and international capital mobility: A trade policy analysis, *Journal of Development Economics* 46, 181-193.

Lall, S. (1978): Transnationals, domestic enterprises, and industrial structure in host LDCs: A Survey, *Oxford Economic Papers*, 30, 217-248.

Lansbury, M., N. Pain and K. Smidkova (1996): Foreign direct investment in Central Europe since 1990 : an econometric study, National Institute of Economic and Social Research Nr. 156, 105–114.

Levinsohn, J. and A. Petrin (1999): When Industries become more productive, Do Firms? Investigating Productivity Dynamics, NBER Working Paper 6893.

Li, B. (1996): *Ausländische Direktinvestitionen und kumulative Verursachung*, Universität Kiel, Diss.

Lichtenberg, F and B. van Pottelsberghe de la Potterie (1996): International R&D Spillovers. A Re-examination, NBER Working Paper 5668.

Lipsey, R.E. [1994]: *Outward Direct Investment and the U.S. Economy*, NBER Working Paper 4691.

Lipsey, R.E., M. Blomström and E. Ramstetter (1995): Internalized Production in World Output, NBER Working Paper No. 5385.

Mansfield, E.M and A. Romeo (1980): Technology transfer to overseas subsidiaries by U.S.-based firms, *Quarterly Journal of Economics,95*, 737-750.

Mansfield, E.M, M. Schwartz and S. Wagner (1981): Imitation Costs and Patents: An Empirical Study, *Economic Journal 91*, 907-918.

Mansfield, E.M. (1961): Technical Change and the Rate of Imitation, *Econometrica*, XXIX, 741-66.

Mansfield, E.M. (1968): *Industrial Research and Technological Innovation*, New York, Norton.

Marczewski, K. (1998): Efektywna protekcja celna (Effective Tariff Protection), in: *Foreign Trade Research Institute (ed.): Poland's Foreign Trade Policy 1997-1998*, Warszawa.

Markusen, J.R. (1995): The boundaries of Multinational Enterprises and the Theory of International Trade, *Journal of Economic Perspectives 9, 2*, 169-189.

Markusen, J.R. and A.J. Venables (1999): Foreign direct investment as a catalyst for industrial development, *European Economic Review 43*, 335-356.

McAleese, D. and D. McDonald (1978): Employment Growth and Development of Linkages in Foreign-Owned and Domestic Manufacturing Enterprises, *Oxford Bulletin of Economics and Statistics*, Vol.40, 321-339.

Messerlin, P.A. (1994): Central European Countries' Trade Laws in the Light of International Experience, CEPR Discussion Paper No. 1044.

Meyer, K. (1994): Business Operations of British and German Companies with the Economies in Transition: First Results of a Questionnaire Survey, London Business School Discussion Paper No. 19.

Morck, R. and B. Yeung (1992): Internalization. An Event Study Test, *Journal of International Economics 33*, 41-56.

Nadiri, M.I. and S. Kim (1996): International R&D Spillovers, Trade and Productivity in Major OECD Countries, NBER Working Paper No. 5801.

Nadiri, M. I. (1993): Innovations and Technological Spillovers, NBER Working Paper No. 4423.

Neary, P. (1988): Tariffs, quotas, and voluntary export restraints with and without internationally mobile capital, *Canadian Journal of Economics 21*, 714-735.

Nelson, R. (1990): What is Public and What is Private about Technology?, Columbia University, mimeo.

Nelson, R. and H. Pack (1995): The Asian Growth Miracle and Modern Growth Theory, mimeo.

Neven, D. (1994): Trade Liberalization with Eastern Nations. How Sensitive?, CEPR Discussion Paper No.1000.

Nyatepe-Coo, A. A. (1998): Foreign Direct Investment and Economic Growth in Selected LDCs, 1963-92; in: Levy-Livermore, A (ed.): *Handbook on the Globalization of the World Economy*; Edward Elgar U.K. USA:, pp. 87-99.

Nyman, S. and A. Silberstone (1978): The ownership and control of industry, *Oxford Economic Papers*, Vol. 30, No. 1, 74-101.

OECD (1992): *OECD Detailed Benchmark Definition of Foreign Direct Investment*, 2nd. edition, Paris.

OECD (1994): *Assessing investment opportunities in economies in transition*, Paris.
OECD (1995): *Taxation and Foreign Direct Investment. The experience of the Economies in Transition*, Paris.
OECD (1998): *Competition Policy and Intellectual Property Rights*, OECD Roundtables in Competition Policy No.17.
Ozawa, T. (1992): Foreign Direct Investment and economic development, *Transnational Economies*, Vol.1, no. 1, 27-54.
Pack, H. (1997): The Role of Exports in Asian Development, in: Birdsall, N: and F. Jaspersen (eds), *Pathways to Growth: Comparing East Asia and Latin America*, Inter-American Development Bank.
Pack, H. and K. Saggi (1999): Exporting, Externalities, and Technology Transfer, World Bank Working Paper 2065.
PAIZ (Polish Agency for Foreign Investment) (1999): *Status of Foreign Direct Investment in Poland at the end of 1997*, http://www.paiz.gov.pl/
Parente, S.L. and E.C. Prescott (1994): Barriers to Technology Adoption and Development, *Journal of Political Economy*, No 2, Vol. 102, 298-321.
Park, W.G. (1995): International R&D spillovers and OECD economic Growth, *Economic Inquiry*, vol. XXXIII, 571-591.
Patel, P. and K. Pavitt (1995): Patterns of Technological Activity: their Measurement and Interpretation, in: Stoneman, P (1995) (ed.) *Handbook of the Economics of Innovation and Technological Change*, Blackwell, Oxford UK & Cambridge USA, 14-51.
Plum, M. (1995): *Auswirkungen von Direktinvestitionen in Empfängerländern*, Bergisch Gladbach: Josef Eul Verlag.
Pohl, G., R.E. Anderson, S. Claessens and S. Djankov (1997): Privatization and Restructuring in Central and Eastern Europe, World Bank Technical Paper No.386.
Porter, M. E. (1990): *The Comparative Advantage of Nations*, New York (Free Press).
Ramachandran, V. (1993): Technology Transfer, Firm Ownership, and Investment in Human Capital, *Review of Economics and Statistics*, 75, 664-70.
Ramachandran, V. and M. K. Shah (1998): Firm Performance and Foreign Ownership in Africa: Evidence from Zimbabwe, Ghana, and Kenya, The World Bank, mimeo.
Rauch, J.E. and J. Watson (1999): Starting small in an Unfamiliar Environment, NBER Working Paper No. 7053.
Reuber, G.L., H. Crookell, M. Emerson and G. Gallais-Hamonno (1973): *Private Foreign Investment in Development*, Oxford: Clarendon Press.

Rivera-Batiz F.L. and L.A. Rivera-Batiz (1991): The effects of direct foreign investment in the presence of increasing returns due to specialisation, *Journal of Development Economics 34*, 287-307.
Rodríguez-Clare, A. (1996): Multinationals, Linkages, and Economic Development, *American Economic Review*, Vol.86, No.4, 852-873..
Rodrik, D. (1997): TFPG Controversies, Institutions and Economic Performance in East Asia, CEPR Discussion Paper No. 1587.
Rojec, M. (1997): The development Potential of Foreign Direct Investment in the Slovenian Economy, Vienna: WIIW.
Roldos, J. (1997): Potential Output Growth in Emerging Market Countries: The Case of Chile: IMF Working Paper WP/97/104.
Romer, P.M. (1987): Growth based on increasing returns due to specialisation, *American Economic Review*, 77, 56-62.
Romer, P.M. (1990): Endogenous Technological Change, *Journal of Political Economy*, vol.98, no.5, 71-102.
Scherer, F.M. (1991): Changing Perspectives on the Firm size Problem, in: Z.J. Acs and D.B. Audretsch (eds*), Innovation and Technological Change: An international Comparison*, University of Michigan Press, Ann Arbor, 24-38.
Schmidt, K-D. (1995): Motives of large multinationals investing in small transition countries: a literature review, Kiel Working Paper No. 668.
Scitovsky, T. (1954): Two Concepts of External Economies, *Journal of Political Economy*, 143-51.
Segerstrom, P.S, T.C.A. Anant and E. Dinopoulos (1990): A Schumpeterian Model of the Product Life Cycle, *American Economic Review 80*, 1077-1091.
Sjöholm, F. (1997): Technology Gap, Competition and Spillovers from Direct Foreign Investment: Evidence from Establishment Data, Stockholm School of Economics, WP Series in Economics and Finance, 1997-12-11.
Sjöholm, F. (1998): Productivity Growth in Indonesia: The role of Regional Characteristics and Direct Foreign Investment, Stockholm School of Economics, WP Series in Economics and Finance No.216.
Smarzynska, B.K. (1999): Composition of Foreign Direct Investment and Protection of Intellectual Property Rights in Transition Countries, The World Bank, mimeo.
Spence, M:E. (1976): Production selection, fixed costs and monopolistic competition, *Review of Economic Studies 43*, 217-236.
Stoneman, P. (1995) Introduction, in: Stoneman, P (ed.), *Handbook of the Economics of Innovation and Technological Change*, Blackwell, Oxford UK & Cambridge USA, 1-13.
Taylor, M.S. (1993): TRIPS, Trade and Technology Transfer, *Canadian Journal of Economics 26*, 625-637.

Teece, D.J. (1977): Technology Transfer by multinational firms: the resource cost of transferring technological know-how, *Economic Journal 87*, 242-261.

Thimann, C. and M. Thum (1998): Investing in terra incognita: waiting and learning, *Economic systems 22*, 1–22.

UN (United Nations) (1997): *1996 International Trade Statistics Yearbook*, New York.

UNCTAD (United Nations Conference on Trade and Development) (1992): *The Determinants of Foreign Direct Investment: a Survey of the Evidence*, New York.

UNCTAD (United Nations Conference on Trade and Development) (1995): *World Investment Report 1995: Transnational Corporations and Competitiveness*, New York.

UNCTAD (United Nations Conference on Trade and Development) (1997): *World Investment Report 1997: Transnational Corporations, Market Structure and Competition Policy*, New York.

UNCTAD (United Nations Conference on Trade and Development) (1998): *World Investment Report 1998: Trends and Determinants*, New York.

Varian, H.R. (1992): *Microeconomic Analysis*, 3rd edition, W.W. Norton &Company, New York.

Veblen, T. (1915): *Imperial Germany and the Industrial Revolution*, London (Macmillan).

Vernon, R. (1966): International Investment and International Trade in the Product Cycle, *Quarterly Journal of Economics 80*, 190-207.

Wang, J-Y. (1990): Growth, Technology Transfer, and the Long-Run Theory of International Capital Movements, *Journal of International Economics 29*, 255-271.

Wang, J-Y. and M. Blomström (1992): Foreign Investment and Technology Transfer. A simple model, *European Economic Review 36*, 137-155.

Wang, Z.Q and N.J. Swain (1995): The determinants of Foreign Direct Investment in Transforming Economies: Empirical Evidence from Hungary and China, *Weltwirtschaftliches Archiv 131*, 359-382.

Weller, C. (1999): The Finance-Investment Link in a Transition Economy: Evidence for Poland from Panel Data, ZEI Working Paper B99-04.

White, H. (1980): A Heteroscedasticity-Consistent Covariance Matrix Estimator and a Direct Test for Heteroscedasticity, *Econometrica 48*, 817-838.

Wlodarczyk, W. (1998): Kapital zagraniczny w prywatyzacji polskiej gospodarki (Foreign capital in Polish privatisation), in: Durka, B. (ed), *Inwestycje zagraniczne w Polsce*, Warszawa: IKC.

World Bank (1997): *World Development Report 1997*, Oxford University Press.

Zagozdzinska, I. (1998): Podmioty z udzialem kapitalu zagranicznego w Polsce w latach 1993-96 (Firms with foreign capital in Poland in 1993-1996, in: Durka, B. (1998): *Inwestycje zagraniczne w Polsce (Foreign Investment in Poland)*, Foreign Trade Research Institute, Warszawa, 63-91.

Zukowska-Gagelmann, K. (1997): Economic Theory of Multinational Enterprises and Foreign Direct Investment in Eastern Europe, Universität des Saarlandes, mimeo.

Zukowski, R. (1998): From crisis to transformational recovery: The case of Poland's industry, *Economic Systems 22*, No. 4, p. 367-397.

Peter Lang · Europäischer Verlag der Wissenschaften

Gustav Dieckheuer / Boguslaw Fiedor (eds.)

Aspects of Sustainable Economic Development

Frankfurt/M., Berlin, Bern, Bruxelles, New York, Oxford, Wien, 2000.
VIII, 219 pp., num. fig., tab. and graf.
Internationale Marktwirtschaft. Herausgegeben von Gustav Dieckheuer, Karl-Hans Hartwig und Theresia Theurl. Bd. 1
ISBN 3-631-36986-7 · pb. DM 69.–*
US-ISBN 0-8204-4809-5

Sustainable development has become one of the topics in modern economics. Since the Club of Rome pointed to limitations of economic growth caused by shortage of natural resources and environmental destruction, western industrial countries have made efforts to avoid these limitations and to establish conditions for sustainable growth. This is the background of a collection of articles published in this book. They are focused on theoretical analysis of growth and environment, political activities concerning environmental improvement, and actual problems of sustainable development in Poland.

Contents: Are there Lessons from the German Wirtschaftswunder for the Transitional Economies? · Sustainable Development and the Paradigm of Modern Neoclassical Economics · International Free Trade and the Problem of Environmental Protection

Frankfurt/M · Berlin · Bern · Bruxelles · New York · Oxford · Wien
Auslieferung: Verlag Peter Lang AG
Jupiterstr. 15, CH-3000 Bern 15
Telefax (004131) 9402131
*inklusive Mehrwertsteuer
Preisänderungen vorbehalten